THE
INDEBTED
SOCIETY

THE INDEBTED SOCIETY

Anatomy of an Ongoing Disaster

James Medoff
and Andrew Harless

Foreword by John Kenneth Galbraith

Little, Brown and Company
Boston ▪ New York ▪ Toronto ▪ London

FIRST EDITION

The authors are grateful for permission to include the following previously
copyrighted material:

Data for Figures 3.1, 3.2, 7.1, 11.2 and Table 11.2 from The Conference
Board's Help Wanted Index. Reprinted by permission of The Conference
Board.

LIBRARY OF CONGRESS CATALOGING-IN-PUBLICATION DATA

Medoff, James L.
    The indebted society : anatomy of an ongoing disaster / by James
Medoff and Andrew Harless.
        p.   cm.
    Includes index.
    ISBN 0-316-56586-5
    1. Debt — United States.   2. Corporate debt — United States.
3. Debts, Public — United States.   4. Consumer credit — United States.
5. Cost and standard of living — United States.   I. Harless, Andrew.
II. Title.
HG3711.U6M43   1996
336.3′4′0973 — dc20   96-20338

10   9   8   7   6   5   4   3   2   1
MV-NY
DESIGNED BY JEANNE ABBOUD

Published simultaneously in Canada by
Little, Brown & Company (Canada) Limited

PRINTED IN THE UNITED STATES OF AMERICA

To
Leslie Miller Medoff
and
Cathy Harless

Contents

Acknowledgments

A
s is appropriate given the book's title, we are indebted to many individuals. John Kenneth Galbraith, Robert Solow, and James Tobin provided many insights and much support. We are most appreciative.

We also wish to acknowledge the very significant contributions of Maureen Steinbruner and Anne Sesler of the Center for National Policy. They taught us much about life within the Washington beltway.

We are most appreciative to our writing and editorial assistant, Kathy Wahl. All of our readers will benefit greatly from her contributions.

Many people from the real world have been most generous with their insights and their data. In particular, we thank Tom Nardone of the Bureau of Labor Statistics and Carol Courter of the Conference Board.

In addition, we would like to thank William Phillips of Little, Brown and Helen Rees, our literary agent, for helping make this book much better and more readable. They also made the lives of the authors more enjoyable.

Last but most certainly not least, this book has been built largely on the backs of our Harvard research associates and assistants. To name some: Kit Ekman, Edwin Lin, Edwin U, and Martin Van Denburgh.

While many others have given generously to us, we alone are responsible for our interpretation of the Indebted Society's problems and for the solutions that we propose. Hopefully, we will pay back some of what we owe.

Foreword

by John Kenneth Galbraith

Economics is at its best when talented economists address topics of high current importance with three supporting qualifications — namely, imagination, high technical competence, and the ability and diligence to bring empirical support to their findings and conclusions. All these qualities are admirably evident in this exceedingly interesting volume.

The subject is debt in its numerous and compelling manifestations, and particularly as it bears on personal and larger social well-being. The last is especially important. This is no antiseptic technical treatise along with the relevant data. The authors start, continue, and end with a strong and compassionate concern for economic well-being, and specifically for that of the least fortunate members of the larger economic community. This concern is evident in every chapter and, indeed, on every page.

The central theme, as already noted, is debt and the economic effect of burgeoning public, corporate, and personal debt in the United States. Medoff and Harless are far from happy about the latter; they see it as acting against the interests of the poorest of citizens. In the early chapters they devote themselves to diagnosis and in the later ones, to remedy. That is good: before one knows what is right, there must be a clear view of what is wrong.

I do not find myself in full agreement with all that is here proposed; the ethos of the economics profession allows, even compels, disagreement with one's most admired friends and colleagues. I've never quite believed that public borrowing by absorbing savings denies private investment. Perhaps it encourages employment, output, and so adds to income and savings. And there is the claim of all who genuflect to the Federal Reserve that it can by lowering interest rates alone make way for more investment. But these are matters for further discussion. This is a highly important piece of work, good as to controlling purpose, method, and result.

It is now some sixty-five years since I took up economics as a basic academic pursuit. Over those years it has not been without its critics.

Does the subject change as its world changes? Does it have an internal dynamic of improvement, of empirical understanding, of needed public action? Books such as this show that the subject can be abreast of the times and capable of improved understanding, and not alone for economists but for all those who are intellectually involved at large. No one who reads of the accumulation of public, corporate, and personal debt and seeks its meaning can ignore this work. And I repeat what I earlier observed: it is economics at its concerned and empirical best. I am pleased, indeed honored, to write this introductory word and recommendation.

Part One

FROM AFFLUENCE
TO DEBT

1▪Unsettling Trends

WHAT HAPPENED TO THE FEELING that Americans were the most prosperous and blessed people in the world, with a future as brilliant and full of promise as a sunlit dawn? Perhaps some readers continue to experience that feeling. But the majority of readers more likely are plagued by nagging suspicions that America is about to awaken to a gray and uncertain morning. Evidence mounts to support the conclusion that a permanent cloud cover is forming over the American dream. No longer does the average American worker believe that lifetime employment with one company is possible. No longer does the average American believe that he or she can financially survive a serious illness. Parents worry about the safety of their children at school and about the quality of the education that their children receive. Mothers and fathers work long hours at jobs that barely allow them to make ends meet. Every worker is victim to the recurring nightmare that one day his or her employer will become one of the growing number of corporations in which workers are expendable.

The average American senses a rent in the fabric of society, not only at the personal level but also at the government level. Services that citizens once took for granted are being cut and eliminated. The supports that allowed families to prosper in the good times and survive in the bad are crumbling. The voices of ordinary Americans seem not to be heard over the din of downsizers, demagogues, and doomsayers. There is one notion, however, that the majority of Americans agree upon — that America is at a crossroads.

The political developments of the past ten years show that Americans are eager for a change, but uncertain of what that change should be or how it can be executed. A variety of interest groups vie for the reform platform, and modern-day medicine men hawking everything from cures for fiscal disaster to restoration of morality peer from the covers of magazines in corner markets and proselytize on the TV or talk-radio circuit. Some of the answers proffered by these contemporary prophets might be right. Some are surely wrong. One thing sorely lacking is a systematic examination of what is wrong and what can and should be done about it.

THE INSIDIOUS EFFECTS OF DEBT

Most Americans, when asked what is wrong with the country to-day, give answers that do not include the word "debt." More likely, they include words like "violence," "unemployment," "crime," "lack of family values" — the list goes on. The following chapters show, however, that the effects of debt bear a strong relationship to many of the problems plaguing America.

One easily understood example of this relationship is the case of the highly indebted firm seeking to service its debt by terminating workers. Often these workers are middle-aged men with families accustomed to a certain standard of living. This comfort is suddenly interrupted. In another time, such a worker might spend a short period of time unemployed and then be rehired or land another job with comparable wages and benefits. Today this is not the case. Temporarily unemployed workers are becoming rarer and rarer, and permanently displaced workers are becoming the norm. Even those lucky enough to obtain new employment must accept positions that pay much less and that often do not include such benefits as a pension plan or health insurance. Consequently, the family often evolves into a two-income household, with both parents working to make the same salary as one parent was previously able to earn. It is generally agreed that effective parenting is a full-time endeavor. With both parents working, full-time parenting becomes a physical and emotional impossibility.

In the late seventies and early eighties, latchkey children were considered a minority and worthy of society's sympathy and concern. In the nineties the child who comes home from school to milk and cookies, whether prepared by a mother or by a father, is the rarity. It is not a radical notion that adolescents with too much free time and too little guidance often find decidedly antisocial ways to spend their time. Some critics ask, "Where are the parents?" We answer, "At work."

This simple vignette could take other routes to its conclusion. For instance, the pressure of the husband's long-term unemployment might undermine the marriage and result in divorce. The children could then find themselves with less economic support and role-model guidance. In addition, the couple would become part of the growing statistics of broken marriages in America. It is not difficult to imagine that the problem which started with the husband's lost job could have some serious implications for the family unit and the children's future. We do not suggest that this relationship is causal in the same way that too much sun on the skin causes a burn. What we do argue is that certain groups have used debt to further their interests in opposition to those of ordinary Americans. Debt has played a leading role in the drama of declining real wages, diminishing job opportunities, and dwindling concern with the plight of America's poor. A climate has thus arisen in which high divorce rates, an explosion of juvenile crime, and plummeting self-esteem for Americans of all ages and financial status are fast becoming the norm. These phenomena, in turn, have broad and profound effects on the citizenry of this country, their pocketbooks, their lives, and their future.

A SHORT HISTORY OF OUR INDEBTEDNESS

It may come as a surprise that we do not believe debt to be, universally and forever, a bad thing. Under appropriate circumstances, and in proportion to the situation, debt can be very people-friendly. We would not suggest, for instance, that students forgo borrowing to pay tuition and drop out of college en masse. Nor would we counsel against borrowing to buy a house to live in, a car with which to conduct one's business, or the equipment needed to improve a firm's productivity. History has taught us that even an extreme level of debt can sometimes be better than the alternatives. Who would question the borrowing necessary for the United States and its allies to defeat Nazism?

The problem is not that all debt is bad, but rather that wherever debt exists, it has consequences. Since the mid-1970s the United States — through its households, firms, and government — has borrowed inappropriately, incurring debt out of proportion with circumstances and without an informed understanding of the consequences. Somebody must pay and, as we shall see, somebody does.

What motivated this wholesale descent into fiscal irrationality? There are a number of factors, but in our view, the most important has been the dramatic slowing over the past twenty-five years of U.S. productivity growth. Productivity — the ability to make things — is what enables a nation to live well without borrowing. Between 1949 and 1973 American productivity more than doubled. The same number of workers could literally produce twice as much in 1973 as they could in 1949. Since the mid-1970s productivity has barely budged. As productivity stagnates, so do wages and profits. Consumption, unfortunately, has not stagnated, and consumption continues to feed private debt.

The private-debt nightmare epitomizes the opposite of the very positive American dream, in which economic well-being increases with successive generations. In 1958 John Kenneth Galbraith identified affluence as a quintessential characteristic of modern America. When Galbraith wrote *The Affluent Society*, the most critical question confronting society was what to produce. In our own time the most critical question is how much to consume.

History and human nature have combined to force government heavily into the red. Historically, actual or perceived overtaxation has led to wars and revolutions. In a democratic society, losing a reelection bid is the more common result. Nevertheless, the needs of the nation, many of which require public funding, have continued to rise. Spending more, but taxing less, has left the government with one alternative — borrow to cover the deficit. At times in the past, with a cooperative monetary policy, government borrowing has been extremely beneficial. In this respect, in fact, World War II was a blessing in disguise because it justified the deficit spending and the monetary accommodation necessary to lift the United States from the Great Depression. Right now, with an inhospitable monetary policy, government borrowing is at best an ineffective tool and at worst a disastrous drain on the nation's resources. Far from encouraging investment, low taxes on the rich have supported a buying binge that commandeered the very resources America might have used to invest in the future.

The lenders — those who live by creating debt — silently but forcefully echoed the slogan of the tax cutters. "No new taxes!" became "No new jobs!" If more people were working, America could produce more and perhaps satisfy both the desires of today and the needs of tomorrow without importing its needs and desires from abroad. The lenders, however, would not hear of it. More new jobs — more demand for labor — might mean rising wages, which might ultimately mean higher prices. To those who receive fixed interest payments, higher prices are the worst of all disasters. Even the slightest risk of inflation must be avoided. To America's now-powerful lender class, employment is the enemy.

Most consumers would probably point to the federal government as the cause of, or leader in, debt accumulation. The historical sequence of events shows otherwise. Throughout the 1960s and early 1970s, while consumer and business debt was rising rapidly, government debt was actually declining relative to what the nation produced. Only during the 1980s did government debt start to grow more quickly than the economy. It was the demand for tax relief by indebted citizens that led the government so deeply into debt. The Reagan revolution spilled no blood but shed gallons of red ink.

THE INDEBTED SOCIETY

Thirty years ago a family in America, enjoying growth in its real earnings, borrowed money to buy a house or a car, or to finance a college education. Firms borrowed dollars to invest and, in so doing, became more productive and increased their market shares. The government borrowed in time of crisis and when a broad consensus recognized the need for an economic stimulus.

Life in the Indebted Society is very different. Families borrow to maintain lifestyles eroded by falling wages. Firms under pressure to service their current debt forgo investments in future productivity. And the government borrows solely to meet interest payments. Today one can hardly imagine a world in which these three groups are not way over their heads in debt. Families now owe money for their children's education, the new TV, the refrigerator, the lawn mower, the very shirts on their backs. The corporation owes money for a newly acquired subsidiary (which it bought at twice the fair price) or because its new owner bought it with no money down. The government owes money for everything under the sun and finds itself caught in a downward spiral of borrowing more to service the current debt.

Thirty years ago, neither firms nor politicians used (or could use) massive indebtedness to justify their actions or inaction. Since 1980 firms, politicians, and others have regularly used debt to rationalize conduct that has been damaging to workers and to the poor. The country's lenders have been able to use their fear of inflation to justify the high real interest rates that strangle America's workers, block the creation of jobs, and stunt America's growth. Debt, directly or indirectly, has decayed the very soul of America.

The Indebted Society undertakes the tasks of identifying and explaining both the motivations and the underlying causes of the crisis now facing America. We start with a detailed examination of what is wrong and why, and then we move on to propose the steps that must be taken to solve these problems. Our argument is that debt — family debt, business debt, and government debt — is the underlying cause of the economic insecurity felt today by most Americans. Although debt is really only an abstract idea, it has taken on tremendous power. Later we outline the broad conditions of life in the Indebted Society — where it is and where it is going — and the steps that our nation must take in order to escape from these conditions. First, however, we must understand how America has stumbled into this dark and savage forest.

2 · The Unconfident Consumer

P EOPLE BORROW MONEY for two basic reasons. First, they borrow to buy assets, such as houses, farms, factories, stocks and bonds, inventories for resale, and so on. Normally, one expects these assets to provide a financial profit or some other long-term benefit. A house, for example, provides the owner with shelter, and a farm or factory provides income. Second, people borrow to buy goods or services for short-term consumption, which, for our argument, means within five years. This category includes autos, air conditioners, television sets, home computers, clothing, and most other consumer goods. The debt used to buy these things normally requires monthly payments and is called "installment debt."

Before the invention of credit cards, consumers borrowed the money to finance such purchases from finance companies or from banks. The installment loans these institutions gave consumers were most often specifically earmarked for the item purchased. That is, when the consumer approached the lender, the questions of where and for what the money was to be spent were negotiated as part of the loan transaction. Credit cards, when they appeared on the scene, took away the element of forethought from borrowing transactions. Once the consumer had the card in hand and entered the store, the nature and price of the item bought were between the consumer and the card limit. There is much debate about the cause-and-effect relationship between credit cards and impulse buying. However, one thing is clear and beyond dispute. Since the introduction of credit cards, the debt level of the typical American has risen far out of proportion to his or her income.

In 1969 the total credit card debt of American consumers was $2.7 billion. In 1994 the comparable figure (in 1969 dollars) stood at $74 billion. What are the factors that contribute to this astounding increase in the debt level of the average American? What effect does this indebtedness have on the economy and on the individuals saddled with this debt? To answer these questions, we examine the history of consumer credit and the philosophical and economic factors in modern-day America that foster, and even encourage, consumption by credit.

A Brief History of Consumer Credit

Consumer credit is not a new concept. References to credit exist in the Code of Hammurabi, which came into being about 1750 B.C. Nor is credit a new idea in the United States. Borrowing to finance assets has always been an important part of capitalism. Borrowing to support consumption, however, is a more recent development. The Provident Loan Society of New York, a charitable group formed in 1894, undertook the first large-scale foray into consumer lending. It offered loans to needy borrowers at an interest rate of 1 percent per month. This interest rate was in stark contrast to the rates of 20 percent or more (also per month) charged by the lending alternative, the "loan shark." Provident's sponsors reaped rewards for their charity. At one point, the certificates issued to contributors paid a 6 percent annual dividend and traded on the New York Stock Exchange.

In 1910 Arthur J. Morris, a lawyer practicing in Norfolk, Virginia, opened the Fidelity Savings and Trust Company. The Fidelity was the first major commercial business devoted solely to personal lending. Morris successfully expanded his idea to other cities and was able to attract millions of dollars in outside capital. In 1928 National City Bank became the first commercial bank to enter the consumer loan business. The amounts lent by these early finance companies seem tiny by today's standard. The legal limit of loans, for example, was $300 (in 1937 dollars) with repayment schedules of five to twenty months. In the two decades before 1937, personal-finance company receivables increased from $20 million to nearly $365 million (again, in 1937 dollars). From 1933 to 1937 between 17 percent and 23 percent of nonfarm families and individuals in the country obtained credit from personal-finance companies. During this period various retailers, hotels, airlines, and restaurants began to extend credit to their customers. These businesses were not likely to see a profit from the credit operation. Rather, they used credit to enable and encourage a customer to buy their products and to foster customer loyalty to their product line.

The rules of the credit game changed radically in 1949, when Alfred Bloomingdale, Frank McNamara, and Ralph Snyder came up with a new type of credit card — the third-party universal card. They called their invention the Diners Club card. The card was originally conceived as a convenience to such people as traveling salesmen, who could use it to charge business meals and other travel expenses while on the road. With earlier credit cards, each card was specific to a certain business and could not be used at several different places or across state lines. The introduction of the Diners Club card solved these problems and had some other important effects. There now was a third party, other than the buyer or seller, in the transaction. This third party viewed credit as a product to be marketed and sold. Of course, the third party also expected to turn a profit. In 1958 American Express and Carte Blanche joined the fray and introduced universal credit cards. However, these cards did not offer the option of revolving credit, meaning that balances run up during the billing period were due at the time of billing and could not be spread over time. But the revolving credit market expanded enormously after 1958, when two large banks launched credit card operations — the Bank of America and the Chase Manhattan Bank.

The use of universal credit cards grew rapidly. In 1966 the operations of several large bank credit departments were combined into two national credit card companies, BankAmericard and Interbank Card Association (issuer of Master Charge cards). By 1978 more than 11,000 banks had joined one of the two systems, and 52 million Americans carried at least two bank credit cards. BankAmerica changed its name to Visa in 1976. Master Charge became MasterCard in 1980. From 1969 to 1981 the number of banks involved in MasterCard and Visa rose from 4,461 to 12,504, and from 3,751 to 12,518, respectively.

Despite this rapid growth, issuers of credit cards reaped only marginal profits in the 1970s. Banks were keenly aware that the economies of scale directly affect profits. They tried many marketing devices aimed at increasing the number of cardholders, and at inducing cardholders to use the cards more often and to maintain outstanding balances. BankAmericard and Intercard, for example, undertook a mass mailing of unsolicited cards in the late 1960s. Banks hawked cards with no annual fee or reduced interest rates on revolving credit. The lenders were also aware that profits go up quickly as more cardholders use the revolving-credit feature and do not pay the entire balance due each month. In an effort to exploit this advantage, banks increased the credit limits of cardholders and offered credit cards to consumers who, in different times, would have been considered poor risks. The marketing strategies paid off. By 1984 bank credit card operations were outperforming all other forms of bank debt. Today 90 percent of all bank card revenues come from consumers' using their cards on a revolving-credit basis. There is one other factor that helped bring about this increase in profitability — the rise in interest rates in the early 1980s.

UPWARDLY MOBILE INTEREST RATES

As part of the Federal Reserve's anti-inflation policy of the early 1980s, interest rates on all types of debt rose to levels unprecedented in the post–World War II years. At the same time, Congress removed many of the regulations that had governed the banking business. This deregulation allowed banks across the country to attract depositors by offering high interest on deposits and then passing those high rates on to borrowers. Briefly, during 1980, the demand for consumer credit fell abruptly. It is not clear whether this drop was in response to the higher interest rates or to a hortatory speech in which President Carter decried the inflationary impact of credit card use. Whatever its cause, the decline was short-lived. Interest rates rose again with no effect on consumer borrowing.

The banks learned an important lesson during this period: consumers continue to incur debt no matter what the rate of interest charged. Thus, even when the federal funds rate (the interest rate that banks charge one another for overnight loans) fell from more than 14 percent to less than 9 percent between June and December of 1982, the interest rate on credit cards remained high. Moreover, between 1980 and 1992, as the federal funds rate fell from 13.4 percent to 3.5 percent, the average credit card interest rate rose from 17.3 percent to 17.8 percent. The ability of banks to borrow money at a fairly low interest rate and to relend it at a high interest rate further spurred the lenders' foray into the high-risk markets. In the eyes of today's banks, almost anyone is a worthy credit card risk. Defaults by the less creditworthy are more than offset by the income generated from high interest rates.

A few numbers tell the story of just how much high interest rates and the market expansion mean to the profits of universal credit card issuers. The percentage of total installment payments accounted for by consumer credit debt increased from 16.9 percent in 1983 to 25.3 percent in 1986. In 1984, 22 percent of all credit was revolving credit (on which monthly interest was due). This percentage kept on rising until it reached 36 percent in 1993. American consumers owed $2.7 billion in credit card debt in 1969, $22 billion in 1980 (in 1969 dollars), and $74 billion in 1994 (also in 1969 dollars). In 1993 the receivables for the credit card industry as a whole were up by about 400 percent from 1983. In 1980, 41 percent of consumer charges were made with universal credit cards; by 1990 that figure had risen to 78 percent.

It is clear from the numbers that both the use of universal credit cards and the revolving-credit option that the cards offer are now a part of the American way of life. For several reasons, however, the consumer behavior revealed by the statistics is puzzling to economists. This behavior seems to challenge several long-held beliefs about how the economy works and about how consumers make choices.

Consumer Behavior

A simplistic model of the standard thinking about how consumers behave is that they spend when times are good and hold on to their money when times are bad. According to this model, increased spending occurs when unemployment rates are low, productivity is high, and the economic forecast is for clear skies and smooth sailing. Spending declines when unemployment rates are high, productivity is low, and the economic forecast includes tropical storms and high seas. The point is not that economists agree that these expected consumer behavior patterns are what is best for the economy. Most economists would say that the needs of the economy and expected actions of consumers are at polar opposites.

When the economy is not using its full productive capacity, consumption serves as a helpful stimulus. It spurs firms to use more capacity — that is, to hire more people and to activate unused plant and equipment. Under these conditions, borrowing to support consumption would be seen as a positive act. On the other hand, when the economy *is* using its full capacity, consumption creates a demand that domestic resources cannot fill. The pressure of consumer demand for more goods and services diverts resources toward producing for consumption, thereby reducing the amount of domestic resources that can be used for investment in future productive capacity. If firms choose to invest anyway, the mixture of high investment and high consumption leads to borrowing from abroad. This borrowing is needed to finance domestic investment in future production and to keep up with consumer demand for more goods and services. As you can see from the description of consumer behavior in good times and bad, consumers often choose to do just the opposite of what economists would recommend for a healthy economy. Consumers spend when times are good, i.e., when the economy is using its full capacity. They cut back on spending when times are bad, i.e., when the economy is not fully using its labor and capital.

A third variable in the production/consumption formula is the net amount of national saving — total saving minus total borrowing. Thus, consumers can choose, in the good times, to spend their entire excess income on goods and services or to save some portion of that income. For the individual, saving is an investment in the future. For the nation, saving makes domestic resources available for firms to invest in future productive capacity. When savings decline, firms must replace these resources by borrowing abroad or by forgoing investment altogether. One of the most troubling aspects of the rise in consumer borrowing rates is the corresponding fall in consumer saving rates. The level of individual saving in the United States is falling at an alarming rate, especially when compared with the increase in debt levels during the same period. The number of families with savings accounts fell from 61.7 percent in 1983 to 43.5 percent in 1989. The money owed to credit card lenders rose from $350.3 billion in 1980 to $470 billion in 1991 (in 1980 dollars).

CREATURES OF HABIT

The huge increase in credit card debt in the United States over the past thirty years does not fit neatly into any of the usual models of consumption. The 1970s and 1980s were lean years, in relative terms, for the American consumer. Real wages for most U.S. workers either stagnated or fell during this period. By 1991 the real income of the average American was a mere 5 percent higher than it had been in 1973. Productivity growth in the economy as a whole slowed from 2.8 percent during the period from World War II to 1973 to an average of less than 1 percent since 1973. Job security for many blue-collar workers in the manufacturing sector became a vague memory. By the 1980s white-collar middle managers and technocrats increasingly found themselves out of a steady, well-paying job and in the uncertain world of temporary and freelance consultant work.

So why did consumers continue to buy with credit when all indicators told them that things were not good and that the future was not rosy? Clearly, part of the reason was the newfound willingness of banks to lend to high-risk borrowers. It may be easy to see how a poor credit risk would welcome a first credit card, even with interest charges near 20 percent. It is much harder to understand why those consumers who were used to credit card interest rates of 7 percent kept on charging when the interest rates rose into the teens. A simple answer may be that the consumers "needed" the items bought on credit. But this answer ignores the likelihood that this class of consumer was in a financial position either to buy the item outright or to save and purchase the item without resorting to the use of credit.

One way to explain this seemingly incongruous behavior on the part of American consumers is to borrow a concept used by theoretical economists to explain fluctuations in the stock market. In trying to explain why investment in stock does not increase sharply during a downturn according to the "buy low, sell high" maxim, these economists introduce the concept of "habit."[1] The habit model, as it relates to consumption, presupposes that a person resists any downward change in his or her consumption level.[2] It also presupposes that habit is formed over time and is slow to change. A recession poses the threat of a downward change in consumption, and people are not eager to add to this threat by investing in risky assets like stocks. In our model, the habits of the consumers of the 1980s and 1990s were formed during the rapid growth of the 1950s and 1960s. However, since 1970 growth has not met the habit expectation of the American consumer.

Americans are struggling harder and harder to maintain a standard of living that is dictated by habit. That is, they are spending as if their incomes have kept pace with the growth of the 1960s, when in actuality

their incomes clearly have not. Because habit resists change and because the creature of habit acts in ways that reduce the effects of
change, American consumers are left with little choice. They have to
borrow in order to support a level of consumption consistent with a
lifestyle they have come to anticipate (see Figure 2.1). The psychological by-products of this tug-of-war between yesterday's hopes and
today's reality are increased frustration and anxiety. Subsequent chap-

FIGURE 2.1 CONSUMING MORE
BUT ENJOYING IT LESS

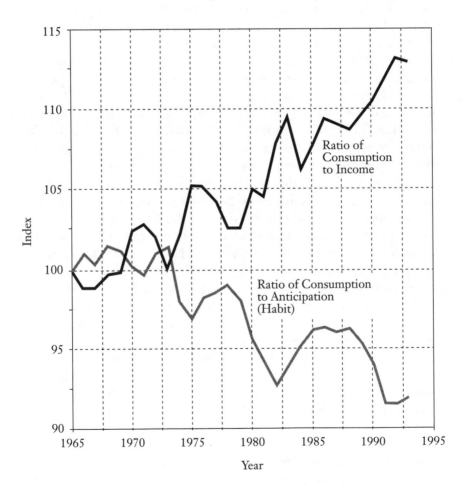

ters examine the specific ways in which frustrated expectations affect behavior and lifestyle.

Declining Confidence and Increased Consumption

Another sign of the enormous rift emerging between the reality of the American consumer's financial status and the fantasy needed to maintain high levels of debt is found in the declining Consumer Confidence Index. This index is kept by the Conference Board, a business membership organization with a twofold mission of improving the business enterprise system and enhancing the contribution of business to society. The Conference Board keeps a number of statistics. The Consumer Confidence Index reports the results of a monthly survey of consumers about their views on the availability of jobs, the chance of their making major purchases, and the general state of business. During 1969 the Consumer Confidence Index held an average value of 133. From 1970 to 1996 the index has never exceeded 118. During 1994 the index averaged less than 91, only 68 percent of its 1969 level. As stated previously, the classic model for consumer behavior is that when times are good, people borrow in expectation of more good times. The 1990s' conundrum is that when times are bad, people borrow to make up the gap between expectation and reality. In itself, this pattern is not a problem, because over the business cycle, it is good that people continue to borrow during a recession. But the pattern becomes a problem when the economic downturn extends beyond a cyclical phenomenon and becomes a long-term trend (as it has). Over time, consumer borrowing starts to tie up more and more resources that could be better allocated to investment.

The use of credit cards to make ends meet during periods of part-time work or unemployment is one aspect of the severed link between consumer confidence and consumer credit. One way to see this severed link is to compare the Consumer Confidence Index and the Normalized Help Wanted Index.[3] In years when many help-wanted ads appear in the nation's papers, consumers report high confidence levels. The reverse is found in years when few help-wanted ads appear. This link between job availability and consumer confidence is thus very tight. No such link exists between job availability and consumer debt. With jobs more and more scarce, consumer debt has kept on rising.

There are no statistics on how many out-of-work Americans use credit to obtain necessities. New developing markets for credit card use suggest the number is increasing. Many supermarkets now provide the option of using credit to buy groceries, and credit card purchasing has been introduced in fast-food restaurants and taxicabs. Another booming credit card market is for the payment of medical bills. The under- and unemployed might not have been the targets for the rapid growth in credit card use. Nonetheless, it is undeniable that the innovations mentioned make it much easier for consumers strapped for cash to survive — one more day, one more month, or one more year — by borrowing.

THE BIG PICTURE

What conclusions can we draw about the marked increase in consumer debt over the past thirty years? And how does this debt affect the larger economy? The answers to these questions become clear as the stories of government and corporate debt unfold, and as we examine in depth the links among the three groups that make up the Indebted Society. For now, however, we offer some general observations.

The rise in consumer debt is mirrored by a fall in consumer savings. This is a major development. Not only is the economy in general worse off for neglecting its savings, but the individual consumer also finds him- or herself between the proverbial rock and a hard place. Thrift, and the saving that thrift engenders, serves several important functions. For the economy as a whole, savings provide a domestic pool of funds from which to draw for investment in future production and growth. For the individual, savings provide a safety net to fall back on in bad times, such as during a period of long illness or unemployment. Without savings, Americans must find other ways to bridge the gap between income and expenses when the times get rough. Unfortunately, it appears that more borrowing is fast becoming the solution to this problem.

A second important side effect of the increase in credit card debt, especially at interest rates much higher than those applied to other types of debt, is the loss of regulatory control over credit. Under current conditions, the Federal Reserve Board cannot effect any reliable changes in the amount or timing of debt increases or credit use. Therefore, a situation exists in which billions of dollars flow into and out of the marketplace without regulation, checks, or balances. We can only imagine the long-term effects of this outlaw monetary system. But it is foolish to believe that it will have no effect on the typical American family. In later chapters, we examine those effects that have already appeared. For now, however, we leave you holding the ticking bomb and move on to a topic that polarizes the nation — government debt.

3 · Voodoo Politics

L ET US HAVE the courage to stop borrowing to meet continuing
deficits. Stop the deficits."[4] It may be difficult for some to believe that those words were spoken by Franklin Delano Roosevelt during his 1932 campaign for the presidency against Herbert
Hoover. The identity of the slogan's originator is surprising for two
reasons. First, it points to the fact that deficit busting is not a new
theme in political rhetoric. Second, after his election FDR presided
over an enormous increase in government spending, with an accom-
panying increase in the deficit. At the time, deficit spending was just
what the depressed economy needed. Times have changed. Nonetheless, politicians continue to curry votes by promising a balanced budget and by decrying deficits. Voters, however, are more concerned
with increased taxes than the actual level of government spending.
The chances of an incumbent staying in office increase when taxes
are low.

Thus, there is a constant pressure on any elected government to
keep taxes low. This pressure on the government becomes particularly strong when stagnant incomes put pressure on family budgets.
And while the exact nature of government spending is not foremost
in the voters' minds at election time, it is clear that proposed reductions in the services that taxpayers are used to receiving can meet with
widespread opposition. These basic interactions between government and its citizens largely occur outside the larger economic picture. They are marked by the dynamics of self-interest and often
appear ignorant of or unresponsive to long-term repercussions of tax
policy on the economy as a whole. In any given era, therefore, there
is a struggle between political expediency and long-term economic
goal setting. Since the 1930s two distinct economic philosophies have
mediated this struggle. The first is demand-side economics; the second may be loosely termed supply-side economics.

DEMAND-SIDE ECONOMICS

Demand-side economic theory was pioneered by John Maynard Keynes in the 1930s. A basic premise of this economic view is that a free-market economy is inherently unstable. This assumption is in direct opposition to classical economic theory, which posits that free-market economies are self-regulating, self-sustaining, and self-stabilizing. Keynesian theory focuses on the demand aspects of the economy, with the belief that government policy can manipulate aggregate demand to achieve full employment. Classical theory, on the other hand, holds that government intervention in the market causes the very problems it proposes to solve.

In 1964 President Johnson signed a tax cut that represented the first self-conscious attempt by the federal government to apply demand-management policies to the U.S. economy. The tax cut proposal came at a time when there was already a sizable budget deficit. The tax cut, Johnson and his advisers argued, would stimulate private spending, which in turn would spur employers to hire more workers, who would subsequently spend more, thus encouraging even more employment. The tax cut worked as expected. Between January 1964 and November 1966, the U.S. unemployment rate fell from 5.6 percent to 3.6 percent. Because the newly employed workers paid taxes — instead of getting government unemployment benefits — the federal budget moved into surplus. Johnson, it appeared, had worked magic: by cutting taxes, he got rid of the deficit.

But problems arose when the success of the 1964 policy went to the president's head. With the economy seemingly under control, Johnson at once undertook the tasks of ending poverty in the United States and ending communism in South Vietnam. Both these programs required substantial government spending, but Johnson waited until 1967 to seek increased taxes to meet the shortfall created by increased expenditure. In hindsight, it is evident that the modest tax increase enacted in 1968 came too late to halt the inflationary forces that had been building in the United States.

The post-Johnson political and economic landscape continued to be shaped by demand-side policies. Even Richard Nixon, himself a product of classical laissez-faire economic theory, remarked that "we are all Keynesians now." Nixon proceeded to abuse monetary policy in much the same way that Johnson had abused fiscal policy. Soon after Nixon came to the White House in 1969, the nation began to fall into a recession. Starting in 1970, Nixon lobbied the Federal Reserve Board to cut interest rates and to keep them low. This lobbying included public appeals, veiled threats, rumors planted in the press, and repeated office visits by White House staff. Nixon also made it easy for the Fed to cut interest rates by abandoning the gold standard and imposing wage-price controls. Under the gold standard, keeping interest rates high encouraged foreign investors to keep their dollars on deposit in the United States instead of asking for gold. The end of the gold standard removed this barrier to low interest rates. Wage-price controls temporarily removed the threat of inflation, thus negating the other major argument against low interest rates. The Fed cooperated. By Election Day 1972 the recession was a distant memory.

Conditioned to prosperity by the postwar growth spurt of the 1940s and 1950s and by the booming policies of the Johnson-Nixon years, Americans expected a steadily increasing standard of living. The ball stopped rolling, however, in the early 1970s, and incomes began to stagnate. Several events challenged demand-side policies and made it clear that factors other than those identified by Keynes could have profound effects on the economy. For example, the decision by the OPEC nations to embargo sales of oil to the United States and Europe pointed to the importance of price effects in overall economic functioning. Yet, notably, in the very years OPEC was accused of single-handedly causing inflation to defy gravity, the U.S. labor market was also at its post-1950s tightest.[5] The events of the 1970s, combined with a growing unease on the part of the electorate, provided a platform for the development of a new theory intended to jump-start the economy in the 1980s. Elements of the new theory were used by Ronald Reagan to win the presidency and were implemented, with mixed results, during his eight-year administration.

Supply-Side Economics

Supply-side economic policies manage to combine the tax-resistant tendencies of the electorate with the classical economic theorists' bias against government interference in the economy. A basic tenet of supply-side economics, as practiced by Reagan, is that lower taxes result in higher revenues. Supply-siders base this prediction on the ability of tax cuts to stimulate supply and increase the economy's potential. The tax cuts proposed by demand-side theorists, such as the cut implemented in 1964, work by stimulating demand and exploiting more of the economy's current potential.

The supply-side mechanism proposed by Reagan found little support among economists. To most, it sounded like nonsense. Lower tax rates could make the economy more efficient, most would agree, allowing it to produce a little bit more with the same resources. But this increased efficiency could not possibly be large enough to replenish the revenues lost through the tax cut. In addition, Reagan's supply-side view did not take into account the effects of his proposed policies on the demand side of the economy. In other words, Reagan did not acknowledge that a tax cut would create an increase in demand. George Bush's characterization of the Reagan proposals as "voodoo economics" is but a small indicator of the general sentiment expressed toward the proposals. However, voters struggling to maintain their standard of living were not anxious to entertain the skepticism of economic technocrats. In 1980 the failure of demand-side policies was evident at every store window, and the stagnation of living standards was evident in every home. Supply-side economics was an idea whose time had come.

For the health of the economy's supply side, Reagan's policies turned out to be just about the worst thing that could have happened. Investment did not increase, growth continued to stagnate, and the federal deficit ballooned to new dimensions. To counter these effects, a true supply-side economist might have argued for raising taxes, rather than lowering them. Higher taxes would have meant less government borrowing. Reduced government borrowing would have made more funds available for private investment. More private investment would have meant more capital, more productive resources, more supply. The increased savings by the government would have far outweighed the slight effect of higher tax rates in discouraging savings and investment. The fact of the matter is that the United States was lucky the Japanese and other overseas investors were able and willing to take up some of the supply-side slack by investing in a country that was not investing in itself.

The boondoggle of supply-side policies continued into the Bush presidency. The phrase "voodoo economics" was gone from Bush's vocabulary. Ignoring a deficit that seemed out of control, Bush made a campaign promise of "no new taxes." Bush administration insiders admitted privately that the low-tax policy was political hocus-pocus and not a serious attempt to deal with the country's economic problems. By 1988 the vast majority of economists (including many of Reagan's former advisers) agreed that supply-side economics had failed. But political strategists saw that it had succeeded. The Great Communicator had communicated a valuable lesson to U.S. politicians: less taxes mean more votes. The very failure of Reagan's policies on the economic front became a reason for their continued political success. Struggling to maintain a rising standard of living in the face of stagnant incomes, voters in 1980 had been all too willing to accept tax cuts on faith. Still struggling in the late 1980s, Americans were understandably loath to give up the borrowed fruits of Reaganomics. It was not until 1990 that congressional Democrats were able to back Bush into a corner and force him to support a compromise deficit-reduction proposal that included a tax increase. Unfortunately, the damage had already been done. In 1981, the year Reagan took office, the public debt was 26.5 percent of the gross domestic product (GDP). That debt-to-GDP ratio barely exceeded the postwar low of 24.5 percent set in 1974. In 1993, the year Bush left office, the public debt was a staggering 51.9 percent of the GDP.

The deficit created by supply-side policies also took its toll on U.S. workers. Reagan proposed that lower tax rates would reduce the deficit. The reality of his policies was an increase in the deficit. This increase in the deficit did not bode well for wages or for unionism in this country. The U.S. government was forced to borrow more from abroad to finance the larger deficit. In order to attract the funds it needed, the United States offered interest rates higher than those offered by other countries. The value of the dollar rose as a result of the higher interest rates. The strong dollar made it difficult to sell American manufactured goods abroad. Consequently, manufacturing industries, such as steel, autos, and machine tools, declined during the early 1980s.[6] Service-producing industries, such as those providing temporary services and health care, prospered because they did most of their business domestically and, therefore, were unaffected by the strong dollar. Workers were adversely affected in two ways by the decline in manufacturing. First, the wage-and-benefit packages of manufacturing jobs typically were better than those found in the service sector. Second, unionism was stronger in the manufacturing sector. The decline in manufacturing jobs, therefore, coincided with a decline in wages and in trade unionism as the workforce shifted from manufacturing to services.[7]

Thus, the tax cuts caused deficits, the deficits led to high interest rates (relative to interest rates abroad), the high interest rates strengthened the dollar, the strong dollar weakened manufacturing, and the decline in manufacturing weakened the organized labor movement. Ironically, the demand-side effect of the tax cuts — in the form of increased government borrowing — was what ended up causing an increase in aggregate supply. This result was accomplished when workers did more work for the same wages, not because they got to keep more of what they earned after taxes, but because they were less likely to be in unions and more likely to be in search of a decent job.

The Role of the Federal Reserve System

Thus far, the ups and downs of the economy and the policies that underlay these fluctuations have been pinned on politicians, particularly the president. However, there is in the United States a powerful force that is not elected and that exerts a huge influence over the functioning of the economy. The body in which this force resides is the Federal Reserve System (or the Fed, as it is commonly known). The Federal Reserve System was created in 1914 for the primary purpose of protecting the country's financial stability. It is composed of a national Board of Governors and a nationwide network of "Reserve Banks." The Board of Governors has the power to set interest rates by controlling the supply of money available to banks. The power that the Fed has to influence presidential election results cannot be overstated. By manipulating interest rates, the Fed controls the availability of jobs. The availability of jobs bears a direct relationship to who gets elected. Figure 3.1 shows a strong positive correlation between changes in help-wanted advertising and voter behavior. Figure 3.2 is illustrative of another important correlation — the one between past changes in interest rates and present changes in help-wanted advertising. What is clear from these figures is that whoever controls interest rates controls the job market. The Fed, at least in the short run, controls interest rates.

Richard Nixon was keenly aware of the Fed's power in 1960. Nixon blamed the tight money policies of Fed Chairman William McChesney Martin for his defeat in the election. A decade later, when Nixon finally won the White House, he fired Martin at the first opportunity and replaced him with an ally, Arthur Burns. As noted previously,

Nixon took no chances with the Fed. He engaged in an intense campaign of political pressure on Burns to cut interest rates and to keep them low. As we shall see, the symmetry, or lack thereof, between presidential economic policy and the policy of the Fed can serve to undermine or enhance the presidential agenda.

For Nixon, the policies of the Fed worked to his advantage. From August 1971 to February 1972, the federal funds rate fell from 5.6 percent to 3.3 percent. During 1972 the Fed's Board of Governors (dominated by Burns) rejected twenty-two recommendations from Federal Reserve Banks to raise the discount rate (the rate the Fed charges on loans made directly to commercial banks). As a result of the low interest rates, jobs were plentiful by election day. Nixon's policy of using political pressure on the Fed to ensure his own reelection was arguably the most critical cause of the 1970s' inflation.

Nixon's enemy at the Fed, William McChesney Martin, had facili-

FIGURE 3.1 JOB AVAILABILITY AND VOTER BEHAVIOR
1956–92

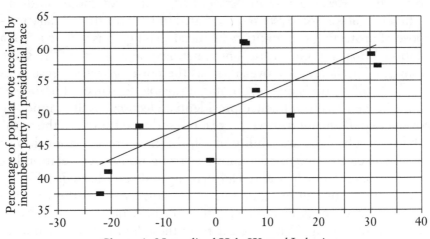

Change in Normalized Help Wanted Index in two years
up to election year

Note: The diagonal line across the chart is intended to show the general tendency of the data, to summarize the statistical relationship between the two variables. The line was generated by a standard statistical technique called linear regression, which we use in many of the charts in this book. In general, an upward-sloping regression line indicates a positive relationship, a downward-sloping line indicates an inverse relationship, and a horizontal line indicates no relationship at all.

tated Johnson's tax experiment by keeping interest rates relatively low. As the tax cut (and the anticipation of continued low taxes) stimulated buying, the demand for borrowed funds by consumers and businesses rose. This demand produced an upward pressure on interest rates. Martin allowed interest rates to rise somewhat, but not enough to dampen significantly the effect of the tax cut. As the economy improved, tax revenues rose, and the federal deficit did not become a problem.[8]

Reagan's experience with the Fed was very different. Reagan and his allies never described their tax cut as a demand-management policy. Their objective was not to give businesses more customers so that they would hire more workers, but to get workers to do more work and investors to put more money into businesses. However, Reagan ignored the demand-side effects that the tax cut would have on the economy. The increase in consumption that resulted from the tax cuts had two potential outlets — an increase in prices (inflation) or an increase in jobs. Since the outcome is difficult to predict, the Fed tries to prepare for either possibility. At the time of Reagan's tax cuts, the economy was already facing high inflation. Therefore, the Fed was more concerned with reducing inflation than with creating jobs. Under the supply-side theory that Reagan espoused, the Fed's demand-side policies were not relevant to the success of his program. This theory was wrong.

FIGURE 3.2 INTEREST RATES AND JOB AVAILABILITY
MONTHLY DATA 1955–94

Change in
Normalized
Help Wanted
Index over
12 months

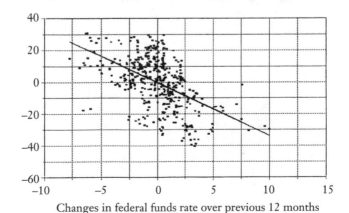

Changes in federal funds rate over previous 12 months

Determined to keep inflation low, the Fed (under Chairman Volcker) felt that high interest rates were necessary to counter the demand stimulus from the Reagan tax cut. By ignoring the potential demand-side effects of his supply-side policy, Reagan became caught in a conflict between these effects and the will of the Fed. To reduce inflation, the Fed tightened the money supply forcefully just as Reagan's tax cut was starting to stimulate demand. To pursue its policy of reducing demand, the Fed had to fight not only the economy's inflationary momentum but also the potential stimulus of a major tax cut. The resulting high interest rates made it very hard for the government to borrow just as its borrowing needs were rising to record levels to meet expenditures for which tax revenues were not keeping pace. Furthermore, the deep recession induced by the Fed's tight money policy meant that the tax base was reduced just as the declines in tax rates were taking effect. This monetary tightness also caused interest rates to remain high. After the recession, the Fed continued to keep interest rates high relative to the inflation rate. If the Fed had accommodated Reagan's tax cuts by keeping interest rates low, the deficit might not have become a problem. With lower rates of interest, the need to service government debt would have been smaller, and the desire to invest stronger. However, Reagan knowingly supported the Fed's war on inflation, which, in combination with his supply-side policies, produced the disastrous deficits.

These examples show that the Fed plays a major role in determining the ease with which a president carries out economic policy and also the ease with which a president is reelected. We have more to say about the Fed in chapter 7. For now, we move on to the third player in our ménage à trois of debt — the corporation.

4 · Bond Capitalism

FOR BETTER OR WORSE, American capitalism has taken on a new look. At one time, it was a system based on owning. It is now a system based on owing. Consider some statistics. In 1958, the most debt-burdened year of the 1950s, interest payments by nonfinancial corporations (those not specifically in the business of borrowing and lending) were only 4.6 percent of total cash flow. In 1985, the least debt-burdened year of the 1980s, interest payments were 15.9 percent of cash flow — more than three times the 1958 level. The ownership of a firm is measured by its outstanding equity. Before 1984 net equity issues by U.S. nonfinancial corporations were positive in most years. They have been negative in every year since. Corporate debt ratios, which had been roughly constant from World War II until the late 1970s, increased dramatically during the 1980s.

Although 15.9 percent is not a huge proportion, there are several reasons why it can be enough to have a profound effect on corporate structure and policies. First, there are other major demands on a firm's cash flow. For example, to stay in business, a firm must replace its equipment as it wears out. Also, its stockholders often expect regular dividends. Second, firms cannot expect that their cash flow or their debt service requirements will be constant. Cash flow will fall in some years, and interest rates will rise in some years. Therefore, a firm's decisions must account for the good times and the bad. A firm with a 15.9 percent interest-to-cash-flow ratio must plan for a year when that ratio may be closer to 100 percent. Third, 15.9 percent is only an average. Therefore, many firms have much higher debt-to-cash-flow ratios, and the behavior of these high-debt firms may set industry norms that affect the behavior of lower-debt firms.[9]

In fact, we do find a lot of variation from one sector to another. The goods-producing sector saw the largest debt increases during the 1980s. In manufacturing, the largest goods-producing industry, the ratio of debt to the total amount produced was only 1.7 percent in 1977. By 1992 that ratio was up to 36 percent.

Media coverage of the debt boom has focused on the character of individuals such as Michael Milken. Many people resort to epithets about greed, avarice, and amorality. These sentiments certainly have their place in any description of the fortunes made and lost in the risk-laden eighties. There are also those who argue that corporate debt is a good thing because it forces managers to run more efficient shops. Bolstering this argument is the fact that the need to meet interest payments reduces the ability of managers to use corporate resources in pursuit of their own interests. However, there are fundamental and structural factors that helped to bring about the enormous shift from equity to debt in American business. A few of these factors are discussed below, along with some of the effects of increasing corporate debt on the employees of the corporations.

The Tax Advantage

The U.S. tax code provides a simple incentive for debt financing: corporate profits are taxed at a fairly high rate, while interest payments on loans are considered a deductible expense. Thus, one of the best ways to avoid taxes on profits is to avoid profits. Consider, for example, a hypothetical firm worth $1,000,000 with 100,000 shares of stock outstanding. (Each share is worth $10.) The firm makes $200,000 per year in pretax profits that are taxed at a 50 percent rate, netting an after-tax profit of $100,000. This leaves each shareholder with a share of profits valued at $1, or a 10 percent return on the $10 share value.

Now suppose the company borrows $500,000 at a 10 percent interest rate. The firm uses this money to buy back half its outstanding shares at a market value of $10. To service the loan, the firm must now pay $50,000 per year to its creditors — leaving a pretax profit of $150,000. Taxed at the 50 percent tax rate, the firm is left with $75,000 in after-tax profit. Since there are now only 50,000 shares outstanding, each shareholder realizes a profit of $1.50, or a 15 percent return on the original $10 stock value. This seemingly magic formula is called leveraging.

As long as profits are taxed heavily, there is an incentive for corporations to finance with debt.[10] The incentive for debt financing was particularly strong during the 1970s when inflation rates rose. In a high-inflation economy, a large part of the interest payment merely serves to compensate the lender for the decreased purchasing power of the principal. To the tax man, an interest payment is an interest payment, and it is all deductible. Therefore, debt financing is particularly advantageous. (When our earlier example is cast in an economy with 10 percent inflation, that 15 percent real return becomes 20 percent.)[11] In the United States, the inflation of the seventies may have been the spark that ignited the conflagration of corporate debt. When inflation was low and the tax advantages of debt financing were smaller, there was no compelling reason to abandon the tradition of equity financing. As the inflation rates rose, the tax advantages of debt financing began to outweigh any perceived disadvantages.

Takeovers, LBOs, and Changing Attitudes

Tax advantages, of course, are only one of several factors fostering the increase in corporate debt levels since the 1960s. There is also a changing ethos in the American boardroom. Older businessmen remembered the Great Depression of the 1930s, in which high debt levels had usually meant bankruptcy. As these older men retired, the memory of the depression faded. Economists also became more confident that a depression was preventable. Older businessmen had a sense of tradition, in which excessive debt was taboo. An increasingly egalitarian society began to open the corridors of corporate power to those who would challenge that stodginess. As the need for new ideas supplanted the love of "tried and true," the four-letter word "debt" was uttered more freely.

Debt, it seems, always supported the latest fad in corporate structure. In the 1960s and 1970s, "diversification" was the word of the day. Steel producers borrowed money to buy radio stations, and construction firms borrowed money to buy textile makers. In the 1980s stock analysts learned to pronounce the word "diworseification."[12] Diversity was out. Now deal makers used debt to break apart the unhealthy conglomerates. The leveraged buyout, or LBO, became a common means to bring about such corporate divorces. In an LBO, a buyer (often an insider) uses borrowed money to buy up a firm's outstanding stock. The buyer pledges the firm's assets as collateral. During the mid- to late 1980s, LBO artists were often able to repay the debt quickly by selling off divisions of a firm to an eager stock market.

Increasingly, debt was used to effect control. If the leaders of a midsized company wanted to extend their empire, they sold bonds and bought another midsized company. The result was a large company with a large debt load. If the leader of a large company wanted to wrest control from uncooperative shareholders, he or she went to the bank, borrowed money, and bought out the shareholders. If an outsider didn't like the way a company was run, he or she secured financing (generally debt financing) and made a tender offer. When insiders were intent on keeping control, they loaded the balance sheet with debt, to make a takeover more difficult and less attractive.

Meanwhile, investors began to see that the riskiest of debt securities were not really as risky as they had thought. Bond salespeople produced studies to show that defaults were not a frequent occurrence, even for low-quality ("junk") bonds that offered interest rates much higher than "investment grade" bonds. A broad market for newly issued "junk bonds" was born. Previously, junk bonds had usually come into being only when the credit of a higher-quality issuer deteriorated. The issuer's outstanding bonds would thus become junk bonds. In the 1980s it became acceptable to issue "junk" as "junk." (The issuers, and their underwriters, generally preferred the term "high-yield" to "junk," but the phrase "junk bonds" stuck in the public's memory.)

Mergers and acquisitions increased dramatically in the 1980s — fivefold from 1980 to 1988. During this period leveraged buyouts increased by an even larger degree. Some theorize that the hostile takeovers and leveraged buyouts of the 1980s point to a larger power struggle, the outcome of which will determine to whom corporations will be accountable in the future.[13] Margaret Blain argues that "takeovers and financial restructurings were devices the financial markets used to discipline corporate managers and pressure them to increase cash flows and to pay out more money to shareholders and other investors."[14] Blain finds the incentive for redirecting a firm's excess cash flow in the increased cost of capital in the 1980s. This rise was prompted by an increase in real interest rates. Thus, when the interest rate on "safe" investments such as government securities rose from between 0–2 percent to 6–8 percent in the 1980s, investors demanded a higher return for "risky" investments such as corporate stocks. Restructuring and buyouts provided this higher return by enabling owners to squeeze more profits out of workers, managers, and tax collectors.

The Impact of Corporate Debt

Regardless of the motivations of a particular firm to incur debt in excess of its equity, the pressure that debt payments exert on a firm's operation are fairly predictable. Recent research shows a strong relationship between corporate debt and the sensitivity of employment to the business cycle. Steven Sharpe shows that, in a given industry, firms with more debt have a greater tendency to reduce employment during recessions.[15] Other research shows that this relationship holds across the spectrum of manufacturing industries. Anecdotal and media accounts of the increase in mergers and buyouts also reflect the impression that when the stockholders and deal makers profit, the workers suffer.

Several commentators give credence to this view, some from the perspective of workers and some from the perspective of owners. Michael Jensen, for example, argues that any loss of employment resulting from reorganization serves to increase the efficiency of the organization.[16] In Jensen's view, the fact that a firm has employees making good wages is an indication of inefficient management. That inefficiency is corrected through the pressure imposed by debt on managers to economize and reduce expenses. (In the fantasy of neoclassical economic theory, this ends up benefiting workers in the economy at large. Too bad we live in the real world.) Others posit that the negative effects on employees resulting from takeovers involve a breach of trust between the employer and employee. This breach of trust, they argue, may have detrimental long-term effects on the firm's efficiency.[17]

There is no dispute, however, that the increase in indebtedness among U.S. firms has profound effects on the workforce. Subsequent chapters focus on the specific effects on workers and the specific groups of workers most adversely affected. It is clear that the repercussions of corporate debt linger long after firms reduce their actual debt. Corporations learn slowly. They unlearn even more slowly. During the 1980s and the recession that followed, American corporations learned how to deal with their high debt levels — cut jobs aggressively and hold wages down. During the 1990s debt levels have fallen moderately, and the merger-and-acquisition frenzy of the 1980s has slowed. But corporations continue to behave as though debt levels have remained constant. The new corporate culture is characterized by a "downsizing" mind-set.

High debt levels gave corporate America permission to treat employees like commodities. The need imposed by debt service was used to justify this attitude. This mentality has leaked into the boardroom of corporations that are not heavily leveraged, so that firms in fairly strong financial positions act as if they have problems. Old habits die hard. It will take a massive shift toward equity financing to break the momentum of the debt service culture. Later chapters outline concrete suggestions for motivating this shift. For now, we continue our morbid review by discussing the effects of the new corporate culture on America's workers.

Part Two

LIFE IN THE INDEBTED SOCIETY

5 · The Immobile Worker

THE ALL-TOO-FAMILIAR HEADLINE reads "Last week, Mobil Corp. posted soaring first-quarter earnings. This week it announced plans to eliminate 4,700 jobs." This combination of high profits and workforce reductions puzzles many and angers some. A worker reacting to the news sums up the confusion. "It just doesn't make a whole lot of sense. You could see them cutting back personnel and doing different things to get out of a bind, but just to make profit, I just don't understand."[18]

These two quotes clearly illustrate the role of corporate debt in the changing world of the worker's relationship to the employer. Job reduction began when the level of debt service payments forced corporations to reduce labor costs. Many firms had to cut costs just to stay afloat without angering stockholders or creditors. Initially, mass layoffs were met with bad press and political blustering. But as time went on, the shouting in opposition to downsizing became a whisper. Corporate managers realized that no excuse was needed to make workers the pawns in a redistribution of income — from labor to capital — that marked the 1980s and continues today.

The stage was thus set for the fate of the workers at Mobil to be duplicated in countless workplaces across the country. Pink slips appear in the pay envelopes of employees who spent a major portion of their adult lives at one job — and who were certain that they would retire from that job. The effects of the job loss on these workers and on the lives of those who depend on their incomes are often devastating, not to mention the feelings of paranoia and anxiety that overcome the workers lucky enough to avoid this round of the cost-cutting ax. A survey of downsized firms reports a decline in morale among remaining employees in 80 percent of firms surveyed.[19]

Employee lunchrooms echo with the fears of workers wondering when it will be their turn to get the boot. What can be done to avoid termination? Does working harder make them irreplaceable? Once-friendly coworkers become competitors in an uncertain game to get the few crumbs left. The atmosphere in the workplace becomes one in which fear and distrust are ever present forces. What long-term effects does this atmosphere have on productivity, growth, and the human spirit?

The repercussions of downsizing account for only a portion of the bad news dished out to workers in the eighties. New entrants in the job market are less and less assured of stable, long-term employment. They can barely hope for wages that give them a real chance at the American dream. Even during "good times," jobs are not plentiful in most regions. For those jobs that appear, the pay and benefits offered are seldom enough to support a family, live the lifestyle, or purchase the goods associated with success and well-being in a consumer society. Much of this decline occurred because the growth of low-paying service-sector jobs outpaced the growth of higher-paying jobs in the manufacturing sector. As Table 5.1 shows, the pay of service workers has remained between 9 percent and 19 percent below the pay of those working in manufacturing since the 1970s. The current differential is 9 percent. Real hourly earnings, however, have fallen in both sectors since 1973, further compounding the loss to workers. Table 5.2 shows that jobs in the rapidly growing service sector are less likely to provide either a pension or health insurance when compared with the more unionized manufacturing sector. Recent public debate has addressed the implications of the increasing percentage of Americans without health insurance, and of the increasing cost of health care in general. Few discuss the long-term effects of the lack of adequate health care. Imagine the cost of caring for generations of the elderly

TABLE 5.1 SERVICE-SECTOR HOURLY EARNINGS AND
MANUFACTURING-SECTOR HOURLY EARNINGS
35 MONTHS AFTER 4 CYCLICAL TROUGHS BETWEEN 1973 AND 1994

35th month after trough	Feb. '94	Oct. '85	Feb. '78	Oct. '73
Real service earnings	$7.25	$7.09	$7.46	$7.49
Real manufacturing earnings	$7.95	$8.52	$9.17	$8.82
Service/manufacturing earnings ratio	.91	.83	.81	.85

Source: Bureau of Labor Statistics: Establishment Survey; James L. Medoff, "The Labor Market: February 1994," Center for National Policy, March 1994.

who were denied access to health maintenance during their work lives.

Another little-publicized effect of the mixture of downsizing and rising profits is the erosion of pension and health benefits for retired workers. Even those who have given a lifetime of work effort to a firm with the expectation, and the implied promise, of a decent standard of living in retirement are seeing their benefits put on the corporate chopping block.

We see in later chapters that debt in general — not just corporate debt — has helped to produce a society that is harmful to working people. Here we simply take a look at the conditions that America's working people now face. We look separately at the problems of diverse groups of workers. No worker — whether male or female; young, middle-aged or old; unionized or nonunionized; educated or uneducated — has totally escaped the effects of the corporate descent into debt. The resultant mania for budget trimming and cost cutting became rampant in the 1980s and continues relentlessly into the 1990s.

THE PLIGHT OF THE MIDDLE-AGED MALE WORKER

The Bureau of Labor Statistics routinely examines a section of the unemployed population referred to as "displaced workers." This category includes those workers who have become unemployed because of plant closings or relocations, insufficient work, or the abolishment of their positions or shifts. An examination of this category of unemployed workers can be informative for a couple of reasons.

TABLE 5.2 EMPLOYEES COVERED BY FRINGE BENEFITS
(PERCENTAGES): MARCH 1992
EMPLOYEES COVERED BY:

Plans	Health Insurance	Pension
All sectors	54%	38%
Manufacturing	74%	56%
Services	46%	30%

Source: Bureau of Labor Statistics: Household Survey; James L. Medoff, "The Labor Market: February 1994," Center for National Policy, March 1994.

First, the category does not include voluntary job leavers. Second, to be counted as displaced, a worker must be over twenty years of age and have worked at the same job for at least three years. These limiting criteria ensure that younger people new to the workforce who may be "shopping around" for a suitable job are not able to skew the findings. The Bureau has kept statistics of this sort for every two-year period since 1984.

Several tendencies emerge from the statistics. The first is the disproportionate number of men in the ranks of displaced workers. For example, in the 1987 survey, men were found to be one and a half times more likely than women to have been displaced. A second pattern is the concentration, especially in the 1980s, of displaced workers in the goods-producing industries. The 1984 survey showed that nearly one-half of the displacements occurred in goods-producing jobs. (This is striking because goods-producing industries employ less than one-fifth of employed workers.) Although these tendencies hold over the years of the surveys, the proportions decrease. Thus, in the 1992 survey, the percentage of displacements in goods-producing jobs fell to one-third. The percentage of women workers in the ranks of the displaced increased with each successive survey, but it is still smaller than proportionate.

The number of *middle-aged* men counted among the permanent job losers was also high compared with other workers. This is partly because male workers tend to be found in manufacturing-sector jobs. That they were also middle-aged means that their earnings were likely in the higher brackets for that particular firm or industry. If the decision to lay off is between a comparably skilled younger worker and a more highly paid middle-aged worker, the pressure for profits argues for keeping the younger one. In a time of lower corporate debt levels, a sympathetic manager may easily resist that pressure. In our own time, the manager sees little choice. Moreover, since women still tend to get lower wages than men, the victim is more likely to be male. Other important changes in the landscape of the manufacturing sector have also favored the dismissal of the middle-aged worker.

A foul wind blew through the manufacturing sector as a result of high debt levels engendered by the 1980s' merger-and-reorganization frenzy. That wind cleared away in one gust the hard-won benefits and job security that trade unions had fought to bring to manufacturing jobs. During the 1980s wage-and-benefit concessions became the norm when union contracts were renegotiated. In 1985, for example, a third of all workers covered by new collective-bargaining agreements saw a total freeze or cut in wages.[20] Fringe benefits were also eroded, not only in the manufacturing industries but across all job and employer categories. The proportion of employers' contributions to fringe benefits such as health insurance steadily declined, while the portion of the cost of coverage paid by employees to the insurance plans increased.

In addition, many employers were able to substitute lump-sum payments for the historically standard cost-of-living raises in union contracts. This form of wage increase did not translate into a higher hourly wage and need be paid only if the employer did "well" during the year, a totally subjective standard. Thus, employees' wages remained stagnant, with only the promise of a raise that was ultimately at the employer's discretion. Another mechanism used by many firms to lower the cost of labor was the institution of a two-tiered wage system, with newly hired workers being paid at a rate lower than the lowest level of the wage scale in effect for existing workers.

One effect of this mixture of wage takebacks and benefit erosion was to increase the pressure to get rid of more-experienced workers. When firms paid the same wages and benefits to all employees in a given job, the decision of whom to terminate might have been a hard one. When newer workers receive lower pay and benefits than older ones, the decision is easy.

In earlier times firms seemed to feel a commitment to their workers. Firms treated wages and benefits as a "quasi-fixed" cost over the long term of the employment relationship. Young workers accepted relatively low pay, even during good times, because they expected to earn much more later in life. In today's highly indebted firm, the need to meet fixed interest payments effectively forces managers to treat labor costs as variable. Accordingly, managers must reconfigure their workforce to maximize the ability to take on or let go workers with ease and with minimal expense. Often this reorganization involves getting rid of middle-aged male employees. More generally, it involves extensive use of overtime hours and temporary services instead of hiring new workers. Small wonder, then, that middle-aged males and others have a hard time finding new jobs when their old ones are cut.

WHITE COLLARS PROVIDE LITTLE PROTECTION

While the initial rounds of job loss occurred among blue-collar workers in the goods-producing industries, the reaper has more recently been spotted clearing a path through white-collar workers across sectors. The Bureau of Labor Statistics reports that between 1981 and 1986, more than 780,000 managers and professionals lost their jobs to plant closings and permanent layoffs. Additionally, the largest increase in the number of displaced workers reported in the Bureau's 1994 survey was among managers and professionals and technical, sales, and administrative support workers.[21]

The blight appears to be spreading. In earlier survey years, non-manufacturing-sector workers typically found reemployment opportunities with relative ease and often obtained new jobs similar in pay to the jobs they lost. Those tendencies have disappeared. Among displaced workers from service-industry jobs, reemployment declined from 80 percent in 1990 to 66 percent in 1992.

THE BLEAK FUTURE OF THE YOUNGER WORKER

It is true that the younger worker probably got to keep his or her job. But at what cost? During the period between 1963 and 1973, the proportion of new employment paying middle-level earnings was 78 percent. By the period ended 1986, the percentage plummeted to 26 percent.[22] Younger workers are also financially responsible for more of their health care costs and retirement investment. Many employees at large- and medium-sized establishments were once covered by health insurance plans funded entirely by employers. From 1980 to 1993 the fraction so covered dropped from 72 percent to 32 percent.

Younger workers face a growing disparity between the wages paid to those at the bottom of the scale and the wages paid to those at the top. One result of this growing disparity is the virtual disappearance of jobs near the middle of the male distribution.[23] Moreover, through the 1970s and 1980s the average real hourly wage of a production worker actually fell about 0.4 percent a year.[24]

The future of the young uneducated worker looks particularly bleak. Jobs that typically require less than a college education exist mainly in the goods-producing sector, which happens to be the one that took on the most debt during the 1980s. It is no coincidence that it also has had the largest drop in real wages. Furthermore, these are the very jobs that are disappearing altogether, thereby greatly limiting the realistic career choices for non–college graduates entering the workforce.

Not that life is easy for the more-educated worker. This worker's plight is revealed in a recent study of New England families from 1989 to 1994. The study found a drop in real family income even for families headed by someone with a postgraduate education. It also found that couples earning more than $80,000 per year worked an average total of 90 hours per week. Paul Harrington, who worked on the study, sums it up: "They are doing better by working like crazy."

Younger workers are less likely to be covered by pension plans in the employment setting. Adding to this general decline in pension coverage is the trend among employers to offer defined contribution plans, as opposed to the more traditional defined benefit plans common among older workers. The benefits ultimately paid under a defined contribution plan depend on the yield of the plan's investment. Thus, they cannot be predicted with great accuracy over the long term. Defined benefit plans, on the other hand, guarantee a certain benefit amount to the worker upon retirement. Employers offering defined contribution plans typically require workers to contribute to the plan and often leave the choice to participate up to the employee.

Among full-time employees at medium and large private establishments, the percentage covered by defined benefit pension plans fell from 84 percent in 1980 to 56 percent in 1993.[25] The percentage covered by employer-provided defined contribution plans has also fallen since 1986. Declines have been most pronounced among younger workers, particularly males under age thirty-five. The long-term ramifications of this change in pension coverage are distressing.

The provision of a pension by an employer can be viewed as a commitment to a long-term employment relationship. Technically there is an amortization of wages over the length of the relationship, and an agreement on the part of the employee to defer some wage benefit to the future. The movement away from pension provision by employers is an indication of an unwillingness to commit to the employment relationship. This reluctance is consistent with the indebted firm's aforementioned need for flexibility. The economic retirement needs of the workers without pension benefits will be excessive — forcing these generations of retirees either to continue working after retirement age or to depend heavily on Social Security and other governmental benefits in order to survive.

All this assumes that our young worker has found a job already. Easier said than done. Although the number of young people competing for jobs has declined since the late 1970s, the number of new jobs advertised has declined even more. In November 1993, two and a half years into a business upturn, fewer want ads appeared in U.S. newspapers than at the depth of the 1980 recession. Later we consider some reasons why the Indebted Society has effectively ignored the need for new jobs.

WOMEN IN THE WORKFORCE — THE GOOD NEWS AND THE BAD NEWS

The period from the 1970s to the present witnessed a dramatic increase of women in the workforce. There was some good news for women workers in the 1980s. During the downsizing and reorganizations of that decade, in which males joined the unemployment lines in large numbers, most women managed to hang on to their jobs. (We realize this provides no comfort to those who didn't.) One explanation for this "good luck" is that women workers tend to be concentrated in the service-producing industries. As noted, those industries suffered fewer layoffs and firm closings than the goods-producing industries in which male workers are concentrated. Another explanation is that women tend to have lower wages than men in comparable jobs. For this reason, managers under pressure to cut costs are more likely to terminate men.

There was additional good news for women workers since 1970. While male wages stagnated, or even fell, the wages of women workers went up. This increase is attributable, at least in part, to the rise in the number of hours worked by women and the rise in the experience and educational levels of women over this time span. However, even within educational categories, women did better than men. College-educated women in particular earn considerably more now than their 1970s' counterparts. Since women were paid less than men to begin with, there was "more room" for women's wages to go up. In the 1980s competitive pressures finally forced some narrowing of the wage gap.

The bad news, as far as wages are concerned, is that the gap still exists. Women continue to be paid less than men for comparable work. Women also continue to congregate in the service industries in less-than-managerial positions. While male workers in manufacturing reaped the fruits of union membership during the 1960s and 1970s and continue to benefit somewhat from the lingering effects of unionization, women were never invited aboard that train in great numbers.

More recent developments find women quickly joining men in the downward slide of wage stagnation and job insecurity as the number of permanent layoffs in the service sector increase. Displaced women workers are less likely to find another job than their male counterparts. Women workers are less likely to be covered by an employer-provided health insurance plan or pension program. While the percentage of women earning wages above $40,000 per year increased dramatically, the total number of such fortunate females amounted to a meager 0.9 percent by 1986.[26]

Who Is to Blame?

From our account thus far, it would appear that greedy stockholders and Scrooge-like managers are solely responsible for the decline in the status of the American worker. But to stop our inquiry with these two culprits would leave us with less than half the answer. In order to come to any meaningful conclusions and to see the full picture, it is necessary to examine who or what it is that lends the money to corporations, individuals, and governments. Who are the lenders waiting impatiently for the interest check that is draining the lifeblood from America's industries and her workers? How does the presence of a large body of lenders change the way society functions?

6 · The Lenders

"NEITHER A BORROWER NOR A LENDER BE." Most readers recognize this admonition. Some may even endeavor to follow its proscriptions. Yet, in the aftermath of the debt explosions in the private, corporate, and government sectors, few Americans can honestly claim to be neither. More than would care to admit it are likely both.

So far, this book has concerned itself mostly with borrowers. Corporate borrowers treat their workers badly. Consumer borrowers and tax-cutting government borrowers divert resources away from investment. We have much more to say about borrowers. For now, however, we shift our focus to lenders. In the days before our society went into debt, lenders were not particularly important. In the Indebted Society, lenders are a major force. Yet as citizens of that society, we have little sense of either where this force resides or what effects it has.

IMAGES OF LENDERS

The word "lenders" conjures up different images for different people. Some may see Shylock extracting his pound of flesh or the nineteenth-century banker walking grandly down the avenue with his top hat and vest-pocket watch. Others may see the friendly, modestly dressed loan officer from the bank down the street. These images represent "retail lenders" — that is, those whom borrowers approach directly to obtain loans. In some sense, however, these so-called lenders are only intermediaries in the lending process. The traditional commercial bank, for example, conveys funds from depositors to borrowers but does not generate those funds from within itself. Moreover, this traditional form of intermediation through retail lenders represents only one segment of the overall loan market.

A focus on those who supply funds, rather than those who distribute them, produces a different perspective on the process and a different set of images. Many of these fund suppliers, for example, lend directly by buying bonds. In its traditional form, a bond represents a loan from the bondholder to the bond issuer, who makes interest payments at regular intervals as the holder redeems the attached coupons. Thus, thinking of lenders from this perspective, some imagine the barber's wife clipping coupons or Uncle Joe bragging at the holiday dinner table about the killing he made in the bond market.

One may also think about people who are less directly involved in the lending process but who nonetheless derive much of their income from interest on loans. Our society has developed a set of sympathetic images for these people, images far removed from Shylock and the top-hatted banker. There is, for example, the bereaved widow in her black dress, and the weeping orphans who must live off the interest on father's life insurance settlement. There is the feeble old man who walks with the assistance of a cane and receives a modest but adequate fixed income from his pension or annuity. Although the pension or annuity is not itself a loan, it is supported by the interest on bonds owned by the pension fund or annuity provider. The widow, the orphans, the feeble old man — these are not images typically associated with the word "lender," but they often come to the forefront when the political interests of lenders are threatened.

A less sentimental individual may find some less sympathetic images for those who receive interest income. Bear in mind that most interest income goes to those whose overall income (including interest) is above average. Bear in mind also that a majority of elderly Americans have Social Security — not pensions or annuities — as their main source of income. A more representative image for interest earners may be that of a retired business magnate playing golf with his financial adviser. Given the tremendous importance of institutions in today's financial marketplace, we may also suggest the image of a power-suited young bond trader staring at a Quotron with cold ambition and scheming to bilk the U.S. Treasury out of one sixty-fourth of one percent of $10 billion.

The reality, of course, is more complex than any of these images. To discover who the lenders really are, we must examine the process of lending in contemporary America.

The Lending Process

The ballooning of debt has several anomalous results. New and more "creative" financing arrangements emerge. A market for the distribution of bonds develops. Investment funds are pooled. Bets are taken on the market's performance. Through these developments, a huge engine of debt financing, refinancing, and speculation runs with the same intensity and metaphorical power as the machines that marked the advent of the Industrial Revolution. The soot of the coal furnaces that filled the air in the eighteenth century is replaced by a spiraling cloud of paranoia of those with money to lose in the marketplace of the late twentieth century. This paranoia sets the rules of the investment game, and its repercussions are felt as shock waves throughout the entire society. Yet, naming or controlling this devilish power eludes us.

The easily identifiable top-hatted banker, the barber's wife with her scissors, or Uncle Joe is replaced by layers of investment consultants, financial analysts, mutual fund managers, pension fund administrators, portfolio strategists, hedge fund operators, and a shrinking group of individual investors. Under these layers we may find our maligned financier, and much to our surprise, the enemy could well turn out to be someone we know very well. In one way or another, at one level of the financial hierarchy or another, many of us are both borrowers and lenders.

To better understand the process, let us first return to the obvious "lenders" — the banks. In this context, when we say "banks," we mean commercial banks — institutions whose business, in theory, is to take deposits from the public and to make loans from those deposits. (Investment banks play a very different role in the lending process.) Also, when we say "banks," we can for practical purposes include savings and loan associations, finance companies, and various other institutions whose lending function is similar to that of commercial banks.

Commercial Banks

Although commercial banks are the most obvious example of lenders, their position in the world of lending is a complex one. As noted earlier, they do not primarily lend their own money. By taking deposits, banks are, in effect, borrowing money from depositors; so a bank is a borrower as well as a lender. Today banks do much of their borrowing not from depositors but from international investors, through repurchase agreements, Eurodollars, and the like. Much of their lending is only temporary. After a bank originates a set of loans, it often sells them off to investors or to an agency that packages loans for resale. Thus, private borrowers find themselves owing money to Fannie Mae, Sallie Mae, Nellie Mae, or Freddie Mac. These agencies, in turn, issue securities that represent an interest in a package of loans. The banks themselves become more like storefronts. Borrowing money from a bank is often like buying milk in a grocery store: the store does the selling, but the milk comes from somewhere else entirely.

Nonetheless, banks do keep some loans on their books. Banks still hold some deposits that are due on demand. And even when banks borrow in financial markets, they usually do so on a short-term basis. Their loans, on the other hand, are often more long term. To the extent that commercial banks function in this traditional role, their business is to convert short-term loans into long-term loans. That is, they borrow money today, lend it out for a period of years, and hope that they can borrow more money tomorrow to replace it while they are waiting to be repaid. When a bank lends out money at a fixed long-term interest rate, it is speculating that short-term interest rates will stay low enough to make the loan profitable.

Increasingly, the role of commercial banks has begun to blur with that of other speculators and investors. Interest rate swaps, bond futures contracts, and other "financial derivatives" enable all types of players in the financial markets to assume the risk and reward that come from the spread between short-term and long-term interest rates. Meanwhile, bank trading departments participate more and more aggressively in the derivatives markets. A commercial bank may, for example, sell off its normal financial risk and then use a currency swap or some such exotic vehicle to speculate on the value of the yen. Outside observers (including bank regulators) have a hard time keeping track of who owns what.

Given the complexities of today's commercial banking business, we cannot really say who the ultimate lenders behind the bank lending process are. What we can say is that commercial banks do typically hold a big stake in the process and that they are well aware of both their own stake and their role in the front lines of the lending process. The top hat and pocket watch are gone, but the banker is still around.

Individual Investors

The second obvious group of lenders in the Indebted Society is individuals who lend money. Individuals have the opportunity to act directly as lenders by buying bonds. The direct participation of U.S. households in the bond market has fluctuated over the past twenty years. In 1976, for example, households composed 21 percent of the total of bondholders. This percentage fell to 7.2 percent in 1983 and rose to 12.1 percent by the end of 1987. The current trend is for household involvement in direct lending through bond purchase to fluctuate downward.

Several factors can explain the decline in the percentage of households participating in bond markets. The most relevant is the enormous increase in the participation of organized forces in the market, such as pension and mutual funds. The concentration of bond buying in managed funds partly reflects the growth of the bond market itself over the past twenty years. With so many bonds available, the bond-buying game seems to have become too complex to warrant the direct attention of most individuals. This expanded market share of funds also coincides with an increased concern with pension planning as the population ages. Because they are perceived as a stable source of income, and because many pension plans still promise fixed payments such as those provided by bonds, bonds are a staple asset for pension plans.

Despite the decrease in the percentage of households directly investing in the bond market, the number of individuals depending upon income produced by interest-bearing corporate and government bonds has grown enormously over the past twenty years. This increase partly reflects the growing proportion of the population that now collects at least a portion of its annual income from pension plans. During the period from 1950 to 1975, the percentage of workers covered by pension plans managed by or partially subsidized by their employers rose from 26 percent to 52 percent of the full-time private wage and salary labor force. The coverage rate for younger workers has slipped since 1975, but increasing numbers of covered individuals have been reaching retirement age. By the year 2017 the proportion of retirees in the general population is projected to grow from 12 percent to 20 percent. If pension planners continue to perceive bonds as a stable source of retirement income, the percentage of the population receiving income indirectly from bonds is therefore likely to continue growing.

Despite the increased fraction of the population receiving income indirectly from interest-bearing assets, the distribution of interest and other capital income (income from investments rather than from work) is still heavily skewed toward the rich. The top 20 percent of the families in the United States receives a much larger percentage of its income from capital returns than the remaining 80 percent of families. Income from investment constitutes nearly half the income of the top 1 percent of families.

Now and Future Lenders

The value of the market created by pension funds has experienced phenomenal growth since 1970. Though not all the money in pension funds is invested in bonds, the historical perception of the bond market as a safe haven for investment dollars makes it attractive to fund managers and future retirees — so attractive that pension funds now hold 27 percent of the total outstanding corporate bonds.

From 1975 to 1987 pension plan assets in the United States increased by an astounding 445 percent. The assets of pension funds are invested in a variety of financial markets, including the bond market. Direct pension fund holdings in corporate and foreign bonds increased from $6 billion (in 1987 dollars) in 1950 to more than $464 billion in 1987. It is apparent from these statistics that the livelihood of current retirees and the future expectations of today's workers are more closely tied to the burgeoning debt market than most are aware and some are willing to admit.

Financial Wizards

Mutual funds are not new to the financial marketplace. The first mutual fund in the United States was organized in 1924. What *is* new is the rapid growth both in the absolute number of funds and in the size and distribution of fund assets. These assets currently total $1.6 trillion, with bond funds accounting for $510 billion of the total. The number of bond funds increased from 8 in 1972 to 1,662 in 1992. Through these funds, large groups of individuals and institutions pool their money to invest in large portfolios of bonds.

This increase illustrates both the astounding growth of bond mutual funds and their potential for influence. The number of equity funds — those that invest in stocks — increased from 463 to 1,432 during the same period. As one observer has noted, "There are more mutual funds investing in stocks, for example, than there are underlying stocks to invest in."[27] The increase in bond mutual funds is all the more striking because, unlike stocks, bonds are by their nature not very different from one another. A bond issued by an auto company pays the same kind of interest as a bond issued by a food company. The argument for pooling assets to provide a diverse portfolio is one that applies mostly to stocks. While the explosion of stock mutual funds has been extreme, the explosion of bond mutual funds has been even greater.

Mutual funds allow individual investors to diversify holdings in equities and bonds while controlling risk and minimizing overhead expenses. Fund managers devote 100 percent of their time to the investments under their control, as opposed to pension fund managers, who must often divide their time between the investments and administrative tasks. And mutual fund managers are under enormous pressure to add value to the returns generally obtained in the markets in which they work. In other words, the managers are expected to turn a profit on the profit in the case of equities or to avoid a loss in the case of bonds. A brief look at one of the largest mutual funds in the United States is illustrative of the magnitude and importance of these distinctions.

Fidelity Investments, headquartered in Boston, Massachusetts, reportedly controls at least $300 billion in total mutual funds. The total value of Fidelity's mutual funds tripled in the 1990s, and Fidelity owns large shares of an array of U.S. corporations, including American Express Co., Motorola, and International Business Machines. Even though Fidelity's bond funds hold a diverse portfolio of bonds, their sheer size sometimes allows them to hold large portions of the outstanding bonds of individual firms. For this reason, Fidelity has been able to exert control in reorganization decisions of companies, such as Macy's, in which it was a major debt holder. In addition, Fidelity holds the largest market share of employer-sponsored 401(k) plans and other similar retirement plans. Its accounts include such giants as AT&T and General Motors. Fidelity boasts that during the first eight months of 1995, seventy cents of every dollar of customer money received came from retirement accounts.[28] It is not surprising to discover that the owner of Fidelity, Edward C. Johnson III, is the fourth-wealthiest man in the United States.

Investment Banks

No discussion of the lending process would be complete without mentioning the role of investment banks. Unlike commercial banks, investment banks do not take deposits from the public. Investment banks are not really in business to lend money, although providing temporary financing is part of their operation. Their primary purpose is to find buyers for stocks and bonds. A corporation may borrow money by issuing bonds, and generally those bonds are issued through an investment bank. Thus, while an investment bank is not itself primarily a lender, it is often in the business of selling debt.

During the 1980s investment banks were notoriously aggressive in promoting the use of debt. Investment banking firms like Kohlberg Kravis Roberts were instrumental in making corporations aware of the tax advantages of debt and in convincing the public that high-yielding debt securities did not pose a serious risk of default.

Despite the debt-mongering role taken on by many investment banks during the 1980s, it would be a mistake to think that the investment banking community was united in the belief that debt is good. Some of the most strident warnings about the dangers of debt came from one Henry Kaufman — nicknamed Dr. Doom — who spent most of the eighties as the chief economist at the investment banking firm of Salomon Brothers. A central focus of Kaufman's warnings was that debt poses a major risk to the stability of the financial system.

7 ▪ Financial Stability

I N THE CONVENTIONAL ECONOMIC LITERATURE, the most frequently cited problem with high debt levels is the risk of financial instability. Commentators often picture an indebted society as a house of cards. A slight disturbance to just one of the cards causes the whole setup to topple.

The idea that debt can threaten financial stability is an old one. History provides many examples of financial structures that have collapsed because of debt problems. For this reason, and because debt has always been present, the United States and other nations have developed institutions to deal with potential financial instability. These institutions have met with varying success and have evolved over time. They have often played an important role in society beyond merely protecting against instability.

DOMINOES

D ebt threatens financial stability largely because many creditors are also debtors. Banks are the most common example. A bank is in business to lend money, but it also owes money to its depositors. Many of these depositors themselves owe money, often to other banks.

Banks and depositors are not the only creditors that are debtors. An indebted corporation may owe its bondholders but extend trade credit to its customers. The federal government borrows heavily to fund its budget deficit, yet at the same time makes loans to citizens through various programs. State and local governments often do likewise. Many individuals who owe money on home mortgages also own bonds, signifying that somebody owes them money.

The dual identity of debtors and creditors can create problems when one debtor is unable to make payments. The missed payments may induce a shortage of cash for that debtor's creditor. If the creditor is also a debtor, then the creditor may be unable to make payments on its own debts. The creditor's creditor may then face a cash shortage and be unable to make debt payments. Thus, if many creditor/debtors are operating with limited cushions of cash, one debtor's default can topple a whole string of creditor/debtors like a line of dominoes.

Creditors and debtors can also affect one another indirectly. For example, as we discussed in chapter 4, firms that are heavily in debt are more likely to trim employment when their product markets weaken. Laid-off employees may then default on loans. They will almost certainly curtail their spending. Consequently, other product markets tend to weaken. If these other producers are also heavily in debt, they are similarly likely to trim employment, and so on.

Another example of indirect debtor/creditor effects is the behavior of asset markets such as stocks and real estate. If a debtor is strapped for cash, the debtor may sell assets. If many debtors do so, the value of the assets falls, as it always does when many are trying to sell and few are trying to buy. Reduced asset values have two effects. First, other debtors that need money are not able to raise as much cash by selling assets as they otherwise could. Therefore, they are more likely to default. Second, creditors who have lent against assets see a reduction in collateral values. Often, this induces them to call in loans early, thus forcing their debtors to sell more assets or to call in their own loans (if they are also creditors).

Finally, there is the confidence effect, which can appear primarily in the banking business. Banks usually have commitments to provide cash on demand to depositors. However, at any particular time, they have only a fraction of their total demand deposits available to pay out immediately. Ordinarily, this is not a problem, because depositors do not come all at once asking for their money. However, if depositors begin to question the bank's ability to pay, they may arrive in large numbers to withdraw their money before the bank runs out. This of course strains, and perhaps exhausts, the bank's cash reserves. The belief that a bank is unable to pay can thus become a self-fulfilling prophecy. Weak financial conditions in the overall economy weaken people's confidence in banks and tend to increase the chance of such bank runs.

Through all these channels, high debt levels create the potential for chain reactions. In an economy without the necessary safeguards, the system of debt, credit, and economic activity can therefore resemble a complex arrangement of dominoes, which topples when one critical domino falls over.

PROPPING UP THE DOMINOES

The U.S. economy has many safeguards. Small deposits in banks and thrift institutions are protected by deposit insurance. Workers are protected — up to a point — by unemployment insurance and other income-replacement programs. Incomes in general receive a measure of protection from a progressive tax system that reduces its demands when incomes decline. Highly developed financial markets make it relatively easy for a cash-strapped but fundamentally sound bank or corporation to borrow from those that have excess cash. Regulations limit borrowing against volatile collateral such as common stock. Most important, the United States has a lender-of-last-resort with an effectively unlimited ability to make cash available during times of crisis. The Federal Reserve System, unlike private banks, firms, individuals, or even the U.S. Treasury, can create large quantities of money from thin air.[29]

The Federal Reserve System was primarily created for the purpose of protecting financial stability. Before the founding of the Fed in 1914, the United States frequently experienced banking panics in which widespread runs by depositors could bring the entire banking system to a temporary halt. These panics were typically followed by economic depressions. The creation of the Fed was motivated largely by the need to prevent and assuage such panics.

According to its charter, the Fed was originally established to provide "an elastic currency" and to accommodate "the needs of business and industry." It consists of a national Board of Governors and a nationwide network of "Reserve Banks" that can make loans to banks (and purchase government securities, which ultimately has become a more important activity) with newly created money. The governors were appointed for ten-year terms (later lengthened to fourteen) by the president of the United States and had limited control over the Reserve Banks. Those Reserve Banks are "owned" and partly controlled by their "member banks" — private commercial banks. By changing the supply of money relative to the demand, the Fed is able (although it did not at first seem entirely aware of this power) to control interest rates.

Two factors limited the Fed's effectiveness as a lender-of-last-resort in its early years. First, its policies were constrained by an excessive concern with maintaining U.S. gold reserves to support the national gold standard. Although gold reserves remained plentiful, the Fed found it necessary to push up interest rates whenever reserves began to flow out at a significant rate. (The higher interest rates would encourage people to keep money in the bank rather than demanding gold, which paid no interest.) Second, many Fed officials lacked a sophisticated knowledge of how the U.S. financial and economic system worked. As a result, the Fed failed its first major test. During the years following the 1929 stock market crash, the Fed allowed many banks to fail and did not replenish the contracting money supply. Largely because the Fed failed to respond appropriately, the economic depression that began in 1929 became by far the worst in history, for the United States and for much of the world.

The Fed learned its lesson. Since 1933, although the Fed has sometimes played a game of brinkmanship, it has never seriously shirked its responsibility to maintain financial stability. When push comes to shove, the Fed has always been willing to provide the money necessary to avoid a major nationwide (or worldwide) financial disaster. This willingness is partly because the gold standard no longer constrains the Fed. Although the United States did not abandon the gold standard entirely until 1971, President Roosevelt (and Congress) reduced its force in 1933 by devaluing the dollar and prohibiting Americans from buying and selling gold bullion. Moreover, international cooperation after World War II made the gold standard easier to maintain in conjunction with an independent monetary policy. For the most part, however, the Fed's willingness to play an active role in preserving financial stability probably stems from an increased level of economic and financial sophistication and an increased sense of responsibility for the United States and the world economy.

THE PUNCH BOWL

In fact, the Fed's sense of responsibility now extends far beyond the need to preserve financial stability. The Employment Act of 1946 mandated that the Fed seek "to promote maximum employment, production, and purchasing power." The Humphrey-Hawkins Act of 1978 presented the Fed with specific unemployment and inflation targets. Although the Fed quickly dismissed the Humphrey-Hawkins targets as unrealistic, it has been quite cognizant of its responsibility to minimize inflation and unemployment.

However, Fed economists regard minimizing unemployment as a lost cause. Less unemployment now, they believe, leads either to more unemployment later or to a permanent increase in the inflation rate. This conclusion comes from the widely accepted "natural rate theory," which is discussed in detail in chapter 8. The Fed considers most alternative theories to be temptations from Satan. To be moral, Fed officials seem to believe, a theory must imply strict limits on economic growth.

William McChesney Martin, who was chairman from 1951 to 1970, described the Fed's function through a metaphor with distinctly moral overtones. The Fed's job, he said, is to take the punch bowl away before the party gets too wild. In other words, the Fed should stop the expansion of money and credit before businesspeople and workers get confident enough to start raising prices and wages excessively.

If the Fed's primary role is to preserve financial stability and to fight inflation, how are these functions affected by high debt levels? Economist Benjamin Friedman (not to be confused with Milton Friedman) suggests that high debt levels weaken the Fed's inflation-fighting resolve. Since high debt levels make the system more unstable, they first raise the risk of a depression. The Fed therefore is more concerned with preventing that depression than with fighting inflation. In other words, the Fed is afraid to take away the punch bowl because it might knock over some dominoes in the process.

WATERING THE PUNCH

Although Benjamin Friedman's analysis is a major advance over the simplistic "debt leads to financial collapse" view, we believe there is more to the story. In the end, we draw the opposite conclusion. High debt levels certainly make the Fed more cautious about policies that can cause a severe economic downturn. The question is, which policies ultimately cause a severe downturn? A look at the postwar record shows that such severe downturns occurred only in *reaction* to high inflation rates.[30] Since World War II the Fed has a nearly perfect record at preventing such severe recessions — except when it was deliberately trying to reduce an already high inflation rate.

Think about that. Inflation, indirectly, is what *causes* severe recessions. Specifically, inflation causes the Fed to precipitate those recessions in order to bring the inflation rate back down. The Fed is well aware of what its own likely response will be when the inflation rate gets too high. Therefore, if the Fed wants to prevent a severe economic downturn, it does so by preventing inflation from getting too high in the first place.

We liken the position of the Fed in a high-debt economy to that of a driver without a seat belt. Just as the driver knows that slamming on the brakes may cause him or her to go through the windshield, the Fed knows that sharply tightening the money supply may cause a financial crisis. Does the driver go too fast because he or she is scared to use the brakes? Of course not. The way to prevent having to slam on the brakes is to drive slowly. Similarly, the way to prevent having to tighten the money supply sharply is to keep it from expanding too fast in the first place. Therefore, in an economy with high debt levels, where the Fed's perceived risk of financial crisis is high, the Fed follows a *disinflationary* policy whenever a financial crisis does not seem immediately imminent. In terms of the traditional punch bowl metaphor, if the Fed is afraid to take away the punch bowl, it instead waters down the punch.

In the Fed's worst nightmares, it faces a choice between high inflation and financial collapse. During normal circumstances, the Fed steers away from that danger point by pulling down the inflation rate. When the danger of high inflation is remote, the Fed is quite comfortable averting financial collapse. A case in point is the 1987 stock market crash. Because of the huge oil price decline in 1986, inflation was not a major worry in 1987. When the stock market crashed in October, some prognosticators foresaw another Great Depression. The Fed — and the rest of the world's central banks — calmly pumped a lot of extra money into the system, and there was no depression at all. Inflation rates rose a little bit, but it was not a major problem, because the inflation rate was low to begin with. In our view, the Fed's long-run policy in a high-debt economy is to pursue lower and lower inflation rates that let it react to such financial crises with increasing comfort.

The experience of the 1990s supports our view. In the first year of the decade, consumer prices rose by 6.1 percent. (Excluding energy prices, which were distorted by Iraq's invasion of Kuwait, the increase was 5.4 percent.) During each of the four succeeding years, the inflation rate fell. In 1994 consumer prices rose by only 2.7 percent. (Excluding energy prices, the increase was 2.6 percent, the lowest in twenty-nine years.) Alan Greenspan, the Republican Fed chairman, showed a commendable lack of partisanship by following slow-job-growth policies that cost George Bush the presidency. The Fed did not intentionally cause the 1991 recession, but it did promote a very slow recovery. During the recovery the inflation rate continued to fall. Somebody forgot to add the rum!

LOOKING AT THE WRONG NUMBERS

Under present circumstances, the Fed's disinflationary bias is exacerbated by its fixation on the unemployment rate.[31] In principle, you want a labor market variable that indicates conditions foreshadowing faster wage-and-price increases. The unemployment rate is not really the most reasonable candidate. (The unemployment rate is equal to the number of people looking for jobs divided by the number of people who are looking for jobs plus those who already have jobs.) A better variable would be the job vacancy rate.[32]

Think about it. It's easy to imagine a manager saying, "We've got to raise wages, so we can fill some of these vacancies." It's much harder to imagine him or her saying, "Even though we have no positions open, we are going to raise wages anyway, because nobody is looking for a job." Conversely, imagine a situation where many people are unemployed, but none have the skills that employers want. In that case, the vacancy rate is high, and there is upward pressure on wages, despite high unemployment. Common sense strongly favors the vacancy rate over the unemployment rate as a measure of potential wage pressures.

Unfortunately, the United States does not collect data on job vacancies. A number of economists, including Nobel laureate James Tobin, have decried this oversight. With the federal government in a downsizing mode, however, no remedy appears likely. It is truly unfortunate that the world's largest economy, the one whose policies affect every other nation in the world, has neglected to collect the one statistic that could be most useful for setting those policies.

One nation that does collect job vacancy data is the United Kingdom. The British vacancy rate turns out to be an excellent predictor of changes in the British inflation rate. In fact, once we take into account the vacancy rate, the British unemployment rate becomes useless as an inflation predictor. Evidence from other nations is difficult to interpret, for various reasons, but in general it does not contradict the theory that vacancies are more important than unemployment as a predictor of inflation.[33]

Although the United States has no job vacancy data, it does have a piece of data that provides a reasonably good proxy for job vacancies. The Conference Board, a nonprofit business organization based in New York, takes a monthly survey of the nation's major newspapers in which it tracks the number of help-wanted ads. From this information, it constructs the Help Wanted Index (see endnote 3). In a paper published in 1977, Martin Neil Baily and James Tobin used the Help Wanted Index as a proxy for job vacancies. Since then it has been used by a number of researchers, including us and Bureau of Labor Statistics Commissioner Katharine Abraham. To correct for the increasing size of the overall economy, it has become common practice to "normalize" the Help Wanted Index by dividing it by an index of payroll employment. The Normalized Help Wanted Index does indeed appear to be a better predictor of inflation than the unemployment rate. Figure 7.1 shows what the Normalized Help Wanted Index has done since 1988. It is truly striking that by 1994, a year when numerous economists and Wall Street commentators feared an "overheating" economy, the Normalized Help Wanted Index had barely made up a third of its 1988–92 drop.

Of course, the Fed has reasons for ignoring the Normalized Help Wanted Index. Fed economists argue that many vacancies are now filled by temporary employees who become permanent rather than by applicants who respond to ads, so that help-wanted advertising overstates the vacancy rate. This is undoubtedly true to some extent. Again, it would be nice if we had real vacancy data. But the Fed has a history of looking mostly at the data that support its own agenda. In the 1970s Chairman Arthur Burns ignored very *high* levels of help-wanted advertising. The help-wanted numbers, he argued, overstated

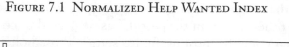

FIGURE 7.1 NORMALIZED HELP WANTED INDEX

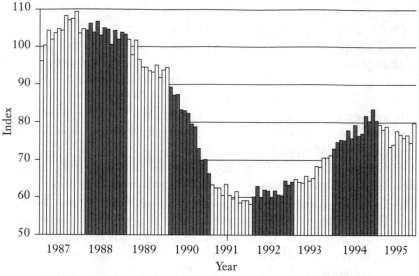

the vacancy rate, because the failures of many small newspapers had shifted more advertising to the major newspapers tracked by the Conference Board. In the 1990s, with a disinflationary agenda, Chairman Alan Greenspan has a new excuse to ignore very *low* levels of help-wanted advertising.[34]

ALAN WHO?

When Yankelovich Partners asked people in April 1994, "Do you happen to know who Alan Greenspan is?" only 29 percent of the respondents correctly identified Greenspan as chairman of the Federal Reserve System's Board of Governors. Another 13 percent said, "Yes," but gave an incorrect identification. And 58 percent responded, "No/Not sure." Thus, the head of one of our Indebted Society's key economic institutions was unknown to the vast majority of Americans. Therefore, his accountability was a nonstarter as a political issue. Moreover, his actions or inactions were relatively unaffected by public opinion. However, they were subject to approval or disapproval by members of the lender class who follow U.S. monetary policy. This anonymity appears most inconsistent with our claims of being a totally democratic society. Nevertheless, Alan Greenspan is not a household name.

Anonymity and secrecy have long been a hallmark of the Fed. Until 1994 it had a policy of keeping its decisions (not to mention its decision process) secret until several months after they were made. Financial markets were left to infer changes in Fed policy from changes in the economic variables it controlled (various measures of bank reserves and short-term interest rates). The theory, apparently, was that the Fed would be more effective if it could fool the markets for a while. In 1994, largely (rumor has it) due to the influence of the new Vice Chairman Alan Blinder, the Fed began to announce its decisions as soon as they were made. The Fed has come out of the closet on Wall Street, but not on Main Street.

The usual argument for keeping the Fed away from the public eye is that it must be insulated from politics. Political forces, it is argued, may push the Fed into easy money policies that produce inflation. To the untrained observer, however, it appears that political forces already had just that effect during the 1970s. Somehow, anonymity failed to shield the Fed from politics. (Fed insiders continue to insist otherwise. Admittedly, there was no "smoking gun" linking easy money to political pressures, but there was certainly "motive, means, and opportunity.") There is one crucial difference between the political pressures experienced by the Fed during the 1970s and those that are contemplated by advocates of anonymity. In the 1970s the Fed felt pressures from opportunistic politicians, not from the American people.

Nonetheless, it is compelling when advocates of an apolitical Fed point to the mess that politics has made of fiscal policy. If monetary policy becomes a political issue, they argue, some presidential candidate will get a crackpot economist to argue that easy money reduces inflation, just as Arthur Laffer argued that cutting taxes would raise revenues. Monetary policy will no longer be able to provide the one anchor that has prevented disaster during these years of record fiscal deficits.

It is not entirely clear to us whether monetary policy has prevented disaster or hastened it. Monetary policy has certainly kept inflation low, confounding the many economists who argued that high deficits and low inflation could not coexist. On the other hand, the deficits would not be such a problem if monetary policy had been looser.

From the very founding of our country, fiscal policy has been inherently political. "No taxation without representation!" was the rallying cry for those who made America a nation. We might have been better off with "No monetary policy without representation." If some unaccountable bureaucrat can control the government's purse strings, perhaps the government will not need to borrow money, and there will be more funds available for private investment. But if citizens consistently vote for easy money, real interest rates will remain low, further encouraging investment. As it is, politics gives us low taxes, which encourage overconsumption, while the government borrows. Meanwhile, an independent monetary authority believes that, out of duty, it must keep interest rates high and thereby discourage investment in the future.

Under the present system, this unfortunate interaction is hard to avoid. If the government plays the role of "good cop" with taxpayers, then the Fed is left to play "bad cop" with the nation's future. Concerns about financial stability, along with the influence of an increasingly important lender class, intensify the Fed's role as disciplinarian. In the end, a large national debt increasingly pushes the government into the "bad cop" role. The nation is forced to confess that it is not willing either to invest in its own future or to take care of its needier citizens. Chapter 9 explores in more detail the ways in which the national debt and continued borrowing have hobbled the government. To fully understand the government's situation, however, we must first look at the ways in which public policy — often implemented through the Fed rather than through the elected government — has come to serve the needs of lenders.

8 · The Political Economy of Lending

As most Americans are well aware, the past thirty years have seen a dramatic increase in debt levels. As many Americans may not be aware, those thirty years have also seen a dramatic shift in economic policies toward ones favoring lenders. We doubt this is a coincidence. It is inevitable that lenders become more important in a society where debt becomes more important. Therefore, it seems likely that lenders also become more powerful. When lenders become more powerful, they have more influence over policy; and the policies chosen naturally reflect that influence.

If the shift toward pro-lender policies is truly because of the increase in debt, then it may be the most important result. The reason pro-lender policies are so important is that, in addition to having effects of their own, they compound the other problems found in the Indebted Society. For example, high interest rates, which benefit lenders, increase the pressure on indebted firms to terminate middle-aged employees. High interest rates also increase the burden of government debt by making the required interest payments larger. Pro-lender policies designed to combat inflation place tight limits on resource utilization in the Indebted Society, so that government borrowing must take resources away from private investment. Through mechanisms like these, which we discuss later in more detail, pro-lender policies compound the problems of the Indebted Society in much the same way that alcohol compounds the effects of sleeping pills.

To investigate the relationship between lenders and economic policy in the Indebted Society, we begin by noting the increased importance of interest income — and, therefore, of lenders — in recent decades. Then we look at the likely political objectives of various lenders. With those likely objectives in mind, we examine extensively the lender-friendly ideas currently guiding economic policy and how the policies arising from those ideas harm other groups. We also consider ways in which the power of lenders over policy manifests itself in the Indebted Society. Finally, we take a look at the broader social effects of the lenders' nemesis, inflation.

The Importance of Lenders

In 1950 lenders were not an important group in the United States. Net interest made up only 1.3 percent of the national income, and interest made up only 4.2 percent of the income of individuals. Figures 8.1 and 8.2 show how that situation has changed. The importance of interest rose steadily throughout the 1950s, 1960s, and 1970s. By 1980 net interest accounted for 8.7 percent of the national income, and interest accounted for 12.4 percent of the income of individuals. Lenders had become an integral part of an increasingly indebted society.

FIGURE 8.1 NET INTEREST SHARE OF NATIONAL INCOME

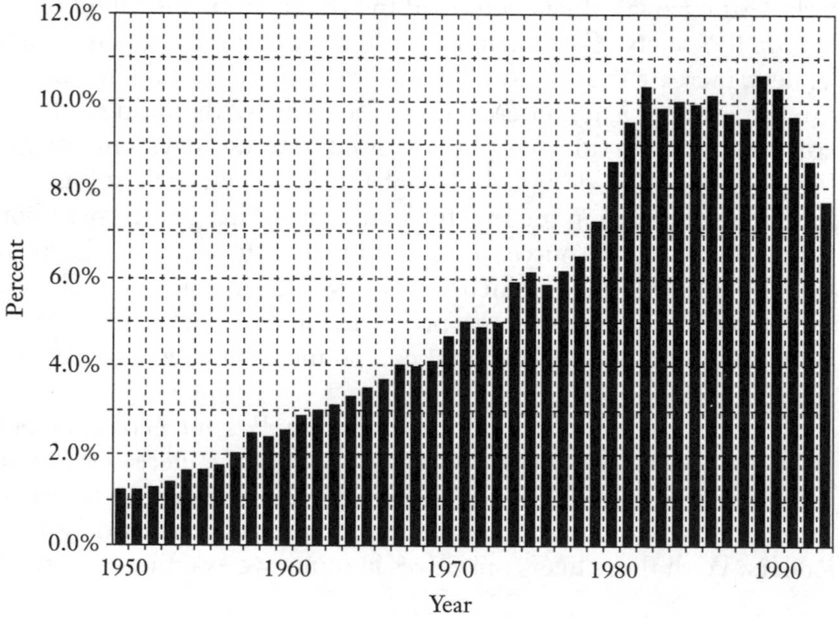

Year

Interest income increased in importance for two reasons. First, money lending increased faster than the nation's productive capacity. Second, interest rates rose, so that a given loan would produce more income. During the 1980s interest rates fell, but interest income continued to increase relative to total income. During the 1990s, nominal interest rates have fallen to levels seen in the mid- to late 1960s, but interest income, relative to total income, has remained above its 1979 level. Lenders continue to claim a significant share of the pie.

Given the changes documented in Figures 8.1 and 8.2, it should not be surprising that America in the 1980s and 1990s has functioned in ways that have tended to advance the interests of lenders. In the 1950s, 1960s, and early 1970s, the powers that be showed a callous disregard for the needs of lenders. In the 1980s and 1990s, the needs of lenders seem to have acquired an almost sacrosanct status. The particulars of this change occupy much of the rest of this chapter. While it is not always easy to find explicit links between the greater quantity of debt and the greater concern for lenders' needs, one can hardly doubt that a connection exists.[35]

FIGURE 8.2 INTEREST SHARE OF PERSONAL INCOME

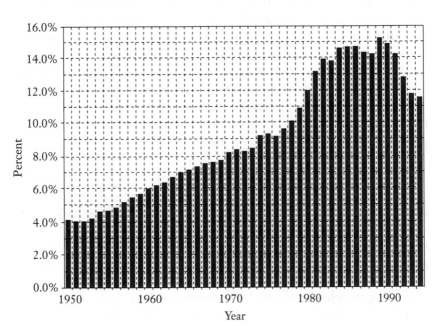

The Needs of Lenders

People who make their living by lending money have, in principle, two overriding concerns. First, they want to receive the highest interest rates they can. Second, they want to make sure that their money retains its purchasing power — which is to say, they want inflation to be as low as possible. To the extent that public policy fosters these two objectives, it is working to the benefit of lenders.

The sophisticated lender recognizes a precise trade-off between the two objectives. If the interest rate that a lender receives rises by the same amount as the inflation rate, then the lender is no better or worse off. The lender can simply set aside the additional interest and add it to his or her principal to maintain its purchasing power. This insight leads to the concept known to economists as the "real interest rate," which is equal to the nominal interest rate minus the expected rate of inflation. Thus, the lender's two objectives can be consolidated into one objective: to obtain the highest possible real interest rate.

The needs of lenders are a little more complicated, though, because not all lenders have the same needs. For example, short-term lenders and long-term lenders are quite different. In terms of the images discussed in chapter 6, the barber's wife is an example of a long-term lender. She keeps the same bond under lock and key for years running, and she clips the coupons regularly. Since she has lent long-term at a fixed interest rate, she need not care about changes in the market interest rate during the term of the bond. She will worry, however, about any possible surprise inflation.

At the other extreme is the short-term lender. Suppose, for example, that the mourning widow is afraid to tie up her insurance money in a long-term bond. She may then choose, in effect, to make short-term loans, perhaps by buying 90-day treasury bills or by putting her money in a money market fund. As a short-term lender, she needs to lend again when the first loan is repaid. (If she has a money market fund, the fund will automatically relend.) Once she has made the decision to be a short-term lender, she is concerned only about changes in the real interest rate, not about inflation per se. If the inflation rate and the nominal interest rate rise by the same amount, the widow can effectively relend on the same terms as before. If the real interest rate falls, she can relend only on less attractive terms.

A lender making a decision between short-term and long-term

lending has a difficult problem. If the lender lends long-term, he or she faces the risk of unanticipated inflation. If the lender lends short-term, he or she faces the risk of lower interest rates. This problem can be solved by making an inflation-adjusted long-term loan at a fixed interest rate. On such a loan, the principal automatically increases as the price level increases.[36] Take, for example, a $1,000 inflation-adjusted bond paying 10 percent interest. If the inflation rate were 5 percent during the first year, then the official principal value of the bond would rise to $1,050 at the end of the first year, and the interest payment for the second year would be $105 (10 percent of $1,050).[37] This process of principal-value and interest-payment readjustment continues throughout the life of the bond. Unfortunately, for reasons that are not clear, borrowers — in particular, the largest borrower, the U.S. government — seem unwilling to borrow on these terms.

Lenders can also switch back and forth between long-term and short-term lending, thereby creating another complication. A long-term lender — a bondholder — may anticipate selling his or her long-term bond to someone else before it is paid off. In terms of the images in chapter 6, Uncle Joe, before he made his killing in the bond market, must have fit this lender profile. (The power-suited bond trader is a more extreme example.) Bond prices depend inversely on interest rates.[38] Therefore, Uncle Joe, once he owns the bond, prefers low market interest rates to high ones. If the market interest rate goes down, Uncle Joe can sell the bond at a profit. If the rate goes up, he can't sell the bond without taking a loss. Such "back and forth" lenders are particularly vulnerable to inflation. For lenders like Uncle Joe or the young trader, inflation is a double whammy. On one hand, by pushing up nominal interest rates, inflation pushes down bond prices. On the other hand, since inflation doesn't affect real interest rates, it is no help when these lenders want to relend the proceeds from their bond sale.

It is important to realize that most people who are lenders can also choose not to be. Other investments — most notably, stocks of various kinds — are always available. Lenders may choose to lend because they have calculated rationally that the terms of a loan are advantageous. More likely, we suspect, they choose to lend because the fixed interest payments give them a false sense of security. Such lenders feel particularly outraged when they see that rising prices have reduced the purchasing power of their interest and principal. However, history suggests that rising prices are normal in a healthy economy. The U.S. economy, like most others, has seen periods of rising prices and periods of falling prices but very few periods when the price level remained stable. In general, the periods of falling prices have been depressions.

More important, perhaps, in a modern economy with a managed money supply, the fear of inflation can inhibit valuable monetary experimentation. Economists have a great deal of general knowledge about how to manage a national economy, but the specifics remain highly uncertain. We know that making "too much" money available by holding interest rates "too low" for "too long" causes inflation to accelerate. We know that making "too little" money available by holding interest rates "too high" for "too long" causes a recession (and causes inflation to slow down). We know that lower interest rates, if they don't produce inflation, encourage valuable private investment, which creates good jobs and raises productivity. We just don't know how much money is "too much" or "too little" and which interest rates are "too high" or "too low." Since the economy is constantly changing, it is unlikely that we shall ever get a definitive answer as to how much is "too much." If we insist on protecting lenders' false sense of security, however, we will invariably err on the side of "too little" money, "too high" real interest rates, and "too little" investment — and we shall never get any real answers.

Unfortunately, lenders' false sense of security has been encouraged by numerous professionals who ought to know better. Financial planners have continued to recommend fixed-income investments to retired people. (A fixed-income investor is essentially making a fixed-rate loan.) Businesses have continued to offer defined benefit retirement plans without cost-of-living adjustments. (The beneficiary of a defined benefit plan is essentially making a fixed-rate loan to the plan's sponsor.) Insurance companies have continued to offer fixed annuities (which are essentially the same as defined benefit retirement plans). In terms of overall risk and return, these lenders are not much worse off than they would be with better-constructed portfolios. For this reason, some economists have argued that the "bonds are safe" fallacy is not a very harmful one. These economists ignore the effects of this "lenders' neurosis" on the rest of society.

Granted, even nonlenders would generally like inflation to be low or zero, *all other things being equal*. The problem is that for lenders, usually, all other things *are* equal. For the rest of us, all other things are quite *un*equal. Lenders, who are usually retired or secure in their jobs, have little to lose from a recession. Lenders don't mind when interest rates are too high. The resulting shortfall in investment may harm the rest of us, but lenders are happy with the extra income. More middle-aged men may lose their jobs because of higher debt service payments, but the people who receive those payments lose nothing. To the extent that our society encourages fixed-rate lending, it encourages the creation of a large power group whose interests are very special.

THE IDEOLOGY OF LENDERS

The Politics of Economics

In our time, economists like to think of their field as a dispassionate science guided by logic and evidence. Looking at the history of the field, however, one finds politics to be an inescapable part. The classical economists Adam Smith and David Ricardo crusaded against government policies that protected the interests of aristocratic landowners while stifling those of the emerging capitalist class. Karl Marx, whom economists usually claim as one of their own, was certainly more concerned with politics than with economics. His theories were designed to support the interests of the working class against those of the capitalists.

In the end, the economic theories of Marx did fall victim to logic and evidence. The name of Marx was tarnished by the unsuccessful and sometimes inhuman policies of his followers. Nonetheless, Marx may have been right about the relationship between thought and politics. Marx's theories had a blatant political purpose, but he suggested that theories in general had political purposes, acknowledged or not. On this point, logic and evidence do not contradict him.

Twentieth-century economists have stumbled more than once because of their pretense to dispassion. The followers of John Maynard Keynes, who dominated the field during the 1950s and 1960s, fell in the 1970s largely because they had not acknowledged their political purpose. They claimed to be servants of truth. They claimed to have theories that would benefit everyone. In fact, the theories of Keynes were a political weapon against the lenders. Those theories justified a policy — government deficits supported by low real interest rates — that helped both workers and capitalists. That policy also risked inflation to an extent its boosters were loath to acknowledge. In the 1970s rampant inflation discredited the Keynesians.

With the battlefield clear and the old Keynesians in hiding, the lenders launched their army. Their general, who still commands today, goes by the name of NAIRU. The NAIRU — the "non-accelerating inflation rate of unemployment" (also known as the "natural rate of unemployment") — is the concept that forms the cornerstone of today's pro-lender theories. According to these theories, the unemployment rate must be kept above a certain magic number in order to prevent an accelerating spiral of inflation. That theory, known as the "natural rate theory," is now accepted as gospel by most economists.

How the Natural Rate Theory Helps Lenders

To see how this theory helps lenders and hurts everyone else, let's look at an example. Suppose you read in the paper that the U.S. unemployment rate had fallen from 6.0 percent to 5.6 percent. Do you consider that good news or bad news? If you are a worker, a property owner, a graduating student, a businessperson, or an incumbent politician, you most likely consider it good news. If you are a mainstream American economist, you consider it bad news. Six percent, contemporary tradition tells us, is the NAIRU. If the unemployment rate goes below 6 percent, the Fed — which by default controls U.S. macroeconomic policy — has overshot its mark. Unless they expect the dip in unemployment to reverse itself, the Fed's governors will find it necessary to raise interest rates.

In the unforgiving logic of the natural rate theory, an unemployment rate held below the natural rate is an invitation to disaster. Whatever the inflation rate is now, it will begin to accelerate and won't stop until unemployment is brought back to (or above) its natural rate. Five percent inflation. Ten percent. Twenty percent. Fifty percent. No rate of inflation is high enough to satisfy the requirements of a too-low unemployment rate.[39]

The critical implication of the natural rate theory is that changes in the unemployment rate are "temporary," whereas changes in the inflation rate are "permanent." Changes in the unemployment rate are literally temporary, because the unemployment rate eventually has to move back toward the NAIRU. For example, if the unemployment rate falls below the NAIRU, inflation continues accelerating as long as the unemployment rate remains so low. Unless the unemployment rate rises back to the NAIRU, the inflation rate eventually becomes so high that the economy can no longer function.

Changes in the inflation rate are "permanent" in the sense that (unlike changes in the unemployment rate), they do not normally reverse themselves. To reverse a change in inflation, policy makers must take deliberate action to push the unemployment rate away from the NAIRU. For example, if the rate of inflation rises from 2 percent to 4 percent, it will remain at 4 percent unless policy makers deliberately push the unemployment rate above the NAIRU and keep it there for a long time.

Thus, to natural rate believers, low unemployment has the character of a vain, earthly pleasure, and inflation has the character of eternal damnation. Inflation, even though the harm it causes at any one time may be small, is infinite in time. That is, the harm from inflation lasts forever (unless action is taken to reverse it). The total harm is infinite. Consequently, inflation must be the overriding concern of policy makers. Unemployment, although it may cause great harm during a certain year, is finite. The unemployment rate eventually moves back to the NAIRU. Therefore, any decline in unemployment below the NAIRU is of limited benefit, and any rise above the NAIRU is of limited cost. Consequently, unemployment should not concern policy makers.

Now, the natural rate theory may be true, or it may be false. Probably, like most economic theories, it is partly true and partly false and partly irrelevant. Whether or not it is true, however, the *theory* affects public policy because policy makers believe the theory and act on the basis of that belief. Since the theory implies that policy makers should concern themselves with inflation, its acceptance benefits those who care about inflation. In particular, then, it benefits lenders. Since the theory implies that policy makers should not concern themselves with unemployment, its acceptance is of little help to those who care about unemployment.

Suppose that the natural rate theory is false, but policy makers believe it. Who is hurt, and who is helped, if policy makers act on this belief? In this case, policy makers keep unemployment unnecessarily high to prevent inflation from accelerating. Workers who must suffer through unnecessary unemployment certainly are hurt. More generally, society is hurt because it has to give up what those workers would have produced. Lenders are helped. Because policy makers see inflation as a permanent risk, they do not allow it to rise, even temporarily. Thus, the purchasing power of lenders' interest receipts is protected. Moreover, since the vehicle used to keep unemployment high is a high real interest rate, lenders enjoy high returns.

Now, suppose the natural rate theory is true, but policy makers don't believe it. Who is hurt, and who is helped? In this case, policy makers keep unemployment low in the expectation that inflation will eventually stabilize. Primarily, lenders are hurt. As policy makers allow inflation to accelerate, lenders see their purchasing power evaporate. Using low real interest rates to stimulate the economy also gives lenders a low return to begin with. Workers, and society in general, are hurt very little, if at all. Wages and everything else rise with prices. When the inflation rate gets very high, policy makers may get fed up and cause a recession in order to get it back down. (Even if they don't believe in the natural rate theory, they may dislike very high inflation and may believe that a recession will cure it.) But the recession just balances out the earlier good times. During the recession many people are out of work. Before the recession, however, jobs were easy to find.

Thus the NAIRU, or natural rate, idea is one that clearly helps lenders, possibly at everyone else's expense. If the theory is true, it helps lenders tremendously but everyone else only marginally (if at all). If it is false but still used to guide policy, it helps lenders and hurts everyone else tremendously. In our view, the real importance of the theory is not in its truth or falsity, but in how its acceptance skews policy to the benefit of lenders. Nonetheless, we can ask whether the evidence suggests that it is true.

NAIRU vs. the Evidence

Surprisingly, given the wide acceptance of the natural rate theory, the evidence is questionable at best. Natural raters argue that an unemployment rate under 6 percent is cause for losing sleep over possible inflationary forces building in the economy. Yet, the unemployment rates in Europe, for example, in the period between 1959 and 1973 were exceedingly low by American standards. The rate in France averaged 2.3 percent. The rates in Germany and the United Kingdom averaged 0.9 percent and 2.0 percent, respectively. During this period, inflation did not spiral out of control in these countries. After 1973 high inflation rates finally appeared, but by that time, unemployment was rising.

In the 1980s the French unemployment rate rose to 9.6 percent; the German, to 7.5 percent; and the British, to 10 percent. A disinflationary effect did appear in these economies when the unemployment rate first reached these levels, but that effect wore off, and the unemployment rates remained high. The European experience is hard to reconcile with the natural rate theory.

The Japanese experience also gives little support. From 1961 to 1968 Japan's inflation rate fell from 8 percent to 3 percent. In 1973 it rose to 24 percent. In 1986 it fell below zero. In 1989 it was back up to 3 percent. Meanwhile, during this whole period, Japan's unemployment rate remained between 1 and 3 percent. Something was causing the inflation rate to bounce up and down like a yo-yo — but unemployment clearly wasn't it.

The case for the NAIRU rests mostly on U.S. data. Yet, American evidence is hardly overwhelming. The United States maintained unemployment rates below 6 percent for most of the fifties and sixties. By 1972 the inflation rate was still only about 3 percent. Not until 1972 did unemployment rates below 6 percent seem to become a problem.

Natural raters have answers for all of this, of course. The U.S. and Japanese evidence supports the NAIRU, they say, when all the relevant factors — like oil prices and changing inflation expectations — are taken into account. Concerning Europe, they just say that the NAIRU changed over time.

This stance leads to a big problem. Even if the natural rate theory is true, nobody really knows what the NAIRU is. Economists can estimate the NAIRU, but what if it changes? Nobody who has seen the European data can believe that the NAIRU is an immutable constant. In any case, one would not expect the natural unemployment rate to be constant in a changing economy. When the NAIRU does change, the change may not be detected for many years. Meanwhile, the Fed may be following a wrong policy. Millions of people may remain out of work unnecessarily.

Of course, natural rate theorists say that this extra, unnecessary unemployment is not really a problem, because it brings a permanent reduction in the rate of inflation. Then, if the Fed decides that the old, higher inflation rate was okay, it can simply allow the unemployment rate to fall below the natural rate for a while. The additional jobs will exactly cancel the jobs lost when the unemployment rate was too high. Unfortunately, by that time, the natural unemployment rate may have changed once again, and the Fed may once again be following a wrong policy.

The natural rate people have a response here, too, but let us not continue chasing our tail. We acknowledge that if the natural rate theory is exactly correct and if inflation is always a bad thing, then policy makers should not be worried about unemployment. But what if the natural rate theory is only *almost* correct? What if, as some economists believe, there is a range of unemployment rates that are consistent with stable inflation — a "natural range of unemployment," if you like. Then shifts in the natural range become a major problem. Policy makers want to keep unemployment near the bottom of the natural range, but without experimenting, they will never know where the bottom is. If the natural range shifts, then the old bottom could be the new top, but policy makers obsessed with a natural rate will never know the difference. Millions of people may be unnecessarily out of work, and there is no long-run benefit.

Furthermore, if the natural rate theory *is* correct, then there will really be no long-run cost to experimentation. If a temporarily "too high" unemployment rate is not a problem, neither is a temporarily "too low" unemployment rate. If we keep the unemployment rate "too low" for too long, we can precisely compensate by keeping it "too high" for the same amount of time. The two differences still cancel out. The only problem is that the inflation rate will be a little bit too high for a little while — which does not seem to us to be a major problem. If the natural rate theory is exactly correct, then policy makers have little to lose by experimenting. If the theory is not quite correct (or, God forbid, completely wrong), then policy makers have much to gain by experimenting — unless their central concern is to please lenders.

The Ironies of Age

Even though the acceptance of the natural rate theory benefits lenders, and even though lenders are on average older than other Americans, the economists most inclined to doubt the natural rate theory seem to be those who are past retirement age. This may seem puzzling, but there are reasons. For one thing, retired economists know enough not to place their trust in fixed-income investments. They choose to be lenders only to the extent that lending furthers their portfolio objectives. Since they recognize inflation as a valid risk, they do not feel entitled to low inflation rates.

More important, perhaps, is that economists over the age of sixty-five are old enough to have lived through the 1930s. The period from 1930 to 1938, the Great Depression, was one in which deflation was the clear enemy, and inflation was really not something to be upset about. To an economist who grew up thinking about the problems of the Great Depression, the prospect of high inflation cannot seem a great terror. Younger economists, on the other hand, lived through the 1970s. To these economists, the Great Depression is an abstraction, but the Great Inflation is a real memory. Having missed the much more painful experience of the 1930s, these economists see inflation as something to be feared.

In particular, economists between the ages of forty-five and sixty-five are too young to remember the Great Depression, but old enough to have been watching the economy during the early 1970s. When that decade began, the economic orthodoxy did not support the natural rate theory, but Milton Friedman — the theory's most vocal advocate — was on record saying that the United States would soon experience a combination of inflation and recession. Today's middle-aged economists saw that prediction come true. Even though it is hardly overwhelming evidence for the natural rate theory, that experience is salient in the minds of those economists. Like everyone else, economists are influenced more by salient events than by dispassionate evidence.

Those middle-aged economists are precisely the ones who have the most influence over policy. Younger economists are regarded as immature and inexperienced. Older economists are regarded as having stale ideas. When middle-aged economists talk, policy makers listen. The message heard today is that high unemployment is necessary to prevent inflation from accelerating.

Sound Money Rhetoric

Those who oppose any policy that risks higher inflation have rallied for many years around the banners of "sound money." However, "sound money" means different things to different people. To the monetarists, a school of economists once led by Milton Friedman, "sound money" means rigorous control of the money supply. From 1979 to 1982 the Fed made an attempt to implement the monetarists' sound-money doctrine. It quickly became clear that it was easier said than done. By mid-1982 the Fed had discovered that not only could it not control the money supply with any precision, it did not even quite know what exactly the money supply was. As it subsequently turned out, neither did Milton Friedman.

An altogether different sound-money doctrine comes from gold standard advocates. Under the gold standard, a nation promises to buy or sell unlimited amounts of gold at a fixed price. Whenever its gold supplies start to run low, it must stop creating money so that demand for gold declines. From the mid-1800s until 1971, the United States spent most of its time on some version of the gold standard. During that period it experienced numerous inflations, deflations, and depressions, including the Great Depression of the 1930s. Perhaps lenders took some comfort in the link between money and a tangible commodity, which may at least have made inflation no more likely than deflation. The link was notoriously flimsy, however. During wartime the gold standard was typically suspended. In 1933 and again (finally) in 1971, the gold standard was suspended for economic reasons. Money was only as sound as our leaders conceded to make it. Thank God. In 1933 it was only because people could no longer trust money buried in the backyard that they were willing to start using their money to hire some of the 25 percent of Americans who were out of work.

More recently the advocates of sound money have focused more on goals than on methods. The goal is to keep down inflation. Their rhetoric has taken on a new imagery. Inflation is like "a genie in a bottle." We must keep the lid on tight. Inflation is "a slippery slope." We must remain on the level ground. Inflation is "a yawning cliff." We must not venture near the edge. All these metaphors, as MIT's Nobel laureate Robert Solow points out, suggest some sort of irreversibility about inflation. However, there is no evidence — there is not even a theory — that inflation is irreversible. The double-digit inflation of the 1970s was reversed in the early 1980s, albeit painfully. The inflation that might result from a slight overshoot of the natural unemployment rate would be much milder. According to typical estimates, if the natural rate is 6 percent and the actual unemployment rate remained at 5 percent for three years, the inflation rate might rise from 3 percent to 4 percent. It would not take a 1982-style recession to reverse that inflation. The lenders, it appears, have lent us some frightening but misleading figures of speech.

Sound-money rhetoric can be particularly damaging (and particularly helpful to lenders) when it comes from the mouths of those who are pursuing "unsound" fiscal policies. The combination of low taxes and tight money — a combination endorsed by the early Reagan administration — has the predictable effect of raising real interest rates. High real interest rates are good for lenders. They are not good for anyone else.

THE POWER OF LENDERS

It should be clear by now that the ideas and policies prevalent among economists today are, to say the least, more beneficial to lenders than to the rest of us. Are today's pro-lender policies just an accident of intellectual history, or do they reflect the increased power of lenders in our society? While we cannot give a completely unassailable answer to this question, we believe the evidence supports the idea that today's policies are the result of lenders' power.

In principle, those who have money to lend also have money to buy influence. Those who have money to lend typically have the leisure to pursue their own political agenda, while borrowers are typically too busy even to recognize their interests. Those who have money to lend, who have been clever enough to gain and keep their money, are clever enough to convince others that the interests of lenders are the common interest. And those who have money to lend, unlike those who only owe money, know they have something to lose. Only those who know they have something to lose fight to keep what they have.

None of these principles has changed in the past forty years, but one thing has. Forty years ago those who had money to lend did not actually lend most of that money. Probably because Americans were less eager to borrow in those days, potential moneylenders instead found other investments — stocks, real estate, collectibles, whatever. The increase in debt has made the rich and influential into a lending class. Today they use their influence to support the needs of lenders, which, as we have seen, may be at conflict with those of the rest of society.

When examining the ideas popular in academia, we should take into account that those who endow universities (not to mention the universities themselves) have more bonds in their portfolios than they did forty years ago, simply because more bonds are available. There should be no question that academic ideas affect public policy. In fact, studies show that Fed officials with academic backgrounds are among the most likely to vote for higher interest rates or tighter money. Most academic economists would like to think that the success of ideas in academia rests purely on their intellectual merit. Universities do try valiantly to shield the academic process from the overt influence of financial sponsors. However, one can hardly doubt that subtle influences persist. Would you be inclined to endow a university that was popularizing ideas damaging to your own financial health? Would you be inclined to promote ideas damaging to the financial health of those who pay your salary? Given the explosion of debt and the consequent importance of lending to the financial health of those with money, we believe the acceptance of pro-lender ideas is no accident.

If the influence of lenders in academia is subtle, their influence on the monetary policy process is less so. Right now the Federal Reserve System has little reason *not* to pursue the interests of lenders. The internal structure of the Fed is closely linked with the rest of the nation's banking system. Just as legislators usually start out as lawyers, Fed officials usually start out as bankers. In the private sector they have spent their lives looking out for the good of lenders; they can't be expected to change drastically just because they move into a public position.

Given that Fed policy-making positions are not permanent, Fed officials have strong incentives to favor the interests of lenders. A high inflation rate, even if only temporary, looks particularly bad on the résumé of a former Fed governor, especially if he or she is looking for a job in private-sector banking. Even relatively liberal Fed governors acknowledge privately that this concern is part of their motivation. A high unemployment rate, on the other hand, doesn't look so bad to most bankers, and the résumé-holder can easily justify it by appealing to the natural rate theory.

Although the Fed's governors are officially appointed by the president of the United States (with the approval of the Senate), the financial community pulls the strings. When making appointments to the Fed, presidents are careful not to upset the financial markets. After all, a market crash in response to a Fed appointment doesn't look very good for the president, and its effects on the economy are believed to be unpleasant.

Even when the president makes a slightly out-of-line appointment to the Fed, a single individual cannot prevail against the culture and tradition of the institution. Former Vice Chairman Alan Blinder, himself hardly an extremist, found this out the hard way. In a speech soon after his appointment by President Clinton, Blinder noted that a fairly large temporary rise in employment would likely involve only a tiny increase in the inflation rate. Because Blinder's remarks suggested that slightly higher inflation might be tolerable, he was instantly vilified by numerous "unnamed sources" within the Fed. In subsequent votes, Blinder acquiesced in the Fed's consensus to a degree that sometimes surprised outside observers.

Perhaps a more obstreperous vice chairman would have acquiesced less readily. However, the appointment of an outspoken individual, even one acceptable to Wall Street, can bring strong opposition from lenders' representatives in the Senate — as President Clinton discovered when he tried to appoint Felix Rohatyn, a successful investment banker with uncharacteristically pro-growth ideas, to succeed Blinder. Senator Connie Mack, representing the state of Florida, mounted a strident campaign against Rohatyn in the Senate Banking Committee, and Rohatyn withdrew his own nomination in disgust. Florida, nicknamed the Sunshine State, might also be called the Lender State. In terms of direct interest income as a fraction of total income, Florida is third among the fifty states. Given the number of wealthy pensioners in Florida, it is likely that, once *indirect* interest income is included, Florida is well ahead of the pack. (As discussed in chapter 6, much of the income from pension plans is provided indirectly by interest on bonds.) It is no accident that one of Florida's senators sits on the banking committee.

Of course, there are some less-wealthy pensioners in Florida, and in other states. When politicians make the case against people like Rohatyn who aren't sufficiently afraid of inflation, the images of poor senior citizens on fixed incomes inevitably appear. As noted in chapter 6, these images are deceptive because poorer senior citizens get most of their income from Social Security, which is fully indexed — perhaps more than fully indexed — for inflation. The widows and orphans also appear. Sympathetic characters, certainly; but are they worthy of a financial safety net that operates at the expense of job-seekers and of economic growth? In any case, inflation-adjusted bonds would provide a more reliable safety net than tight money. Finally, those who advocate intense fear of inflation appeal to a general feeling that rising prices are bad for the average person.

WHO REALLY BENEFITS FROM LOW INFLATION?

Most people believe that inflation harms them. Most economists believe that inflation does real harm to only a few, although it may be inconvenient for the rest. When people see prices going up, and their wages are not similarly rising, they believe that the problem is with prices. In fact, the problem is more likely with wages. If prices stopped going up, then wages would start going down (and probably there would also be widespread unemployment). In the 1990s, as inflation has slowed to a snail's pace, many wages have begun to fall. If inflation is reduced to zero, workers will lose a scapegoat for their declining living standards but will not be any better off.

The general perception that inflation is bad is a relatively recent development. During the nineteenth century, farmers — a much larger group than they are now — generally believed that inflation was to their benefit. Higher prices for their products made it easier to pay their expenses. Workers, who suffered massive job cutbacks during periods of deflation, also tended to welcome inflation. People with money were the only victims of inflation.

More recent economic theory calls into question not only who is harmed by inflation but also who is helped. If inflation is fully anticipated, contemporary economists argue, then it does not hurt lenders, who simply demand higher nominal interest rates to compensate for the inflation. Nor does it help borrowers. Borrowers are equally well off with higher inflation matched by higher interest rates.

However, there is at least one valid theoretical (and practical) reason why even fully anticipated inflation, if moderate, can be beneficial to the economy. American economists have tended to ignore that reason in recent years, but Japanese economists have lately been unable to ignore it. Inflation can be beneficial because it encourages people to invest their money rather than burying it in the backyard. This effect of inflation is known as the "Tobin effect," after economist James Tobin, who first pointed it out to the community of economists. When inflation is relatively high, burying money in the backyard is a very bad idea because the money loses its value. Faced with inflation, even a very risk-averse wealth-holder will choose to invest. When inflation is low or negative (as it has been in Japan recently), there may be nothing to prevent "money hoarding."

Ordinarily, hoarding does not present a problem, because the Federal Reserve System can create new money to replace the hoarded money. But sometimes (notably, in the United States in the late 1930s) investors are so timid that they simply keep hoarding whatever money the Fed creates. In the late 1930s the United States found a solution to this problem. Actually, Hitler and Tojo were kind enough to find a solution for us — the solution was called World War II. Even if a war does not occur, it is theoretically possible to solve this problem by raising public expenditures so that demand increases and investment becomes more profitable. However, in the Indebted Society, raising public expenditures is difficult. But for the existence of adequate inflation, 1991 might have been the beginning of another Great Depression.

The only people who are substantially harmed by fully anticipated inflation are those who must retain large amounts of cash that do not earn interest.[40] Historically, three major groups have fit this criterion: retailers, banks, and criminals. Of these three groups, only criminals still have an unambiguous need for cash. As credit card use becomes more common, retailers no longer need to hold much cash. The amount of cash needed by banks can be adjusted up or down arbitrarily by changing legal reserve requirements, so that any harm from ongoing inflation could be reversed. Criminals, however, have no escape. Criminals cannot generally accept credit cards, because they risk being caught. Since criminals are by definition violating the law, their need for cash cannot be adjusted by changing legal requirements.

There is one primary group that benefits from fully anticipated inflation — taxpayers. Inflation is effectively a tax on cash balances, and it therefore reduces the need for other taxes. In effect, inflation is a crime tax that reduces the need to tax law-abiding citizens.[41]

However, inflation is seldom fully anticipated. People always expect some inflation, but their expectations are seldom realized precisely. If inflation exceeds expectations, borrowers get a windfall. They can pay back their loans with less valuable dollars. If inflation comes in below expectations, lenders get a windfall. They are paid with dollars that are more valuable than expected. Is it a coincidence that, over the past fifteen years, inflation rates have much more often come in below expectations?

9 · Let Them Eat Cake

S O FAR, WE HAVE SEEN how the United States fell into debt and have looked at the effects of high debt levels on working people and on monetary policy, as well as the role of lenders in the Indebted Society. Now we return to the subject of government debt and examine its effects. Again, we find that the debt bomb has already exploded, and America is now living with the consequences.

Debt service payments by the federal government soak up money that could be used to increase productivity and fight poverty. Continued deficit financing also absorbs capital that could be used to create good, productive jobs in the private sector, both here and abroad. Moreover, heavy federal indebtedness is used as an excuse to pursue supposedly "efficient" policies that transfer responsibility for various expenditures to states and localities. For many reasons, state and local governments are likely to be less generous than the federal government.

This chapter delves into the effects of the federal indebtedness described in chapter 3. Four major effects are notable. First, by its impact on private capital accumulation, the rapid expansion of government debt has aggravated the productivity slowdown that began in the 1970s. Second, by encouraging consumption and crowding out investment, tax cuts have accelerated the trend to lower quality jobs. Third, by necessitating inflows of capital to finance it (given the low U.S. saving rate), the increase in government debt has made the United States dependent on foreign creditors and made U.S. goods less competitive. Fourth, government debt has put a crimp on the current government's resources. Now that most of the deficit is used to fund interest payments on existing debt, this resource-constraining effect of government debt has become the most important.

TILL DEBT DO US PART

From 1960 to 1979 the ratio of federal debt to total domestic product fell from 46 percent to 26 percent. The decline was quite sharp during the 1960s, and the ratio remained at a low level throughout the 1970s. After 1980, however, the federal government embarked on a huge debt binge. Within eleven years, the debt ratio was back to its 1960 level and rising.

In order to understand the effects of this debt binge, we must first take a closer look at the forces that spawned it. During the 1970s the American people had faced stagnating incomes for the first time since the Great Depression. Struggling to maintain a higher standard of living, they were piling up new personal debts faster than double-digit inflation could render their old debts insignificant. The United States, leader of the free world, seemed to be at the mercy of Middle Eastern oil profiteers. Caught between rising prices and falling expectations, Americans desperately sought a way out. Supply-side economics offered them that escape.

Supply-side economics had its genesis in 1974, when a man named Arthur Laffer drew a curve on a napkin. The curve, roughly replicated in Figure 9.1, purports to show the relation between tax rates

FIGURE 9.1 ARTHUR LAFFER'S CURVE

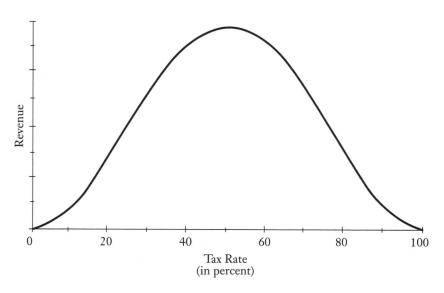

Revenue

Tax Rate
(in percent)

and tax revenues. A tax rate of zero naturally produces no revenue. As tax rates rise from zero, revenues rise in tandem. As rates rise, however, they also have the effect of discouraging the activities being taxed. At some point, this discouragement effect begins to predominate. Beyond that point, rising tax rates actually reduce tax revenues. At the far extreme, a 100 percent tax rate induces people to abandon completely the taxed activities, since they can obtain no benefit from them, and the revenue falls back to zero.

At its extremes, the "Laffer curve" is scarcely open to dispute. A tax rate of zero or 100 percent clearly produces no revenue. Laffer's presumption about the particular shape of the curve between zero and 100 is more tenuous. History suggests that Figure 9.2 is more realistic than the curve that Laffer drew. Nonetheless, Laffer managed to convince people that the curve as he drew it was not only realistic but also relevant. He suggested that the United States was on the far side of the curve and that a tax cut might well result in higher revenues. He convinced, among others, the *Wall Street Journal*'s editorial board, a congressman named Jack Kemp, a presidential hopeful named Ronald Reagan, and finally, it appeared in 1980, a majority of the American voters.

Arthur Laffer and his fellow supply-siders argued, using simplistic

FIGURE 9.2 A REALISTIC "LAFFER CURVE"

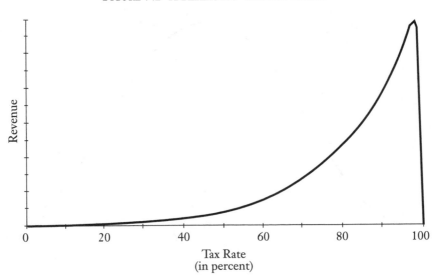

Tax Rate
(in percent)

theories and ignoring empirical evidence, that lower tax rates produce huge increases in productivity and work effort. Let us subject their theories to the test of simplistic empiricism. Figure 9.3 shows a plot of the actual U.S. labor productivity growth rate as a function of the maximum income tax rate for five-year periods from 1950 to 1989. There is a consistent and very strong *positive* relationship. High tax rates seem to be associated with *faster* productivity growth. This is the precise opposite of what Arthur Laffer and his friends would expect! Admittedly, this chart does not prove that there is a relationship. It ignores various complications, such as the effect of inflation. Nonetheless, it does refute the simple "low tax rates produce growth" hypothesis.

What is going on here? Is it possible that high tax rates actually do increase productivity? As a matter of fact, it *is* possible. A "side effect" of high tax rates is that the government collects more revenues. (At this point, nobody can seriously believe otherwise.)[42] When the government collects more revenues, it can spend more money while borrowing less. The additional spending, if it is done well, increases productivity by providing better roads, scientific advances, a better-trained workforce, and so on. The reduced borrowing makes more funds available for private-sector investment, so that the capital stock

FIGURE 9.3 LAUGHER CURVE
FIVE-YEAR INTERVALS 1950–89

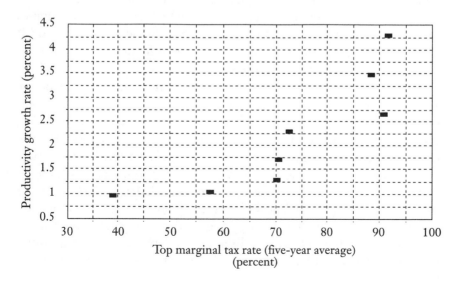

per worker increases. The increased capital raises the average productivity of workers. Overall, higher taxes force people to reduce their consumption, so that more resources are available for investment, both public and private.

Now, one may say, "Even if lower tax rates don't increase productivity, they do encourage people to do more work." The premise is that people do more work if their after-tax wages are higher. A lot of economists have studied how people actually seem to respond to differences in wages, and a couple of conclusions have emerged. First, for men and for single women, wage rates seem to have little effect on how much work they do. Second, married women do seem more likely to work when their wages are higher. Presumably, this difference appears because tradition has assigned men the role of "first earner" in families, so that married men feel the need to work and support their families no matter what the wages offered, whereas married women make a choice based on the relative advantages of working for pay or working in the home.

So, at least as far as work is concerned, some married women probably do choose to increase their taxable income when tax rates are cut. Nevertheless, the likely increase in taxable income is small compared with the revenues lost through lower taxation of the people who would be working anyway. Furthermore, it is probably not a huge loss to society when women *choose* to work in the home instead of working for pay. Some say it is a gain to society. Ironically, social conservatives, who often favor the traditional "homemaker" role for women, also tend to favor lower tax rates, which encourage women to forgo their traditional role. Of course, traditions may change, and it may be that men will start to feel more comfortable in the homemaker role than they have in the past. Then taxes may start to affect men's decision to work for pay. Still, the same underlying principle applies: higher taxes discourage two-income households. If our society decides that tax policy should encourage two-income households, there is a better way to do it than just cutting taxes. The discouraging effect of taxes on second-income earners results largely from the perverse way that tax rates are applied. Personal income taxes, which are charged jointly to a couple, are progressive (that is, the rate rises as income increases). Social Security taxes ("contributions," as they are officially called), which are charged individually to each wage earner, are regressive (that is, the rate falls as income increases). When someone considers contributing a second income to his or her family, he or she faces both a high personal tax rate (because total family income is high) and a high Social Security tax rate (because his or her individual income is not so high). If America really wants to encourage two-income families, it should integrate the two tax systems, not just lower their rates. In any case, we doubt that encouraging two-income families is what most of the Reagan supporters had in mind.

Private Benefits, Public Costs

A very few who supported Reagan's tax cut were "economists" who truly believed in supply-side economics. Some others were serious economists who thought they could convince Reagan and Congress to undertake the severe spending cuts that would balance the tax cut. Many, including the president himself, were naive noneconomists seduced by the siren song of supply-side economics. Others were anti-government cynics — both inside and outside the field of economics — who realized that a large national debt would ultimately force a massive curtailment of public services and social welfare programs. This last group got their way.

The dismantling of government is accomplished by widening one particular category of government expenditure — interest on the national debt. Unlike other expenditures, which benefit the public and the poor, this one benefits only moneylenders. The true "cost" of federal debt service is in the expenditures forgone. Table 9.1 shows that this cost has become quite high. To be more precise, the table shows that debt-related costs have cut sharply into the money available for nondebt-related expenditures.

The indebted federal government faced additional exigencies. Rising

TABLE 9.1 THE OPPORTUNITY COST OF FEDERAL DEBT SERVICE

Years	Federal interest as a percentage of total expenditures
1960s	6.5
1970s	6.8
1980s	11.9
1990s	13.1

Source: U.S. Department of Commerce

health care costs and increasing numbers of Medicare beneficiaries squeezed the government from one end as interest costs squeezed from the other. Politics dictated that any tax increases be small. The government was already borrowing at an embarrassing rate. Cutting spending seemed to be the only viable option. In 1982 federal expenditures other than interest, health care, and Social Security came to 14.5 percent of the nation's total output. By 1994 that figure had fallen to 11.5 percent. "The era of big government," President Clinton told the nation in his 1996 State of the Union Address, "is over."

Lamentably, the era of big government is over, but the era of big government borrowing is still well under way. Now weakened in its ability to provide public services, care for the needy, and invest in America's future, the federal government must still borrow hundreds of billions of dollars per year just to pay the interest on its existing debt. The combination of anemic government spending, heavy government borrowing, and an antigrowth monetary policy puts in jeopardy not only the condition of America's poor and elderly, but also America's long-term productivity growth.

PRODUCTIVITY

In the long run — and usually even in the short run — the only way to raise the standard of living is to raise productivity. Productivity depends in turn on three things: the quality of labor, the amount of capital that labor has to work with, and the technology used to combine them. However, the perceived shortage of resources has led us to cut back on exactly what we need for robust growth.

Capital

Private capital can grow only if there is private investment. Factories and offices do not appear by themselves. When the government borrows money, it reduces the amount available for private investment. The fraction of domestic funds absorbed by government borrowing has risen steadily since the 1970s. During the 1960s only 5 percent of the net change in domestic financial wealth was accounted for by government bonds. During the early 1990s that figure was 38 percent. Although government borrowing also draws in foreign money to supplement the domestic funds, there is still a net reduction in the funds available for private investment.

During the 1960s and 1970s, net private investment (the total amount of private investment minus the amount needed to replace what is used up in the production process) accounted for more than 8 percent of the nation's net domestic product (the total amount produced in the nation minus the amount used up in production). That figure fell to 6 percent in the 1980s and to a mere 4 percent in the early 1990s. The growth in America's private capital stock has thus slowed significantly because of government borrowing.

It is important to realize, though, that government borrowing doesn't have to reduce private investment. Government borrowing uses up *money* that could be used for private investment, but money is just green pieces of paper. The Fed can create as much new money as it wants. The real problem with government borrowing is that the Fed, for fear of inflation, refuses to print enough money to support such borrowing and at the same time allow a high level of private capital formation. In fact, it is our argument that the nation has enough resources to support both a high level of government borrowing and a high level of private investment. It's just that the Fed won't let the nation use those resources.

Since the Fed won't let the nation use those resources, it is almost as if they did not exist. We find ourselves in a paradoxical situation. As noted in chapter 5, we are facing a depressed economy — at least from the point of view of workers. Ordinarily, government borrowing is recommended as a *solution* to a depressed economy. The borrowing occasioned by World War II provided a very effective response to the depression of the 1930s. However, our current depression is different because it is *intentional*. This depression is harmful to workers but quite agreeable for lenders. The Fed, which is now serving the interests of the lenders, works against any force that tries to relieve the depression. Since the Fed works independently of the elected government, that government must view the Fed almost as a force of nature rather than a cocreator of economic policy. We can influence forces of nature — for example, by seeding clouds or by changing our use of aerosols — but when planning day-to-day activities, we have to take forces of nature as a given.

A few economists, recognizing the depressed state of the U.S. economy, maintain that the push for smaller federal deficits is misguided. If the economy grows quickly enough, they argue, then the debt becomes less of a burden. If a larger deficit causes more economic growth, then it could have the effect of reducing rather than increasing the total debt burden. (Moreover, because the nation has more slack resources than policy makers realize, this growth could be accomplished without much inflation, so the nation would not simply be "inflating away the debt.") These economists have forgotten a basic fact of life: you can't fight City Hall. In this case, City Hall is the Eccles Building in Washington, D.C., and the mayor's name is Alan Greenspan. In fact, trying to fight City Hall by deliberately running large deficits only makes the situation worse. Since the Fed lets the United States use only a certain fraction of its resources, any resources consumed by the government have to be taken away from other uses, such as private investment.

But the government is not really using a lot of resources: federal expenditures other than interest, health care, and Social Security have fallen from 14.5 percent to 11.5 percent of the gross domestic product. If the government is actually using up less resources than before, then where are those borrowed resources going? The answer is, into the high lifestyle of wealthy Americans. These resources are also going into the not-so-high but still unaffordable lifestyle of middle-class Americans. The high level of government borrowing is accounted for largely by two things: low personal taxes (compared with what they were before the 1980s) and interest on the national debt. Both these things, it appears, tend to encourage consumption. Tax cuts give people more money to spend, on everything from hamburgers to yachts, and it appears that people reacted to the Reagan tax cuts by doing just that. Similarly, large interest payments give the recipients more money to spend, on everything from VCRs to thoroughbreds, and again it appears that people have done just that. The situation with the federal government is simply an extension of the situation with consumers, as described in chapter 2: America is using too much of its resources for consumption and not enough for investment.

Technology

We must assess not only the size of our stock of capital but also its quality. One of the key mechanisms for improving this factor of production involves private expenditure on research and development (R & D). This R & D has traditionally been a response to both the forces causing investment discussed above and the R & D stimuli provided by the federal government.

Much of these federal stimuli are found in the budget category for "general science, space, and technology," which has been trending downward relative to the gross domestic product since 1968. The Kennedy and Johnson administrations, which recognized the importance of technology to improved standards of living, were able to devote substantial sums to science and technology during the 1960s. Even at their height, however, those substantial sums amounted to less than 1 percent of our national product. Given the potential of technology to improve productivity and enlarge human possibilities, one could certainly argue that even Kennedy and Johnson were too conservative in this regard. In any case, the subsequent administrations — Nixon, Ford, Carter, and Reagan — had other priorities. From 1968 to 1987 this category had fallen from 0.6 percent to 0.2 percent of the gross domestic product (GDP). Under George Bush, science and technology spending began to bud again, if not to blossom. Even so, it never quite reached 0.3 percent of the GDP. Bill Clinton — at least in his rhetoric — would appear to be the most protechnology president since Kennedy. Nonetheless, because of apparent debt constraints, Clinton's technology spending has not even been able to keep pace with that of George Bush.

Basic research by the federal government has also shrunk in importance over the past twenty-five years. During the 1970s federal basic research spending amounted to 0.50 percent of the GDP. During the 1980s it was 0.46 percent. In the 1990s it has been 0.41 percent. Basic research is a prerequisite for good R & D. With less basic research, a given quantity of capital is likely to produce less.

Although the fall in federal basic research spending since the 1970s is not dramatic, the trend is nonetheless troubling. In this time of budget cutting and government bashing, one can hardly hope that the trend will not hasten. With nearly everything being cut, pleas for maintaining research funding are likely to fall on deaf ears. Moreover, the only ones qualified to make the technical case for research funding are the very scientists who would be paid to do the research. Their pleas may appear self-serving.

Yet the importance of basic research to a growing economy and a growing world cannot be overstated. In the history of the industrialized world, the most important contributor to productivity has been not capital investment, not better workers, not more efficient management, but knowledge. Research creates knowledge.

Research is not something that the private sector is inclined to do on its own. Firms have little incentive to support research because the benefits of that research do not typically accrue to the firm that supports it. Take, for example, Windows 95 — the most talked about computer program in history. Windows 95 represents a sophisticated application of the concept of a "graphical user interface."[43] That concept — also applied in Apple's Macintosh and IBM's OS/2, and to a lesser extent in earlier versions of Windows — was not Microsoft's invention. It was not Apple's invention. It was not IBM's invention. The "graphical user interface" concept was developed at the Palo Alto Research Center under support from Xerox. Because of graphical user interfaces, Microsoft will make billions, Americans (and others) will be more productive, and families will find new opportunities for entertainment and personal growth. Xerox will not make a cent.

In the case of graphical user interfaces, the world was lucky. Through altruism or through gross misjudgment, or perhaps through some combination, Xerox was willing to support research whose benefits ultimately accrued to others. Needless to say, the world cannot count on corporate altruism. (The world can probably count on gross misjudgment, but it does not ordinarily have such beneficial results.) The future productivity of Americans and others depends largely on how much they allow their governments to spend on research. In the Indebted Society, that is not likely to be very much.

Labor

Workers' productivity depends both on their skills and on the mix of jobs in existence. Along with decreasing investment in physical capital, there has been less investment in human capital and decreased spending on items that provide the best jobs.

Expenditure on education addresses our three greatest economic concerns. First, it increases the productivity of the workforce. Second, it can reverse the downward trend of the real average wage since 1973. And third, it can provide skills that prevent some near-poor from ending up on the wrong side of the poverty line.

Despite the great value of educational expenditure, since 1970 the growth in federal spending on schooling of all kinds has not kept pace with the overall growth of our economy. During 1970 federal educational spending was 0.93 percent of the gross domestic product. By

1980 it had fallen to 0.86 percent. By 1990 it was down to 0.68 percent.

Recent events do not bode well for federal support of education. Student aid has been targeted for cuts by Republicans in Congress who argue that students should share the burden of reducing the budget deficit. Because college graduates have far greater earning power, these congressmen argue, it is unfair to ask lower-paid taxpayers to subsidize education. The cuts come at a time when steep hikes in student fees and tuition are forcing students to borrow more to stay in school. On some campuses annual student charges more than doubled between 1990 and 1994.

The argument that subsidizing education is unfair to lower-paid taxpayers has a certain superficial appeal. But it ignores several important facts about education and about taxes. For one thing, as the U.S. tax system is progressive, the ones who pay the most are typically higher-paid taxpayers who have more education than the students they subsidize. Moreover, the availability of affordable financing for education helps enable people to move out of the lower-income brackets. An argument analogous to the Laffer curve argument could reasonably be applied to educational expenditure: the more the government spends on education, the less it ends up costing, because citizens move to higher income levels and pay more in taxes.

It is widely recognized among economists that education can be beneficial to society over and above its benefit to the student. Perhaps the most obvious example is the education of a scientist whose discoveries later enrich the broader society. More generally, there are obvious advantages to having educated voters in a democratic country. Countless other examples can be imagined. Thus, even if everyone could afford an optimal amount of education, not everyone would take advantage of it without some encouragement from the government.

Economists have paid less attention to the question of how people choose to use their education, but the availability of student aid is relevant here, too. Students who borrow heavily for education without government help are often constrained in their subsequent career choices. A deeply indebted young doctor, for example, cannot choose to practice in an area where his or her services are sorely needed if that area does not provide sufficient income to service the debt. In general, people may be willing to forgo additional income to pursue careers that, in effect, provide them with moral benefits. This usually means that those careers also provide benefits to others. Increasingly, graduating students do not have that option.

Education, however, does not take place only in school. In 1962 Stanford's Kenneth Arrow, a Nobel Prize–winning economist, offered a novel theory about the development of human capital, labeled "learning by doing." According to this theory, the more workers are asked to produce, the better they become at production. More recently MIT's Olivier Blanchard and (at the time) Harvard's Lawrence Summers have offered a macroeconomic analogue that they called "hysteresis." According to this theory, employing the unemployed makes them more employable in years to come.

We would like to take this line of reasoning a step further. We hypothesize that "good jobs" increase workers' productive skills more than "bad jobs" do. We assess the quality of U.S. jobs by looking at their weighted average compensation. This weighted average is based on the industry-by-occupation mix of jobs. We believe that it affects our country's productivity growth.

This job quality index was developed by one of the authors and is brought out monthly by the Center for National Policy (CNP) of Washington, D.C. The CNP figures for the years between 1980 and 1992 reveal a steady dwindling in the average quality of the jobs available to workers. By "quality" we mean the total compensation, including pay and benefits, associated with a job. "Quality" in this sense would not be said to improve just because people get pay raises, but only if better jobs were created, which unfortunately hasn't been the case. (On the individual level, a clerk who gets a large raise doesn't improve his "job quality," but a clerk who gets promoted to manager does.) Our research shows that the best per-dollar generators of jobs (reflecting both quantity and quality) are private investment and state and local spending. The Indebted Society is not a place where these two activities flourish. The Indebted Society, with its high interest rates and sparse possibilities for intergovernmental grants in aid, does not offer very many good labor market learning opportunities.

The indebted government thus has three strikes against it in the productivity domain. By crowding out private investment (with the help of monetary policy), it slows down the creation of capital. By jeopardizing funding for research, it retards the advancement of technology. By cutting support for education and discouraging the creation of good jobs, it allows the quality of labor to diminish.

Adding Insult to Injury

Although the Laffer curve is now a mere historical curiosity, its tax-cutting agenda is alive and well. In the 1990s those who would cut taxes for the rich have discarded all pretense. Rather than saying, "Cutting taxes will help balance the budget," as they did in 1980, they now say, "Cutting taxes will push the budget further out of balance, but we intend both to cut taxes *and* balance the budget." They would accomplish this feat, of course, by cutting spending more than anyone had previously contemplated. (They invariably admonish us that they merely seek "to cut the growth of spending," not to cut spending itself. "Cutting the growth" is a very powerful concept. If we had "cut the growth" of employment to 1 percent per year over the past forty years, we would now have the highest unemployment rate in history.)

Nor do we hear talk of "tax cuts for everyone," as in 1980. Instead, only the capital gains tax is to be cut. Having learned that it does no economic good to cut taxes for average Americans, the tax cutters now suggest that we do so only for the rich. Cutting capital gains taxes suggests a kinky new version of the Laffer curve. Congress's cutting capital gains taxes almost guarantees an initial increase in revenues. Congress has a history of changing its mind about capital gains taxes. Consequently, whenever a cut passes, those with capital gains are careful to take those gains (and pay taxes on them) before Congress changes its mind and raises the tax rate again. The evidence for any long-term advantage to cutting capital gains taxes is much less clear.

Tax cuts and budget cuts aside, the crowning glory of those who impugn the role of government is "the new fiscal federalism." This ideology holds that, in order to make things more efficient, any single nationwide antipoverty program should be replaced with fifty separate state programs. Replacing one program with fifty is the way to cut big government. It doesn't make a lot of sense until you realize what is really going on. Fiscal federalism will end up cutting big government, not because it makes government more efficient but because it puts states in competition to reduce the size of their antipoverty programs. The federal government can truly serve the people, but state governments have a strong incentive to make some other state do the serving. State budget priorities are always for those things that attract tax-paying businesses away from other states, not things that attract poor people away from other states. The result is what Harvard political scientist Paul Peterson calls "the race to the bottom."

The new fiscal federalism also tends to encourage corruption. State and local governments are notoriously more corrupt than the federal government. Not that the federal government is immune to corruption, but it is much easier to police one government than fifty. The problem of policing *local* governments becomes staggering. One could hardly imagine a corrupt big-city political boss as president of the United States. We should point out here that, whatever his faults, the only corruption of which Bill Clinton as *president* has been accused is covering up former misdeeds as governor. We would much rather have America's antipoverty programs run by President Clinton than by fifty Governor Clintons.

The plight of the poor in the Indebted Society, and the effects of budget cuts and fiscal federalism on that plight, is a subject that is pursued more closely in chapter 11. For now, we turn back to the question of investment and productivity. Does government borrowing, along with a tight money policy and paltry personal saving, condemn this nation to a deteriorating capital stock? Or are there forces that tend to ameliorate this economic decline? As we will demonstrate, there are such forces, but their presence raises new problems.

10 · Foreign Saviors

I T COULD HAVE BEEN WORSE. After fifteen years of $100 billion-plus federal budget deficits, the United States is still here. Most of its workforce is still employed. Good jobs have become scarce but have not disappeared. Productivity growth has been painfully slow, but productivity has continued to grow. Many incomes have fallen in real terms, but some have risen and a great many have held their own. If you had told us twenty years ago about the massive deficits the United States would be running year in and year out, if you had told us about the Fed's determination to fight inflation even when it was nowhere in sight, if you had told us about how much consumers would be willing to borrow even with their confidence at record lows — frankly, we would have predicted much worse.

THE SECRET OF OUR SUCCESS

R emember 1986? The U.S. government borrowed $200,000,000,000 in a single calendar year for the first time in history. Despite the extra money they had from the tax cut, Americans saved less than 6 percent of their disposable income. It was the first time in twenty-three years that the personal saving rate had been so low. The net business saving rate was near zero. Most economists, if they had foreseen such statistics ten years earlier, would have imagined that U.S. investment had dried up entirely. With so much borrowing and so little saving, where could businesses find anything to invest? Yet in 1986 U.S. businesses invested almost $500 billion in new plant and equipment! Not great for a $4 trillion economy with a depreciating capital stock, but quite respectable under the circumstances. How did they manage it?

Well, the United States didn't manage it alone. We had help. Between 1981 and 1995 we had more than a trillion dollars' worth of help. That help enabled America to continue building offices and factories, to continue replacing obsolete machinery, and to continue updating and improving our economy, despite an almost dry pool of domestic savings. The help has a name: the trade deficit. That sucking sound you've been hearing for the past fifteen years is the sound of foreign capital coming to the United States. Nature abhors a vacuum, and the savings vacuum in the United States, powered by budget deficits, tight money, and a need for investment, has been sucking in capital from abroad ever since the first Reagan tax cut took effect.

Yes, the help that America receives from abroad, the help that prevents the U.S. economy from crumbling, is called the trade deficit. You thought the trade deficit was a bad thing? Well, in a way, you're right. The trade deficit does create a lot of problems. Nonetheless, compared with the alternative, a trade deficit is a good thing for a country that faces inadequate national saving and overzealous monetary policy.

How can the trade deficit be a good thing? How can it be good for America when our products are not competitive, when our trading partners don't play fair? How can that be good? To see how the trade deficit can be a good thing, you have to imagine what would happen if it suddenly disappeared. Suppose that everyone in Osaka suddenly decided they had to have a Chrysler minivan. Suppose that everyone in Paris suddenly decided that California wine tasted pretty good. Suppose that everyone in New York City suddenly refused to buy televisions that didn't say "Made in the U.S.A." What would happen?

Here's what would happen first: Chrysler, and Ernest and Julio Gallo, and whatever company still makes televisions in the United States, would start hiring people. Employment would go up. So far, so good. If we lived in a country without powerful lenders, maybe it would end there. But this is the real world. You don't get something for nothing — and in particular, you don't get more employment, period.

More employment means a tighter labor market, and a tighter labor market means that the Fed's early-warning inflation sirens start to go off. What happens next is not pretty. Remember 1994? You thought you were paying just 6.5 percent on your adjustable rate mortgage? Not anymore. You thought you could afford a new car? Check with the bank again. You thought this was the year your business would finally go public? Maybe next year. The Fed will raise interest rates, and it will keep raising interest rates until it chokes off enough employment to balance out the "good news" about the trade deficit. The "good news" turns out to be "no news" as far as jobs are concerned. The only news is that some jobs have shifted into trade-sensitive industries and out of interest-rate-sensitive industries.

This shift turns out to be worse than "no news." Although most of the trade-sensitive jobs are good jobs, so are most of the interest-rate-sensitive jobs. The difference is in what happens to the product. Trade-sensitive jobs may produce goods for export — which means we never see the product again. Or they may produce goods that compete with imports. Most of those are consumer goods — things that help people only in the short run. Interest-rate-sensitive jobs almost always produce things that help people in the long run. Housing is the most obvious example: lower interest rates mean that people can afford to build and buy houses that will stand for decades. A more important example is investment goods: lower interest rates mean that firms can afford to build factories, to buy machines, to develop new products. This growth means better jobs for the future, not just for today. The trade deficit, for all its faults, is what allows a nation of lenders and consumers to create at least *some* good jobs for the future.

THE INDEBTED NATION

Of course, there is a downside: a trade deficit means the nation is borrowing from abroad. The nation as a whole, rather than just its firms or its consumers or its government, is becoming an indebted society. Bear in mind, though, that much of the debt that the United States now owes to the rest of the world is not really "debt." When foreign interests buy into a U.S. corporation, for example, America is not "borrowing" in the strict sense: there is no IOU, and there are no interest coupons. Nonetheless, when people from abroad invest here in this way, the United States becomes indebted: in the future much of the profits of the purchased corporation will have to be sent abroad, just like interest payments. When we talk about borrowing from abroad, we mean it in the broadest sense: U.S. assets, be they treasury bonds or stock certificates or title deeds, move into the hands of foreigners.

Some people say that the trade deficit causes the United States to borrow from abroad. Some say that America's borrowing from abroad is what causes the trade deficit. Really, neither of these statements is true. The "trade deficit" and "borrowing from abroad" are just two names for the same thing. Literally, the trade deficit means that the nation is getting more goods and services from abroad than it sends. The difference between what it gets and what it sends is what it borrows. The other way to think about it is in terms of money: the trade deficit means the United States is sending more dollars abroad than it gets back in payment for goods and services. However, outside the United States there isn't much point in carrying around dollars in your pocket, so those extra dollars come back here to buy assets: bonds, bank deposits, stocks, real estate, whatever.

It isn't so terrible to owe some money to the rest of the world, but it gets a little worse every year. Every year the Indebted Society becomes about $100 billion more indebted. In itself, that's still not a huge problem, because our national wealth is going up even faster than our foreign debt.

Foreign debt becomes problematic, though, when our international creditors begin to worry about whether they will be repaid. Put yourself in the position of a foreign creditor: you're sitting on a stack of U.S. treasury bonds. These bonds promise to pay a certain number of dollars at certain times in the future. But there is no promise about how much those dollars will be worth. In fact, if you're Japanese, you've seen the value of your dollars fall from 250 yen to 100 yen over the past fourteen years. (That's not quite as bad as it sounds, because the cost of living in Japan hasn't gone up much in those fourteen years. Still, it hurts.) On the other hand, if you're British, your dollars may buy a shilling or two more than they did fourteen years ago. Still, you worry about the future. Given that the United States owes so many dollars, and given that it can (in theory) print as many dollars as it wants, what is to stop it from printing so many dollars that they become worthless?

That is what foreign creditors worry about. It isn't America's problem, is it? Well, yes, it is. It is America's problem if America has a Federal Reserve System that cares about stabilizing the dollar. If foreign creditors get too worried about the value of the dollar, their worries become a self-fulfilling prophecy. One thing that the Fed does not want to see is everyone's trying at once to exchange dollars for yen or pound sterling or gold. The image of a "free fall in the dollar" has been impressed on the American psyche, and you can bet that the Fed will go out of its way to avoid having that image become a reality.

A free fall in the dollar would not really be a great disaster for Americans: only those who like to buy foreign products or take vacations abroad would be hurt. But the *fear* of a free fall in the dollar *is* a disaster. That fear is just one more force pressuring the Fed to keep interest rates higher than they should be. Higher interest rates on the dollar encourage foreigners to hold on to their dollars and keep receiving those high interest rates. Higher interest rates also reassure foreign creditors that the Fed has no intention of allowing inflation within shooting distance.

Here we run into the same problem as with the power of domestic lenders — the problem of uncertainty. If the Fed had a perfect model of the economy, it could always stop the economy just before inflation started to go up. Then maybe we could all agree to keep the inflation rate at a certain constant level. Unfortunately, the Fed doesn't have a perfect model of the economy; the Fed's governors have to guess about when inflation might start to rise. If they want to please domestic lenders and reassure foreign creditors, they will always make a conservative guess. They'll never tiptoe near the edge. They will try to avoid even letting unemployment go down to its natural rate (if it *has* a natural rate), because that level would already be in the danger zone.

Again, if you are a thoroughgoing natural-rater and you think inflation is a bad thing, this approach won't bother you: the inflation rate will keep coming down until it reaches zero. (The Fed won't be stupid enough to let it go below zero; at least, we don't think they will.) But if the natural rate theory isn't quite right, if there is a *range* of unemployment rates that are consistent with stable inflation, then the unemployment rate will always be near the top of that range. Millions of people will be — and in our view, millions of people are — unnecessarily out of work.

And interest rates will be too high: not only will too many people be out of work, but too little new investment will take place. A better way to reassure foreign creditors would be for the nation to stop borrowing so much from abroad, for the government to stop running large budget deficits, for the public to start planning seriously for retirement. Then the United States could build good jobs for the future without borrowing the necessary funds from abroad. The dollar might go down (because U.S. interest rates would go down) or it might go up (because the rest of the world would gain more confidence in the United States), but it would not be at risk of a free fall.

Given the U.S. propensity to borrow, the paranoia of international investors is hard to dismiss lightly. At times, that paranoia becomes delusional. In 1994 and 1995, for example, currency traders seemed convinced that the Clinton administration *wanted* a weak dollar. The weak dollar, traders insisted, was being used as a bargaining chip in trade negotiations. The administration never did or said anything (at least, not publicly) to encourage this belief, but attention focused on what wasn't done and what wasn't said. The administration didn't argue vehemently enough for a stronger dollar. It didn't intervene aggressively enough in the foreign exchange market. The abundance of economic evidence, however, indicates that domestic intervention in the foreign exchange market — no matter how aggressive — has little lasting impact on the value of a currency. Nobody wants a weak dollar, but nobody can control the dollar's value.

If America is to transcend our present problems, then we must learn to disregard this paranoia of foreign investors. A weak dollar, even a free-falling dollar, is not necessarily a bad thing. If it encourages Germany and Japan and France and Switzerland to loosen up on their own currencies, it may even be a good thing. But, we repeat, the *fear* of a free-falling dollar — as long as it motivates the Fed to keep interest rates high — is a very bad thing.

There is another issue here. When foreign investors lose confidence in the dollar, they do not necessarily lose confidence in America. One way to deal with worries about the value of U.S. treasury bonds is to exchange them for other U.S. assets, like stocks. The option of owning shares in American industry is becoming very attractive to foreigners now. With American workers, still the most productive in the world, now willing to work for peanuts, there are huge profits to be made here. With the dollar relatively weak in terms of what it can buy in Paris or Tokyo, the advantage becomes even stronger. Not only do American workers work for peanuts, they work for dollar-denominated peanuts. When a firm makes something in the United States, it pays its workers in dollars, which are cheap, but then it can sell the product in France or Germany or Japan and get paid in an expensive currency. Slowly but surely, foreign investors and currency traders are beginning to realize this opportunity. As long as the debt service culture continues to squeeze ever more out of American workers, there really is little danger of a permanent collapse in the dollar. Unless American workers decide they would rather be paid in deutsche marks.

Foreign Trade and the Decline of Labor

Ironically, the craven state of the American working class is partly a result of America's need to borrow from abroad during the strong-dollar years of the 1980s. In chapter 3, we described the "success" of Reaganomics in breaking the labor movement and thereby "raising aggregate supply" (i.e., getting workers to do more work for less money). But there is more to the story.

Back in 1982, just as Reagan's tax cuts were first taking effect, Americans were still worried about their dependence on foreign oil. Apart from oil, however, the United States was more or less self-sufficient. Imported goods other than oil accounted for less than 6 percent of the products bought in the United States. That fraction had barely changed in eight years. Then Americans suddenly developed an appetite for foreign goods. By 1988 those non-oil imports accounted for more than 8 percent of products bought in the United States. The increase was particularly strong among consumer goods.

Why did Americans suddenly want imported products? It's no mystery. During the early 1980s, because of the rising dollar, foreign goods became much, much cheaper for Americans to buy. In 1985, for example, a dollar bought twice as many French francs as in 1980. As the United States recovered from the 1982 recession, consumers increased their spending as usual, but instead of buying only American goods, they included a generous helping of foreign goods on their plates.

The reason for the rising dollar is no mystery, either. The combination of the budget deficits under President Reagan and the tight-money policy under Fed Chairman Volcker gave the United States very high interest rates. These were a signal to investors that America needed to borrow money. People did not want to earn 5 percent on their money in Europe when they could earn 10 percent in the United States, so they all tried to buy dollars. When everyone tries to buy dollars, the value of the dollar goes up, and imports become cheaper for Americans to buy. In 1985, after the Fed moved to a less extreme policy, the dollar began to drop, but the change in American buying habits was well under way. With the dollar strong for several years, Americans had realized that they could no longer afford to shop patriotically. Having given up their illusions of patriotism in consumption, Americans did not seek to regain their innocence as the dollar fell. Moreover, foreign firms that exported to the United States, now that they had a foot in the door, didn't mind getting squeezed a little. Instead of raising their dollar prices as the dollar dropped, they kept prices low and continued to expand their market share.

The ultimate importance of this "import penetration" for workers is not in the trade deficit itself but in the fact that lines of competition have been opened. Even if American manufacturers regain their market share (which they most likely will), they are not playing in the same game as fifteen years ago. The low prices of the mid-1980s caused American consumers to lose their resistance to foreign goods. Even if they now start buying more American goods, they will continue to compare those with foreign goods. "Comparison shopping" in America is now an international phenomenon. Furthermore, the channels of distribution that opened in the 1980s remain open. The massive U.S. borrowing during the 1980s has made it much easier to market foreign goods in the United States. International competition is now a fact of life.

How does this international competition affect American workers? Most people think international competition means that American workers are losing their jobs to foreign workers. But that is not really true. The shortage of jobs in the United States is an *intentional* result of monetary policy, not a side effect of foreign trade. The real importance of foreign competition is for *wages*, not for jobs.

The relevance of foreign competition to wages is most clear in unionized settings. In a closed economy (without foreign competition), when a union pushes for higher wages, management can often grant them because it can then pass the cost on to consumers by raising prices. In economic jargon, we say that "demand is inelastic." In other words, people will still be willing to buy the product at a higher price. In an open economy, like in the United States today, demand is likely to be highly "elastic." In other words, if you raise your price, people will just switch from your product to a foreign product. In this setting, unions have little bargaining power. Management cannot afford to raise prices, because it will lose too many customers. Consequently, management takes a hard line against higher wages. The "monopoly power" of unions, which in earlier times allowed them to push up wages, has little effect when close substitutes for American products are available from overseas.

"Monopoly power" for workers does not exist only in union settings. Even when workers are not represented by a union, they are still organized. They still talk to one another. They can still react in a collective way to what the boss does. When foreign competition was less important, even nonunion workers had some leverage to raise wages. Today nonunion workers have lost what little leverage they had, just as unionized workers have lost their leverage. With the channels of international competition open, we can expect that U.S. wages will continue to stagnate, with or without unions, and with or without a trade deficit.

THE TRADE DEFICIT IN THE 1990S

As for the trade deficit itself, there is good reason to expect that it will soon decline. This is not good news. In 1991 the U.S. trade deficit almost disappeared, but nobody was happy about it. The trade deficit almost disappeared then because the United States was in a recession. Because of the recession, U.S. firms had little desire to invest: why build factories when nobody is buying the products? Since there was so little investment, there was no need to borrow from abroad. Instead, the United States devoted its domestic resources to consumption.

Since 1991 the U.S. trade deficit has appeared again. In 1995 it was more than $100 billion. Nevertheless, the situation in the 1990s is completely different from that in the 1980s. In the 1980s government borrowing and tight money led to a strong dollar, which made U.S. products less competitive and thereby caused a trade deficit. In the 1990s something is missing. The government is still borrowing and money is still tight (at least we think so), but the dollar is no longer strong. By almost any measure, it is cheaper to buy things with dollars than with most other major currencies. This raises two questions. First, with tight money and government borrowing still going on, why is the dollar so weak? Second, with the dollar so weak, why is there a trade deficit?

The first question — why the dollar is so weak — we have already answered: the dollar is weak because international investors have lost confidence in it. But why, with American goods now so cheap relative to foreign goods, does the United States still import more than it exports? The main reason is that most of our trading partners are in recessions. It's 1991 in reverse. With Japan, Canada, Mexico, and Europe all down in the dumps, nobody wants to invest in those places. Consequently, capital is flowing into the United States to finance our continued borrowing.[44] As capital flows in, by definition, so do goods and services. To put it another way, with investment demand so low in other countries, they have no use for U.S. products right now, no matter how cheap they are. In the 1980s America financed its borrowing straightforwardly: we raised interest rates so the rest of the world would lend to us. In the 1990s we have the convenience of financing our borrowing with the world's "leftover capital."

This situation is likely to change. Eventually, foreign economies will recover and will need their capital at home. Demand for U.S. products will pick up, and the trade deficit will fall. Our foreign saviors will desert us. At that point, something has to give. A struggle will take place between high investment, high consumption, and low employment. Three outcomes are possible:

1. (worst and most likely outcome) the Fed will raise real
   interest rates to choke off investment[45]
2. (better and less likely) Americans will start to save more of
   their money and reduce their consumption
3. (best but least likely outcome) the Fed, and America's
   economists, will finally come to its senses and let
   employment rise to levels that might scare the lenders

If you are an optimist, you can still hope for what's behind door number 3. We'll explore these options in Part Four of this book, "The Road Back to Affluence." For now, we continue our tour of the Indebted Society with a look at the rotten deal that debt has made for underprivileged Americans.

11·Out of Luck

BLESSED BE YE POOR, for yours is the Kingdom of God. Evangelists, take heart: the Indebted Society is supplying plenty of citizens for the kingdom of God. Among U.S. religious denominations, only Roman Catholics still outnumber the 38 million Americans living below the poverty line. Childhood poverty in particular has reached shocking proportions: as of 1994, 22 percent of U.S. children — more than one out of five — lived below the poverty line. Between 1978 and 1994 the poverty rate among children rose by an average four-tenths of a percentage point per year, and there is no reason to expect a leveling of this trend anytime soon. Projecting out to the year 2020, the vision becomes frightening: nearly a third of America's children living in poverty. For such is the kingdom of God.

Obviously, poverty has been around since long before the Sermon on the Mount. Even in the United States, poverty is not a new problem. During the 1930s, by some estimates, a full two-thirds of the population lived in poverty. Between 1933 and 1973, however, a growing U.S. economy — with some help from government assistance programs — lifted millions out of poverty. Between 1959 and 1973, despite a growing population, the number of Americans living in poverty fell by more than 16 million. Economic growth has continued, albeit more slowly, since 1973. Yet, between 1973 and 1993 not only the absolute number of poor but also the rate of poverty has shown an alarming increase: in 1973 barely 11 percent of Americans fit the official definition of "poor"; by 1993 that figure had risen to more than 15 percent. Our increasingly Indebted Society has also become increasingly poor. How and why has this happened?

JOBS AND POVERTY

In biblical times, as well as in preindustrial America and in much of the developing world today, the poor were mostly people who worked but had little to show for it. In a modern economy the poor are often those who do not have the opportunity to work. Accordingly, economists have long recognized a connection between poverty and the business cycle. During low points in the business cycle, when many people are looking unsuccessfully for work, poverty is high. The Great Depression, with its low point in 1933, is an extreme example. Typically, at high points in the business cycle, when unemployment is low, the poverty rate reaches a temporary trough. In 1973, for example, the economic boom — the same one that had aided Richard Nixon's reelection — helped bring the poverty rate to its all-time low of 11.1 percent.

The experience of the past thirty-five years, however, does not suggest a simple connection between poverty and unemployment. Figure 11.1 shows graphically the observed relationship between the poverty rate and the unemployment rate from 1959 to 1994. The figure perhaps has more value as abstract art than as evidence of any link between poverty and unemployment. The horizontal line across the middle indicates that even our computer could find no relationship.

Contrast Figure 11.1 with Figure 11.2, which substitutes the Normalized Help Wanted Index (described in chapter 7) for the unemployment rate. Apparently, there *is* a strong relationship between job availability and poverty: when jobs are plentiful, as evidenced by high levels of help-wanted advertising, the poverty rate is typically low; when jobs are scarce, the poverty rate is typically high. More careful econometric analysis has confirmed that declines in help-wanted advertising are more closely linked to rising poverty than are increases in the unemployment rate. With this in mind, look back at Figure 7.1. The recent economic recovery has not been accompanied by a strong increase in help-wanted advertising. Highly indebted firms are not eager to take on new commitments by hiring new workers. It should not come as a great surprise, then, that this recovery has done nothing to reduce poverty: between 1991 and 1994, as business conditions improved, the poverty rate *rose* from 14.2 percent to 14.5 percent.

The link between poverty and a scarcity of advertised jobs is more than a mathematical correlation. The absence of available jobs means that unemployed people must search a long time to find a job. For those without other sources of income, the difference between a short job search and a long job search is the difference between inconvenience and poverty. During the 1990s, although the rate of unemployment has not been unusually high, long job searches have become the norm. In 1993, according to a monthly government survey of households, the average unemployed person had been jobless for four and a half months. One out of five had been jobless for more than six months. In 1977, at a comparable point in the business cycle, the average unemployed person had been jobless for slightly more than three months, and only one out of seven had been jobless for more than six months. After 1977 the average duration of unemployment fell precipitously, as it usually does when an economic recovery gets well under way. After 1993, by contrast, the average duration continued to rise, probably because of the scarcity of new jobs.

FIGURE 11.1 UNEMPLOYMENT AND POVERTY
1959–94

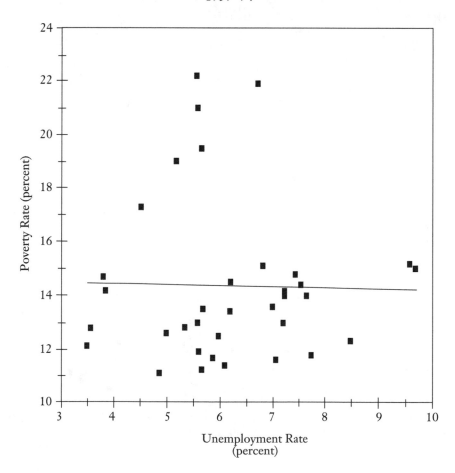

The trend to longer spells of unemployment was accompanied by a greater prevalence of white collars among the jobless (see chapter 5). Although the popular image of white-collar workers is one of relative wealth, the reality is more complex. Many white-collar workers, particularly those in clerical, technical, and sales occupations, have relatively low wages. This group — low-paid white-collar workers — is one for whom long spells of unemployment pose a particularly high risk of poverty. These people are not likely to have other sources of income, nor are they likely to have much savings to fall back on. Table 11.1 shows the percentage of unemployed low-paid white-

FIGURE 11.2 JOB AVAILABILITY AND POVERTY
1959–94

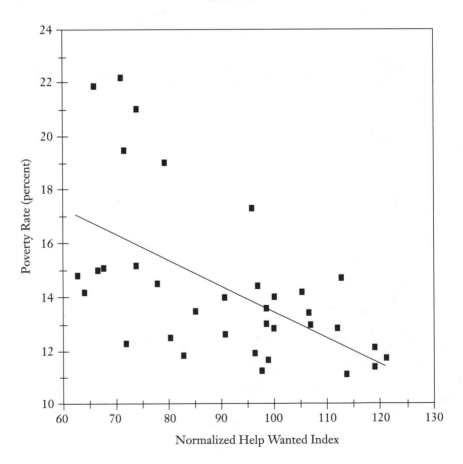

TABLE 11.1 PERCENTAGE OF UNEMPLOYED
LOW-PAID WHITE-COLLAR WORKERS*
ON LONG SPELLS OF UNEMPLOYMENT**

Year	Percentage
1971	22
1977	28
1982	30
1983	37
1984	29
1992	37

Source: J. Medoff, Brookings Papers on Economic Activity, 2: 1993, pp. 334–35.
Notes: *Primarily those in "clerical" or "sales" jobs
  **Fifteen weeks or more

collar workers on long spells of unemployment (fifteen weeks or more) at various times since 1971. Clearly, this group has found it harder and harder to find the new jobs that would enable them to avoid poverty.

Even those who do find new jobs end up closer to poverty than they would have in earlier years. Between 1979 and 1991, while median earnings of all workers fell by 5 percent, median earnings of recently hired workers fell by 11 percent. (We define "recently hired workers" as those with less than one year at a firm.) Back in the 1970s, when unemployment was largely attributable to temporary layoffs, a person waiting to return to his or her old job might be unwilling to accept a near-poverty job. In the 1990s the most common reason for unemployment has been the permanent disappearance of jobs. Near-poverty looks like the better choice when the alternative is true poverty. Unfortunately, in the Indebted Society, poverty is too often the only choice.

Even "finding work" per se cannot be counted on to raise one above the poverty line. Labor force statistics show more than a million adult Americans who work part-time but live in poverty because they cannot find full-time work. Several million — disproportionately, single mothers — work full-time but do not earn enough to keep their families out of poverty. One full-time income at today's minimum wage is not enough to support a two-person family above the poverty line. Even two full-time incomes at the minimum wage cannot support a family of five. As far as the labor market is concerned, many Americans — both with and without jobs — are just out of luck.

The War Is Over

How much is the government doing today to help reduce poverty? Quite a lot, it turns out, for the elderly and disabled, but very little for anyone else. Department of Commerce statistics suggest that almost 7 percent of Americans are kept out of poverty only by their Social Security income. Thus, most older Americans without substantial private incomes are able to escape into near-poverty. By contrast, about only 1 percent of Americans are kept out of poverty by means-tested government cash transfers such as welfare payments. Even though about 15 percent of the official poor would be reckoned slightly above the poverty line if the cash value of their Medicaid benefits were fully taken into account, by any definition poverty is on the rise, and the poverty rate is much higher than it was twenty years ago.

Thirty-two years ago, in his 1964 State of the Union address, President Johnson declared "an unconditional war on poverty." After five years of that unconditional war (helped along by rapid economic growth), the poverty rate had fallen by five percentage points, and the number of poor had fallen by nearly 12 million. Throughout the 1970s the poverty rate remained below 12.5 percent (compared with 19 percent in 1964), and the number of poor remained below 27 million (compared with 36 million in 1964).

In 1981 President Reagan declared, in effect, that the war was over. Not that we had won, but that the goal of defeating poverty was not worth fighting for. Although there should always be a "safety net" for the "truly needy," the poor in general were to be blamed for their own poverty. Trying to improve their lives would only bring dependency and make the situation worse. However, it appears that the particular programs cut by the Reagan administration could not have been the ones that were aggravating the problem. In the most recent statistics, there are more poor people in America than there were in 1964, and the poverty rate hovers near 15 percent. At the 1989 business cycle peak, the poverty rate was higher than during the 1975 recession.

Nonetheless, Americans believe — increasingly and by huge margins — that the government is doing *too much* to help the poor. In a 1984 Roper poll, Americans were asked, "What do you consider a more serious problem in America today — families who are *not getting enough welfare benefits* to get by, or families *getting more welfare benefits than they need?* Forty-nine percent said that "families getting more than they need" was a bigger problem; only 29 percent said that "families not getting enough" was a bigger problem. When the same question was asked in 1994, 58 percent said that "families getting more than they need" was a bigger problem, and only 21 percent said "families not getting enough" was a bigger problem. These numbers may be shocking to anyone of liberal inclinations. In the Indebted Society, however, they should not be surprising.

From people who are working ever harder for ever lower real wages, one cannot expect sympathy for those who — however miserably — are able to survive without working. From people who tiptoe daily near the downsizing precipice, one cannot expect compassion for those who — according to the myth popularized by conservative extremists — becruise the narrow world with welfare Cadillacs. From people who have seen government go deeply into debt without raising *their* standard of living at all, one cannot expect support for programs that use the government's scarce resources to help *others*. The boundless social possibilities imagined during the middle years of this century have faded as the stars might fade while one descends into hell. The damned are not known for their compassion.

THE LOCAL FRONT

In accordance with the will of the Indebted Society, the dismantling of antipoverty programs continues. But "cutting" such programs has gone out of fashion. Instead, the goal is to make them "more efficient" — a laudable goal, given the present fiscal circumstances. The way to make these programs more efficient, we are told, is to transfer responsibility to state and local governments. The most frequent assertion is that it is not efficient to require all of the country's myriad governments to do the same thing ("all wear size-six shoes"). Moreover, it is frequently asserted that states and localities, when acting independently, are much more innovative and creative, in toto, than Big Brother acting by himself.

But what, in the 1990s, are the likely distributional consequences of greater local government control? This is the same concern that should have been addressed in October 1972 when Congress passed the State and Local Fiscal Assistance Act (P.L. 92-512).

It appears that the poor and near-poor were likely to fare worse under Richard Nixon's "revenue sharing" ("super" block grant) program than under the tied ("categorical") grants in aid that the federal government offered states and localities at the time. An analysis cowritten in 1974 by one of this book's authors estimated the costs and benefits of the revenue-sharing program to the poorest sixth of the population. These people, the study found, would suffer a third of the costs and get at most about only a sixth of the benefits. The northward march in the poverty rate since 1973, along with a general increase in inequality, suggests that the study's expectations have been realized.

In the early seventies, the federal government was much more pro-poor in how it "tied" grants than the states and localities were in spending unrestricted funds. The same is true today. When state and local governments spend as they wish, they do far less for the poor than when Washington dictates how funds must be used — most likely reflecting the fact that states and localities want to attract employers and not poor people.

Richard Nixon is now dead. However, untied federal grants in aid are still very much alive. Their likely effects on the poor remain harmful.

Help!

Those who favor the dismantling of government antipoverty programs often tout private support as the antidote to poverty. Have Americans responded to the call for charity? Table 11.2 tells the story. In the 1980s it appeared that they were responding (although not sufficiently to compensate for the cuts in government programs). Combined corporate and personal giving (relative to gross domestic product) rose by almost 19 percent from the 1970s (although it was still down 5 percent from the 1960s). In the 1990s, however, private contributions (relative to gross domestic product) have fallen below even the level of the 1970s. Lamentably, but predictably, the fall in

TABLE 11.2 INDEX OF PRIVATE GIVING/GDP

Years	Index Number (1960s = 100)
1960s	100
1970s	80
1980s	95
1990s	78

Source: U.S. Department of Commerce; Conference Board

private giving came just as the poverty rate was rising to post-1965 highs. Unfortunately, the factors that reduce willingness to give are often the same as those that create the need.

In inflation-adjusted terms, corporate philanthropy fell in every single year from 1988 through 1994, according to the American Association of Fund-Raising Counsel. Firms that face increased pressure from debt service and from the resulting "anything to raise profits" culture obviously cannot afford to give away money.

Surveys conducted by the Gallup Organization for a group called Independent Sector tracked household giving at two-year intervals from 1987 to 1993. Although household giving rose between 1987 and 1989, it fell sharply from 1989 to 1991, and it fell again from 1991 to 1993. In inflation-adjusted terms, the average 1993 household contribution was nearly 10 percent lower than in 1987. As a percentage of household income, however, households gave slightly more in 1993 than in 1987. The problem is that real household incomes declined sharply over that period. In charitable giving, as in other areas, households must run faster and faster just to stay in place. Given the ever increasing burden of consumer debt loads, the prospects for increased generosity are bleak.

Now the government debt problem may even be interfering with private charity. An article in the January 28, 1995, *New York Times* tried to explain the decline in charitable giving compared with the previous winter:

Although the poor local economy is probably the central reason for the decline, the heads of many charities say they believe that cynicism at the

government level is also to blame. The House Republicans' proposal to
slash welfare benefits and eliminate other social programs, they say,
has maligned the poor and discouraged middle-class Americans from
giving.

This piece suggests that the drive to rein in federal spending has, perhaps unwittingly, spawned a general contempt for the poor. If this is
true, it strengthens the already robust conclusion: the ultimate effect
of Reaganomics has been to undermine our country's underprivileged, not just by cutting government help but also by discouraging
the private help that the Reagan administration touted. Whether or
not the link suggested in the *Times* is valid, the dismal economic conditions in the wake of 1980s' policies have certainly done their part to
make giving more difficult. With respect to jobs, government help,
and private charity, a substantial number of Americans are out of
luck, and the situation shows no signs of improvement.

RAGS AND RICHES

The prevalence of poverty and near-poverty in the Indebted Society is symptomatic of a larger problem. Numerous studies show
an increase in overall inequality across the income spectrum. In other
words, the rich got richer, and the poor got poorer. Moreover, the
lower middle class got even lower, and the upper middle class got far-
ther up. In 1978 the 20 percent of households with the lowest incomes got 4.2 percent of total household income, while the 5 percent
with the highest incomes got 16.8 percent of total household income.
In 1993 the lowest 20 percent got only 3.6 percent of total household
income, while the highest 5 percent got a full 20 percent. Similar patterns — increases at the top and decreases at the bottom — are seen
within the remaining 75 percent of households.

This increased stratification is at least partly due to the debt-
mongering policies of the 1980s. By reducing both private and public
investment, those policies ensured both a future of bad jobs for the
lower middle class and a future of high incomes for the capital-rich
upper class. Because capital became scarce, its rate of return rose. Because workers had less capital to work with, their real incomes — on
average — fell. The future of income inequity depends in large part
on how the nation deals with the debt it now has.

A JUST SOCIETY ... NOT

In his classic book, *A Theory of Justice*, Harvard philosopher John Rawls writes that a just society would maximize the well-being of the worst off. He came to this concept of justice by imagining what choices people would make for society if they were separated from their actual roles by "a veil of ignorance." In other words, he imagined the individual making choices from an "original position," before the actual society came to be, without knowing who in that society he or she would become.

In our Indebted Society, most adults have a very good idea of their likely fate. While most are unlikely to be among the worst off, they have fallen far short of their expectations. As a result, the typical American is not receptive to helping the worst off. Rawls's "veil of ignorance" is a powerful philosophical concept. However, to people who have a good idea about how everyone is likely to fare, it is *only* a philosophical concept. And for people whose lot is far below what they had anticipated, its moral power does not resonate.

As long as people in the Indebted Society earn less than expected, they are most unlikely to be generous. For the "not" to be removed from this section's heading, real earnings must again grow vigorously. If not, the Indebted Society will remain "just . . . not."

12 ▪ Family Values

For families in America, the effects of the corporate debt service culture and the associated downsizing movement have often been devastating. Personal debt only increases the stress in the lives of all types of families, and government debt service threatens to limit the use of public funds to help families in crisis. The Indebted Society is not friendly either to families or to values.

In this chapter, we take a look at how the values of the Indebted Society have an impact on families. In general, our society encourages the use of material goods as substitutes for our deeper needs for love and meaningful work. The purchase of material goods has the effect of increasing debt, which exacerbates the conditions that have made love and meaningful work scarce to begin with. The result is increased alienation from spouses and children, who turn to violence more and more frequently to express their despair.

Matters of the Mind

Sigmund Freud believed that individuals' mental health depends greatly on their work and love lives. When either of these sources of psychological well-being is less than desired, problems of either the "heart" or the "head" can be expected. Traditionally, the family is the context in which these needs are satisfied: love is the cornerstone of a healthy family, and work is the means by which adult family members support, maintain, and nourish the well-functioning family. Families and family members, even in highly functional families, have always experienced problems of one sort or another in both love and work. In the Indebted Society these problems have become severe, and deficiencies in love and work have fed one another. One now observes a highly dysfunctional society replete with dysfunctional families.

The attempts of members of the Indebted Society to satisfy their basic needs for success in love and work have frequently involved deeper plunges into debt. Most seem to believe that consumption can provide more satisfaction at a time when they feel that they can't get enough. Don't like your spouse? Buy some silk bedsheets! Don't like your job? Buy a wide-screen TV!

Of course, these actions do nothing to fix the underlying problems. They do, however, impede one's ability to live within one's means. Thus, attempts to reduce the deepest problems have frequently led to deeper debt. Consumption has distracted people from the real needs in their relationships, while the jobs created by consumption spending have been relatively few and generally of inferior quality in terms of pay, benefits, and opportunities for personal fulfillment.

Within the family itself, personal debt has been a frequent source of conflict. While scholarly research on the subject is not abundant, widespread anecdotal experience attests to the strains placed on family relationships by high debt levels. Whether debt comes as a means to obtain substitutes for real personal needs or as a means to obtain necessities during economic hard times, the accumulation of debt weighs on the family. As of this writing, family debt levels in the United States are outstripping family incomes by record amounts.

EXTERNAL STRAINS

Nonetheless, it is not personal debt but corporate debt that has had the most virulent effect on families in the Indebted Society. Corporate financial vulnerability provided the initial justification for most of the purges suffered by America's workers, and the process has snowballed in the culture born thereof. Job loss — especially the increasingly common permanent job loss by middle-aged men — and the scarcity of new jobs have broken the backs of many families.

There is strong evidence, both scientific and anecdotal, that the loss of one's job, like the loss of a loved one, causes depression. In the pre-nineties recessions, job losers were much more likely to be on temporary layoff than is true today. Historically, more than 80 percent could expect to be recalled to their old employers. The lob losses in the nineties have not been "temporary." Job-loss depression is deepened when that loss appears permanent or when the realistic options for reemployment pale when compared with the job lost.

Moreover, the downturn in the nineties (as implied in chapter 5) was the first on record in which the percentage of unemployed white-collar workers *grew*. For the first time the percentage of a downturn's newly unemployed workers with white collars was above the predownturn white-collar percentage. Adding to the job-loss stress of white-collar workers is the fact that these workers tend to earn larger salaries and receive more extensive benefit packages than those whose collars are blue. Loss of wages and benefits, therefore, can prove more problematic to these workers because traditional salary replacement programs, such as unemployment insurance, are likely to fall far short of previous earnings.

As was noted in chapter 5, job losers were most unlikely to find a job as good as the one lost (and certainly not quickly). Firms contemplating their potential financial circumstances are not anxious to take on new obligations by hiring new workers, and the economic policies engendered by the power of lenders have deliberately failed to encourage such new hiring. These facts help us understand the great stress, anxiety, and depression suffered by those who permanently lost their jobs.

THE RISE OF THE TWO-INCOME FAMILY

One of the widely noted side effects of stagnating real wages is the increased number of families in which both parents are employed. According to statistics compiled by the U.S. Department of Labor, the proportion of married families in which both spouses work rose from 47 percent in 1969 to 59 percent in 1993. The proportion of married families in which only the husband works fell from 41 percent in 1969 to 20 percent in 1993. We cite these statistics not to suggest that wives in the workforce is a negative development, but to underscore that it is no longer possible to support a family on one income. In fact, as the rate of two-income families increased, the growth in the average real income of families decreased dramatically.

Given the stresses associated with downsizing and the tenuous nature of stable employment in the Indebted Society, it is evident that many families with both parents working are under considerable emotional and economic pressure. This struggle has caused many marriages to become rocky. In 1993, 7.6 percent of men and 10.1 percent of women reported their marital status as "divorced." These rates represent increases of 0.4 and 0.7 percentage points, for men and women respectively, in just three years, and increases of 2.4 and

3.0 percentage points since 1980. For both men and women, the 1993 rates are more than double what they were in 1970. For men, the rate is more than three times what it was in 1970.

Although this increasing prevalence of divorce can be attributed to any number of causes, at least part of it results from the economic conditions of the Indebted Society. A powerful relationship between permanent job loss and divorce appears in research from a set of data called the National Longitudinal Survey, provided to us by Paul Harrington of Northeastern University. Looking at the sample of men from age eighteen to age twenty-eight (in 1992) who were or had been married and who were in the National Longitudinal Survey continuously between 1983 and 1991 shows that, among those who did not suffer a permanent job loss during the period, only 9 percent had divorced. Among those who did suffer a permanent job loss, a full 14 percent — more than half again as many — had divorced. Male permanent job loss — a phenomenon increasingly prevalent in the Indebted Society — seems to have a very negative impact on marital strength. Losses of all kinds appear in the Indebted Society, and those losses seem to be related.

The consequences of divorce can reverberate throughout the family. After a divorce, the income of most female heads of household decreases dramatically. Reduced earnings coupled with the increased demands of single parenting threatens the emotional well-being of both parent and child. Sara McLanahan of Princeton has provided much evidence on the impact of divorce on children. In an analysis of data from the Panel Study of Income Dynamics, she compares children who are similar in terms of race, sex, parents' education, number of siblings, and place of residence. Several findings emerge. First, children who live with only one parent are 6 percent more likely to drop out of high school than children who live with both parents. Second, teenage girls living with only one parent are 9 percent more likely to give birth (as a teenager) than girls living with both parents. Third, teenage boys and young men from one-parent families are 11 percent more likely to be "idle" — that is, out of school and not working — than their two-parent counterparts.

Does the situation improve when the parents remarry? Unfortunately, the situation seems to get worse. Children in stepfamilies are 10 percent more likely to drop out of high school than children living with their original two parents, and teenage girls in stepfamilies are 13 percent more likely to give birth than those living with their original two parents. The "idleness" risk for males, however, does fall from 11 percent to 5 percent with parents' remarriage.

Professor David Elkind, noted Tufts child psychologist, writes in *Ties That Stress: The New Family Imbalance* that today's home "is no longer a haven, a place for nurturance and protection." He adds in an interview with Linda Matcham of the *Boston Globe* that "it's more like a railway station, with people coming and going. It is not as supportive of children . . . who feel much less protected and less secure."[46] It is not difficult to understand how parents faced with extreme economic and job pressures have little left to give to their children or to each other. Until parents are afforded the time and financial security to reverse the trend, our children will continue to pay an exorbitant price.

HELP FROM UNCLE SAM?

Given the difficult conditions for families in the Indebted Society, one might hope for some help, at least for the poorest families, from their formerly rich uncle. Federal programs to help poor families still do exist, but Uncle Sam's fiscal difficulties are threatening those programs. The three major existing federal attempts to help poor families are the food stamps program, Aid to Families with Dependent Children (AFDC), and the earned income tax credit. All three have recently been seen in the vicinity of the fiscal chopping block.

The welfare overhaul bill passed by the House of Representatives in March 1995 provides a glimpse of what may be in store. That bill would cut welfare spending by $69 billion over five years and would turn dozens of federal programs over to the states in the form of block grants. In addition, the bill would deny cash benefits to unwed mothers under eighteen and set a five-year limit on receiving benefits. It would also deny food stamps to those able to work who do not find a job within ninety days.

All those cuts in welfare for nonworking families are understandable, given the myth that jobs are easy to get and the bizarre idea that poor women who work full-time can somehow still care for their children. After all, why encourage families to be poor by offering them assistance? But it gets worse. Even poor families with working parents are now threatened. The earned income tax credit, which helps poor working people with children by reducing their tax liability, has appeared — and may appear again — as a possible casualty in budget-balancing plans being bandied about in Washington. Legislation already enacted will exclude from the credit families with certain types of income starting in 1996. Some have suggested doing away with the credit entirely. "It doesn't work," they say. Luckily, its recipients do work: for now, they have the good fortune to have jobs.

With the debt service culture cutting existing jobs and lender-friendly economic policies inhibiting the creation of new jobs, Uncle Sam's increasing penuriousness comes at an unfortunate time. For families in the Indebted Society, the maxim is as follows: "One hand taketh away, and the other taketh away."

EATING OUR YOUNG

The rise of a debt culture is extracting a high price from children and young adults in the Indebted Society. The younger generation composes a large group of involuntary lenders. Unlike most lenders, they receive no return for their sacrifice, have little political influence, and most unusual, will themselves ultimately have to repay the loans.

This group that suffers from a sort of "taxation without representation" consists of the more than 100 million Americans under the age of thirty. The lending (or "taxation") of these young people occurs because an elder generation has chosen to spend its money today instead of investing in the future. Some of these elders are parents who feel that consumption is a panacea for all their maladies. Many were told in their youth that they would be richer than their parents. Their spending has been consistent with this expectation, but their incomes have not. As a result, their children may end up poorer than they are.

The spending habits of this group of elders were encouraged by politicians who blithely offered to cut their taxes while assuring them that no cuts in public services were necessary. More recently, another crop of politicians has suggested that America restore to the young their patrimony by cutting child nutrition and education programs. If these children don't starve, and if they are lucky enough to find low-paying jobs when they grow up (instead of living on the street), they will thank the wise statesmen of today for limiting the national debt that will have to be serviced.

In the conventional sense, by passing on debts to its children, the Indebted Society is eating its young. As others have noted, this is particularly true of government debt. Unlike private debt, government debt is not presumed to be payable by those who incur it.

More broadly, however, debt is destroying the prospects of the young. Corporate debt has made jobs scarce and insecure. Personal debt and the culture that promotes it have put the needs of parents before those of children. A generation is coming of age alienated in the present and despairing of the future.

To Borrow and to Borrow and to Borrow

Borrowing comes in several different forms, which have different consequences. It is commonly — and rightly, to some extent — argued that public debt is an unfair burden on the next generation because they have to pay it back even though they didn't borrow it. In fact, this argument isn't always true, because when used wisely, public debt can finance investments that give younger generations the opportunity to produce more. If the additional productivity exceeds the amount of the debt, these subsequent generations are actually better off than without the debt. Moreover, even aside from physical investments, public debt — in combination with an accommodative monetary policy — can improve the functioning of the economy so that it can create jobs for the younger generation. In that case also, the young may be better off for the presence of public debt. This seems to have been the case with the huge public debt taken on during World War II. Before the war, jobs were few, and despite the comparatively low level of public debt, one could hardly envy the young person coming of age in that environment. By the end of the war, the public debt was so high that it exceeded the total that the nation was able to produce in a year. However, the U.S. economy was back in working order. Over the following thirty years, the debt — in some sense — paid itself.

Regrettably, conditions in today's Indebted Society are very different. Instead of the nation using public debt to fight a war, monetary policy has fought a war against the public debt — and lost. As far as producing jobs, the economy still functions much better than in the 1930s but has been hurt, not helped, by public borrowing. Public debt has been used not to finance public investment but to finance tax cuts, so that people could consume more while the government borrowed on their behalf. In this context, the large fiscal deficits that began in the 1980s can truly be said to be a form of fiscal child abuse.

It doesn't stop there. Under the conditions of recent decades, there is a sense in which even private borrowing has to be paid back by the next generation. If people had chosen to save more of their money and borrow less, then more resources would have been available for investment — both private and public. With more investment, the next generation could be more productive, and there would be more good jobs created in the future. By losing the benefit of higher productivity and better jobs, younger people will in effect be paying back the private debts of their parents.

SURVIVAL OF THE LUCKIEST

Unfortunately, what has been borrowed must somehow be repaid. In times of rapid growth, such as the 1950s and 1960s in America, it matters little who gets charged for the repayment, since most have much to spare. In leaner times, such as those that appear to face America over the next several decades, potential payers will struggle strenuously with one another to see who gets charged. Those who survive the struggle will prosper, and those who don't will pay.

In the Indebted Society, we are already seeing the intensity of this struggle. Those who are lucky enough to be well educated or already rich are typically doing very well, and the rest are beginning to pay. Figures 12.1 and 12.2, along with Table 12.1, display the earnings advantages that college graduates enjoy relative to those who did not go beyond high school. Among both men and women, the earnings advantage enjoyed by college graduates has risen sharply from the early eighties to the early nineties. In 1982 the earnings of college graduates were only 40 percent higher than the earnings of high school graduates, a ratio of 1.4. That ratio rose to about 1.6 by 1992, so that college graduates were earning 60 percent more than high school graduates. This equates to about a 14 percent increase in the monetary return on college. When college grads are compared with high school dropouts, the analogous percent increase is about 17.

FIGURE 12.1 EDUCATION AND EARNINGS OF MEN,
1974–92

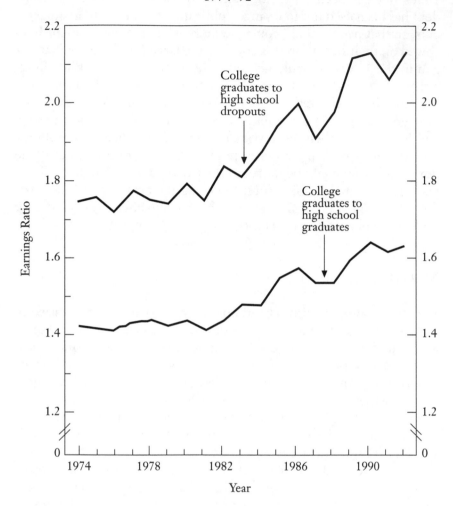

Although education depends partly on individual choices and accomplishment, the opportunity for education and the ability to benefit from it depends largely on a person's socioeconomic background. It is still expected in well-to-do families for the children to follow in their parents' footsteps and get a top-quality education. It is still an uncommon and noteworthy event when someone from a poor family transcends that poverty by getting an Ivy League scholarship. Public

FIGURE 12.2 EDUCATION AND EARNINGS OF WOMEN, 1974–92

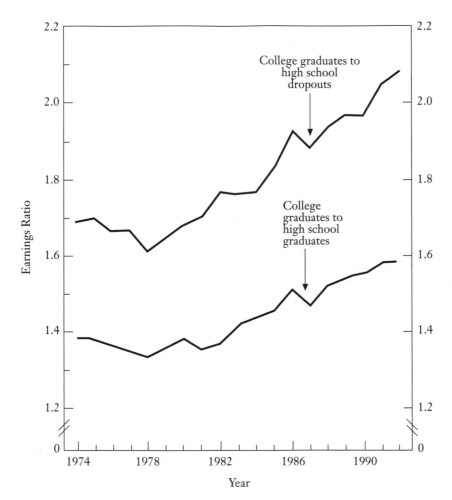

policy can be used to improve the chances for people who begin life on the lower part of the economic ladder, but in the Indebted Society, the chances of public policy being used that way are particularly low. Instead of taking new public initiatives to make education more available and more productive for poorer young people, the pressure of federal debt and interest payments provides a rationale for cutting or eliminating those initiatives that currently exist. Make no mistake

TABLE 12.1 GROWTH IN REAL EARNINGS

Group	Percent change 1979–89	Percent change 1979–92
Gender		
Men	0.7	−3.1
Women	13.0	15.3
Gender by years of schooling		
Men		
0–11	−18.2	−23.3
12	−9.7	−17.0
13–15	−.8	−7.3
16+	9.2	5.2
Women		
0–11	−.5	−7.4
12	4.0	.8
13–15	8.3	7.8
16+	17.3	18.1
Gender by years of potential experience		
Men		
0–9	−1.9	−6.9
0–19	−3.8	−8.5
20–29	2.7	.3
30+	5.5	−2.3
Women		
0–9	10.8	9.0
10–19	14.5	15.9
20–29	16.8	20.4
30+	8.6	11.3

about it, though: the ax falling on educational programs, from Head Start for young children to federal financial aid for college students, does not help the younger generation. All it does is change the distribution of pain within the younger generation. Richer young people, who will ultimately have less to pay in taxes than they otherwise would, benefit when such programs are cut. The poorer young people are the ones who end up paying.

It is also well documented that in the last fifteen years our country's richest workers have gotten *relatively* richer, and vice versa for its poorest. This is true even within educational categories. Among every gender-educational grouping of full-time wage and salary earners above age twenty-five (except women with less than four years of high school), the ratio of the pay of the richest 10 percent of earners to the poorest 10 percent has risen significantly. The top tenth of both male and female earners have enjoyed relative earnings that grew by between 15 percent and 20 percent faster than the corresponding bottom tenth between 1989 and 1993.

Beyond the statistics, looking within groups of young people, we see an increasingly competitive and painful struggle in which everyone hopes to be one of the few winners, but most end up being among the many losers. As a whole, "Generation X" is an unlucky generation. The champions of Generation X, the federal deficit fighters, seem to have twisted the motto of the baby boomers into a new, austere variation: "When the going gets tough, the tough go chopping!" As a result, Generation X+1 may be even more unlucky.

Part Three

THE VICIOUS CIRCLE

13·Productivity Nongrowth

W HAT HAPPENS WHEN AN INDEBTED society is allowed to drift? Do the political tides wash it toward the safety of subsiding debt, or do the winds of economic nature tend to blow it deeper into debt? We find, alas, little reason to think that the problem of debt can solve itself. Rather, the habits that the Indebted Society develops are precisely those that intensify its misery. In the world of real economics and real politics, debt becomes a self-sustaining tendency. The cycle can be broken only by accident or re-solve.

The Productivity Slowdown

W e have referred several times to the productivity slowdown that began in the 1970s. At this point, in order to shed some light on the vicious circle, we take a closer look at that slowdown, what might have caused it, and why it got worse during the 1980s instead of getting better.

Any discussion of productivity has to begin with the business cycle. Productivity shows a distinct pattern over the course of the business cycle, and ignoring this pattern leads to incorrect conclusions. It would be misleading, for example, to contrast the productivity stagnation of the early 1980s with the faster growth of the mid-1980s. Productivity failed to grow in the early eighties because there were two back-to-back recessions. It grew quickly in the mid-eighties because the United States was *recovering* from a deep recession. Productivity *seems* low during recessions because firms aren't taking full advantage of their workers' productive potential. During recessions firms keep a lot of workers that they don't really need immediately, so that they can respond rapidly when the economy improves. When the economy does rebound, productivity seems to grow quickly, because firms put their current employees to work more fully before hiring new ones. To get a clear view of productivity trends, we have to compare periods that begin and end at the same point in the business cycle.

With this precondition in mind, we divide the recent history of the United States into three epochs, each approximately a decade in length, and each beginning and ending at a business cycle peak. The first epoch we call the Age of Affluence. The Age of Affluence began at the business cycle peak in 1957, when Dwight Eisenhower was president, and John Kenneth Galbraith was about to write *The Affluent Society*. We carry the Age of Affluence through to the 1969 business cycle peak, early in the Nixon administration, just after the second edition of *The Affluent Society* came out. During the Age of Affluence, U.S. labor productivity grew by an average 2.9 percent per year, so that American workers could produce 40 percent more per hour of work in 1969 than in 1957.

The period following the Age of Affluence we label as the Time of Transition. The Time of Transition lasted from 1969 to 1979. In 1979 Jimmy Carter was president, prices were rising at a 10 percent annual rate, and cocaine was easier to get than gasoline. During the Time of Transition, U.S. labor productivity grew by only 1.5 percent per year, about half as fast as during the Age of Affluence. In 1979, at the end of the Time of Transition, American workers could produce only 15 percent more than they could in 1969. Even though there was some growth, it was not fast enough to raise standards of living by a noticeable amount.

Finally, the period from 1979 to 1990 we label the Days of Debt. The Days of Debt began with personal and corporate debt already at post–World War II records, but with government debt still near a post–World War II low (as a fraction of the nation's output). By the end of this period, personal and corporate debt had eclipsed their earlier records, and government debt had risen into the stratosphere. Debt had become a central fact of American life. During the Days of Debt, labor productivity growth averaged only 1.0 percent per year — for a total growth of only 11 percent for the entire period.

After the Days of Debt, of course, we find ourselves in the true Indebted Society. Since the United States seems not to have reached another business cycle peak since 1990, the jury is still out on productivity growth in the Indebted Society. Rapidly advancing computer technology provides some cause for hope on the productivity front. At best, however, productivity growth is falling far short of the Age of Affluence. In any case, the fruits of productivity growth in the Indebted Society seem earmarked for the rich. To raise the living standards of ordinary working people, the Indebted Society would have to see productivity growth faster than even in the Age of Affluence.

Now let's review the facts. The Age of Affluence (the 1960s) saw fast productivity growth (continuing, by the way, an established pattern of fast productivity growth from the 1940s and 1950s). The Time of Transition (the 1970s) saw slow productivity growth. Finally, the Days of Debt (the 1980s) saw very slow productivity growth. The big question — the one economists are still asking themselves — is why. Why did productivity growth slow down during the 1970s?

Plenty of answers are available, but none is very convincing. Some say the permissive culture of the 1960s led America's young people to lose their work ethic. Others say the technologies of the twentieth century reached the point of full exploitation, so that rapid progress was no longer possible. Many still suggest that the oil crisis of the 1970s put a sudden brake on productivity growth.

We offer another explanation, which may provide a critical piece of the puzzle: debt had a significant role in causing the slowdown and a major role in continuing it. If current conditions persist, debt will have an ever more critical role in dragging down America's productivity.

Of particular importance here is the role of corporate debt. During the late 1960s, as the Age of Affluence was drawing to a close, American corporations went on a mini–debt binge. In 1969 net interest payments by nonfinancial corporations rose above 10 percent of their cash flow for the first time since World War II. In the recessions of 1970 and 1974, as cash flow dropped because of weak sales, that debt-to-cash-flow ratio rose to higher post–World War II highs. In 1974 the proportion peaked above 15 percent. Later, in the Time of Transition, it subsided, but only because inflation was raising corporate cash flow faster than firms could take on new debt. Nonetheless, 1969 proved to be a Rubicon of sorts. Never again did the corporate debt burden (thus measured) fall to its 1969 level. Although the 1980s deserve the title "Days of Debt," they were really only a continuation of a process that was well under way during the Time of Transition.

The potential productivity-slowing effects of corporate debt were not clear at the time. However, the experience since the 1980s has made clear several mechanisms by which corporate debt can impede productivity growth. Bear in mind, though, that these forces had already started to emerge as the Time of Transition began.

Conserving Cash

Fundamentally, corporate debt is dangerous to productivity because it forces firms to plan for survival rather than to plan for success. An indebted firm must always concern itself with getting through the next recession. Conserving cash to make interest payments, and to have a comfortable margin of safety, takes precedence over improving long-term productivity.

Ownership vs. Control Revisited

To understand the causes and implications of this penny-wise attitude, we must return to the world of Michael Jensen. He argues that corporate debt is a way for a firm's owners to force their managers to maximize profits. In a firm without debt, managers have more freedom to pursue their own interests (and perhaps those of workers). In a high-debt firm, managers live under threat of bankruptcy, and they must act in ways that raise profitability.

There is one big problem with Jensen's argument: the interests of a manager in a high-debt firm are still not the same as those of the owner. In particular, consider the issue of risk. Most stockholders (owners) can afford to take great risks with an individual company because they typically own stock in many different companies. If one stock becomes worthless but another doubles in price, the holder of both stocks is no worse off. Thus, to an investor-owner, a single bankruptcy is not an intolerable risk. To a manager, however, bankruptcy may well be an intolerable risk. The owner has many stocks, but the manager has only one job. If he or she loses that job, particularly under bankruptcy conditions, he or she is in big trouble.

Now consider what this means for the way a corporation is run. Suppose the manager of an indebted firm has a choice between investing in something to improve long-term productivity and saving the firm's cash for a rainy day. With the threat of bankruptcy looming on the distant horizon, that manager will choose to save the cash. Unlike Jensen's manager, this one is not acting in the interest of stockholders. Stockholders can save their own cash in their own banks. They probably have chosen to buy stock instead of saving their money in a bank account because they want a high return, not because they want a perfectly safe investment. The firm won't get that high return by keeping its cash in a piggy bank. Thus, our manager acts in his or her own interest but against the interest of both productivity and profitability.

Now think about the firm without debt. This firm's manager faces much less risk of bankruptcy. If he or she faces a choice between long-term productivity and conserving cash, he or she will more than likely choose productivity. True, as Jensen says, this manager is not acting precisely in the interests of shareholders. For example, this manager may be unnecessarily generous with workers, so as to make friends with them. Nonetheless, this manager is much more levelheaded when it comes to maximizing long-term productivity. The owners of the firm may be better or worse off compared with those who have a more anxious manager, but society as a whole is probably better off.

How Indebted Firms Conserve Cash

All this discussion of owners and managers may sound abstract, but a look at the real world shows that firms in the Indebted Society do behave in ways that can harm productivity. A prime example is the use of excessive overtime hours. In manufacturing industries in 1994, the *average* worker put in a record 4.7 hours of overtime in the *average* week. Before the 1990s that average had never even reached four hours. In some manufacturing industries in 1994, there were reports of workers having more than forty hours of overtime in a single week. A number of studies, in particular those by John Owen, show that workers who are required to work long hours are less productive on a per-hour basis. Owen stresses that fatigue on the job is harmful to both the quantity and quality of what workers produce in an hour. However, managers at high-debt firms cannot afford the risk of hiring new employees, who may be hard to get rid of during the next recession. Therefore, in the Indebted Society, overtime hours have become a popular substitute for hiring.

Another substitute for hiring is the use of temporary help. Figure 13.1 shows the growth of the temporary-help industry between 1982

FIGURE 13.1 TEMPORARY-HELP EMPLOYMENT

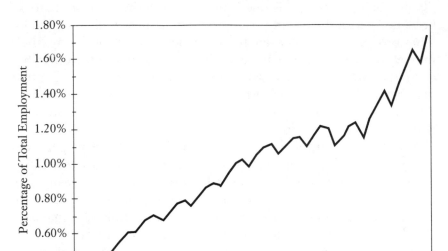

and 1994 (the period for which the government published such statistics). Since 1982 temporary help has been by far the fastest growing industry in the United States. From a productivity point of view, the problem is that temporary workers do not get much of a chance to apply on-the-job learning (or, as economists say, "to develop firm-specific human capital"). As a result, although a firm saves itself from the risk of commitment, it has to retrain workers every time it needs new help. The indebted firm is also less inclined to undertake high-productivity projects that require on-the-job training. Hiring new permanent workers would be too big a commitment, but using "temps" means wasting hours of training on a "one-shot deal."

Even when a firm does hire permanent workers, it is careful to get rid of them before they start eating up too much cash flow. Some people would say those workers are really just being reshuffled to new jobs where they can be more productive, once they are no longer needed in their old jobs. However, a study by the American Management Association (AMA) belies the image of downsizing as a process that increases productivity. In the study of firms that had downsized between 1989 and 1994, the AMA found that only 30 percent reported an increase in worker productivity. Yet 47 percent reported an increase in operating profits. Where did those new profits come from, if not from higher productivity? They didn't fall out of the sky. Usually, operating profits go up in firms that downsize because they get rid of the highest-paid workers and because the remaining workers become too intimidated to ask for raises.

A knee-jerk economist would say this doesn't make sense. The highest-paid workers, Professor Knee Jerk would say, are paid so much because they are more productive than the others. If the firm gets rid of them, it won't save any money, because it won't get as much product out of the lower-paid workers. There is just one problem with that analysis: in any given job, the higher-paid workers are *not* significantly more productive. They are just older. They get paid more because they have had more chances for wage increases over the years. By downsizing away these workers, the firm does not directly affect its average productivity, but it does manage to get the same work done for less money. Indirectly, however, it clearly hurts productivity. In the AMA study, 80 percent of companies that downsized reported a drop in employee morale — clearly not good for productivity. Moreover, when and if the business expands again, it will have to hire and retrain new workers. For the firm's bottom line, the cost of retraining may be smaller than the cost of keeping on highly paid workers. For society, the cost of retraining is definitely higher.

Furthermore, the cost of retraining is only one of many social costs. A much larger social cost may be the breakdown of trust. Economists Andrei Shleifer and Lawrence Summers have studied this issue in the context of hostile takeovers. Recent experience shows that trust breaks down at a more basic level in a number of downsizing contexts. Workers who thought they would have lifetime jobs are suddenly terminated. When younger workers see older workers let go, they learn that firms cannot be trusted. Consequently, they always have one eye on the exit sign. Instead of working to make their firm more productive, they work to make themselves more marketable. To the extent that debt service pressure leads to this sort of general mistrust, it can reduce long-run productivity not only in the individual indebted firm but also in the economy at large. A society in which everyone is just "looking out for number one" is not very productive. Trust is a social resource that is destroyed by these attempts to conserve cash.

Another way that firms try to conserve cash is by putting off new investments in plant and equipment. This tendency is reflected in the high capacity-utilization rates recently seen in the goods-producing sector. In the past, high capacity-utilization rates meant a business cycle peak, a situation of excess demand that led firms to raise prices. High capacity-utilization rates in 1994 led many economists to predict faster inflation, but the inflation never showed up. These high capacity-utilization rates did not mean excess demand; they just meant that goods-producing firms were squeezing every ounce out of their old plant and equipment. This situation also causes productivity statistics to be misleading. Some statistics from the 1990s seem to show a spurt of productivity in goods-producing industries. What they really show is that goods-producing firms are pushing their old plant and equipment to its limits. In the long run, operating this way damages productivity.

Doing More Debt

If corporate debt has the effect of reducing productivity, what effect does reduced productivity have on corporate debt? As we have said before, the productivity slowdown is a major reason for high debt levels — personal, government, and corporate. In the case of corporations, slowing productivity growth reduces the amount of retained earnings available for new investment. When firms want to invest, therefore, they must seek outside capital.

In theory, firms could raise new investment capital by issuing stock. However, when a firm issues new stock, it is asking new investors to share in its future profits. Potential investors then ask the question, "If this firm is going to be so profitable, why does it want to share the profits with us?" So, new stock issued by an existing firm often meets with an unenthusiastic response. On the other hand, when a firm finances new investment by borrowing money, the firm is saying, "We are going to keep all the profits and just leave you with the interest payments." Investors then conclude that the firm's prospects are good. Thus, in the absence of retained earnings to finance new investment by existing firms, debt is the preferred method.

The last few decades have seen an increasing scarcity of retained earnings compared with needed investment. This trend is apparent from figures in the national income and product accounts. (The national income and product accounts are the government's official statistics on how much the nation produces; what the products are used for; and how they are distributed among income categories such as wages, profits, and interest.) Those accounts contain an annual figure called "undistributed corporate profits," which is the amount of earnings retained during a given year, and one called "fixed nonresidential capital consumption," which is (roughly) the amount of investment necessary for firms to replace the plant and equipment that is used up in a given year. Plant and equipment isn't really "used up" the way food is "used up," but the capital consumption figure is a reasonable estimate of how much new investment is needed to avoid falling back on the treadmill. During the Age of Affluence (1957–69), U.S. nonfinancial corporations had undistributed profits equal to 56 percent of their capital consumption. To stay even on the treadmill, then, they needed outside financing for less than half their investment. During the Time of Transition (1969–79), undistributed profits reached only 41 percent of capital consumption, so that about three-fifths of necessary investment required outside financing. During the Days of Debt (1979–90), undistributed profits were only 20 percent of capital consumption. Firms required outside financing for *four-fifths* of the investment needed to maintain their plant and equipment. No wonder there was an explosion of corporate debt during the 1980s.

In the 1990s retained earnings have been less of a problem, because firms have managed to capture a larger share of the pie. Workers have a correspondingly smaller share. This change in income distribution may temporarily ameliorate the corporate vicious circle. However, firms cannot keep taking a larger and larger share of the pie forever. (At least, we hope they can't!) In the Indebted Society, because of a change in corporate culture, the productivity-reducing effects of debt have increased even as corporate debt levels have begun to fall. While the retained earnings side of the vicious circle has become less vicious to firms, the productivity side has become more vicious to society. Figure 13.2 depicts this vicious circle.

FIGURE 13.2 THE CORPORATE DEBT/PRODUCTIVITY NONGROWTH
VICIOUS CIRCLE

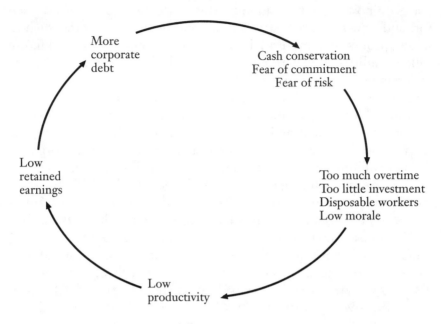

PENNY-WISE POLITICS

A broader vicious circle appears when we consider government debt. Much like indebted firms, an indebted government is inclined to conserve cash in today's budget rather than to invest for tomorrow's productivity. In chapter 9, we discuss various ways in which the federal government cuts spending. The indebted government allows the nation's infrastructure to deteriorate, provides inadequate support for science and technology, and allows our human resources to deteriorate by cutting support for education. The inadequacy of government investment on all these fronts causes productivity to grow more slowly than it should, which in turn leads to lower living standards, lower government revenues, and lower retained earnings. Consumers, governments, and firms have to borrow more to achieve their objectives.

However, in a democracy, the government is by definition the servant of the people. The people may not always feel that they are being well served. Nonetheless, the people's votes determine what sort of government the nation has. A vicious circle involving government cannot persist unless it somehow reflects the preferences of the people. Now we will look at the vicious circle that results from the natural behavior of citizens faced with stagnant incomes. In this context, as we will see, the government is very much, and most unfortunately, a servant of the people — although in the end it does not serve all the people equally.

14 ▪ Savings and Growth

I F WE DO NOT LEARN from our mistakes, it is said, we are doomed to repeat them. If we do not learn from our neighbors' mistakes, it might also be said, we are doomed to repeat *them*. The United States now faces a more frightening possibility: if we do not learn from our neighbors' successes, we may be doomed to repeat them in reverse.

LEARNING FROM OUR NEIGHBORS

I n economics few facts go unchallenged. What appears to be a fact to one economist is seen by another as a misinterpretation. In the comparative study of national economies, one fact cannot be challenged: countries that save a large fraction of their income tend to have quick-growing economies. Japan is perhaps the best-known example. Since the 1960s the Japanese have been saving more than 30 percent of their national income (compared with less than 25 percent for most countries), and their per capita income has grown at a rate of 5 percent per year (compared with less than 2 percent for most countries).[47] A more timely example is Korea. Over the past decade, Koreans have saved 33 percent of their national income, and their per capita income has grown at a rate of 7 percent per year.

At the other end of the spectrum is New Zealand. Since 1973 New Zealanders have saved only 17 percent of their national income, and their per capita income has grown at less than 1 percent per year. Where does the United States stand? Not far from New Zealand. (For reasons that are unclear, English-speaking countries — the United States, the United Kingdom, Canada, Australia, and New Zealand — have tended in recent decades to have relatively low saving and growth rates.)

Why are saving rates and growth rates so strongly linked? The conventional answer given by economists is a simple one: saving leads to investment, which leads to growth. Saving means forgoing current consumption. Every worker who is therefore not needed to help make televisions and evening gowns and ice cream can be put to work making computers and machine tools — things that increase future production. Thus, an economy that saves heavily will produce more in the future: saving causes growth.

Economists have found this analysis compelling. It makes sense. It fits in with the way most economists think. (In fact, the theory relating saving to growth came before the observation of a transnational correlation.) It jibes with traditional morality. It does have some problems, however. First, it clearly doesn't apply in all situations: Americans saved heavily in the early 1930s, but there was no growth. Second, it leaves most growth unexplained: growth occurs more often because of technological change than because of observable investment. Third, it ignores the existence of international trade: why can't a low-saving nation just import its computers and machine tools? Finally, there is the problem of timing: Japan's growth rate peaked in the late 1960s, but its saving rate didn't peak until the early 1970s; Korea's growth rate peaked about 1970, but its saving rate has continued to rise. If saving were causing growth, wouldn't the growth happen *after* the saving?

Undoubtedly, saving does to some extent cause growth, but recent analysis suggests that the relationship is more complicated. Growth, it appears, also causes saving. When an economy grows quickly (as did Japan's in the 1960s), its citizens' income far exceeds their habitual consumption. The economy is always producing much more than people are accustomed to consuming. Therefore, they can consume heavily (relative to their habits) and save heavily (relative to their income) at the same time. They can enjoy an ever improving standard of living while still saving for the future. When an economy grows slowly (as has the United States' since 1973), its citizens' income barely exceeds their habitual consumption. Therefore, they cannot consume very much (relative to their habits) unless they save very little (relative to their income). They can barely maintain their standard of living even if they don't save for the future. (This is the situation described in "Creatures of Habit" in chapter 2.)

A country that grows too slowly saves too little. A country that saves too little grows too slowly. A country that gets caught in this vicious circle is in trouble. Figure 14.1 depicts the vicious circle.

In practice, saving is critically related to borrowing. When we speak of "national saving," we really mean *net* national saving, which is the difference between total saving and total borrowing. Some people save, some borrow, and some do both. Net national saving — the relevant variable for this vicious circle — is the sum of what the savers save minus what the borrowers borrow. In the United States the problem is that the borrowers have borrowed so much that they have absorbed nearly all of what the savers have saved. As a result, the United States is caught in the vicious circle of low saving and low growth.

Interlocking Vicious Circles

Heavy borrowing in the United States has been a cause of low net saving. Nonetheless, heavy borrowing need not imply low net saving. Borrowing is only half the equation. If the savers save *very heavily*, then borrowers can borrow heavily and still leave a large pool

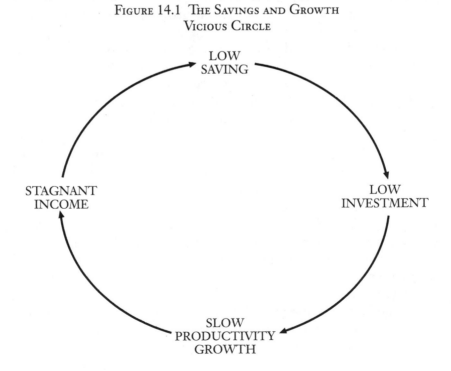

FIGURE 14.1 THE SAVINGS AND GROWTH
VICIOUS CIRCLE

of net savings. In this respect, Japan provides an instructive foil for the United States. Like the Americans, the Japanese made great use of debt during the 1980s. Japan's economy is suffering now from the collapse of its debt structure (much like the "domino" problem described in chapter 7). But Japan is not in the same vicious circle as the United States because it saved even more heavily than it borrowed — much more heavily. Japan's banking system is in trouble, and many individual Japanese are having trouble paying their debts; but unlike the United States, Japan *as a whole* is not in debt. The Japanese owe a lot of money to one another, but on balance Japan is a creditor. In some sense, Japan is an indebted society, but its indebtedness is of a different sort than that of the United States.

Japan's debt is a critical issue for the United States, however, because it is intimately related to America's debt. Japan, because of its own debt situation, plays an important role (a hero's role, for now) in America's vicious circle. The United States plays a complementary role (the role of a very reluctant hero) in the depression that has resulted from Japan's overuse of debt.

To understand what is happening now between the United States and Japan, we have to review what happened during the 1980s. The United States was able to grow, albeit slowly, while going into debt, because it "imported capital" — mostly from Japan. More precisely, the United States primarily imported Japanese consumer goods, so that more domestic resources were available for investment. The Japanese used most of the dollars from their American exports to buy American securities — in effect, to make loans to the United States. Meanwhile, the Japanese were borrowing heavily from one another to buy land, stocks, and various other assets — *including U.S. treasury bonds*. Thus, the United States was able to borrow from Japan partly *because* the Japanese were borrowing so much from one another.

The ability of the Japanese to buy assets with borrowed money resulted in very high prices for Japanese land and Japanese stocks. Those high prices, in turn, enabled more borrowing by raising the value of the collateral. In the 1990s land and stock prices in Japan started to collapse. As collateral values fell, borrowing became more difficult. Since most Japanese could no longer borrow to buy land and stocks, demand declined and prices were pushed down even further. This is a very different kind of vicious circle — the kind the United States experienced during the 1930s.

Like those in the United States during the 1930s, Japanese debtors and Japanese banks have faced a shortage of cash. Cash that was lent aggressively during the 1980s cannot be paid back as expected. Because of the shortage of cash — a shortage of yen, to be specific — it has become more valuable. The yen is more valuable relative to the U.S. dollar, and it is also more valuable relative to many Japanese consumer goods. Japan is experiencing deflation.

Nobody likes deflation. Fortunately, modern central banks know — more or less — how to stop deflation. The solution is to create money at a rapid rate, so that money is no longer scarce relative to goods. As Japan's deflationary situation has become clearer, the Bank of Japan (Japan's analogue to the Fed) has slowly realized that it must create yen at a rapid rate to prevent a more severe deflation. Because the Bank of Japan has been slow to react, it has limited its ability to create money by the usual means — lending at low interest rates. Japanese interest rates are approaching zero, and they can't go much lower.

Consequently, the Bank of Japan has increasingly had to create yen by a different means — by buying dollars. When the Bank of Japan buys dollars, it puts yen in the hands of Americans, who can then use those yen to purchase goods from Japan. This helps to ameliorate Japan's deflation, and it also enables Americans to consume almost as much as they produce even while they are investing heavily. In this way, for as long as it remains convenient, the United States helps Japan out of its vicious circle of deflation and depression, while Japan helps America out of its vicious circle of undersaving and underinvestment. Each motivated by its own self-interest, the United States and Japan are reluctant allies.

The Politics of Self-Deception

Americans themselves are reluctant to take responsibility for their vicious circle. Instead, they have hired an agent to do most of their dirty work. That agent is called the federal government. While individual Americans save, on balance, less than they should, the shortfall is not a huge one. However, their private saving is largely used up by government borrowing. To a large extent, Americans allow the government to borrow heavily on their behalf because they would not feel comfortable doing the borrowing themselves.

Moreover, in the Indebted Society, the government is no longer borrowing for potentially productive projects. During the mid-1980s the U.S. government was in some sense saving what it borrowed. The borrowed money was used — at least, in part — for public investment, so that it was, in effect, saved for the future. If the government saves what it borrows, then it is not, by definition, a net borrower. More recently, however, the government has borrowed just to pay the interest on its existing debt. It is no longer saving in any sense. *Now the government is merely helping Americans pretend that they have more money than they really have.* Taxpayers think *they* have the money that they haven't paid in taxes, while bondholders think *they* have the money that the government pays them in interest. When they make their spending decisions, neither taxpayers nor bondholders seem to take into account that they are really spending borrowed money. By letting the government do their borrowing for them, individual Americans can avoid the blame for their vicious circle.

Human nature dictates that when something goes wrong, we find someone to blame. Based on economists' explanations of the productivity slowdown, one might blame the Rolling Stones or Henry Ford or the emir of Kuwait for stagnant U.S. incomes. However, these are inconvenient choices because they are out of the control of most Americans. Since the U.S. government is elected, citizens can feel that they have some control over it. It is therefore a convenient scapegoat. In 1980, when Americans were already frustrated with their stagnant incomes, Ronald Reagan suggested that they should blame the government. By electing leaders who would cut taxes, they could nail the culprit, and their incomes would rise again.

It didn't work, but that doesn't mean that Americans won't try it again. By exhibiting the primary symptom — large budget deficits — the government may appear (wrongly) to be the source of the problem. It is convenient once again to make the government a scapegoat. The field is ripe for politicians who suggest that America solve its problems by cutting taxes. Cutting taxes has the effect of raising government borrowing and reducing government investment, so as to intensify the vicious circle. In a democracy, tax cutting is a natural part of the vicious circle of undersaving and underinvestment.

Particularly virulent on the tax-cutting front is the wolf in sheep's clothing. The wolf is a large tax cut that is supposedly designed "to encourage saving." In theory, more saving could slow down or reverse the vicious circle. However, if the incentive for saving is a large tax cut, then the resulting increase in government borrowing far outweighs the resulting increase in private saving. Even if the tax cut is offset with budget cuts, those budget cuts reduce public investment by more than the tax cut increases private investment. A tax cut, in whatever guise it comes, is a dangerous exercise in self-deception.

One problem with such self-deception is that it makes one an easy mark. It is easy to fool someone who has already started the job by fooling him- or herself. In the United States the rich have managed to fool the working class. Working people experienced stagnant incomes starting in the 1970s, and they were eager for a tax cut. However, tax cuts almost invariably benefit the rich more than the working class. So did the Reagan-Kemp-Roth cut of 1981. In the end, working people were hurt by the tax cut because the resulting budget deficits absorbed private saving, diminished investment, and reduced the creation of good jobs while allowing existing good jobs to disappear. The working class has thus borne the brunt of the vicious circle. For the rich, the circle has been much less vicious.

DOOMED BOOMERS

Taxes are not the enemy of the American working class, but the payments that working people make to the government have become burdensome, and this burden highlights another aspect of the vicious circle. This burden — reflected largely by payments into the Social Security system — results in large part from an accident of demographics. The so-called baby-boom generation — those born between 1945 and 1965 — suffers and will continue to suffer for the ill-timed fertility of its parents. There are just too many baby boomers and not enough post–baby boomers to support them when they reach retirement. In theory, the problem could have been solved by allowing more immigration to supplement the labor pool available from the post-baby-boom generation. However, the "live inflation-free or die" attitude that has guided macroeconomic policy has led to a shortage of jobs for the post–baby boomers, and as a consequence, they view potential immigrants as dangerous competitors.

Without a large pool of younger workers to pay into the Social Security system, the government had to opt for plan number two: make each individual pay more. The baby boomers have had to substitute money for people. If there will not be enough people to support them when they retire, there must instead be a pool of money. In theory, this pool can be used in either of two ways. First, it can be sent abroad as a sort of nest egg, which the United States can draw down when the boomers retire, by importing what they need. Second, it can be invested so that workers will become more productive, and ultimately fewer workers will be needed to support the boomers when they retire. The first possibility clearly is not happening: the United States is drawing in money from abroad rather than sending it abroad. The second possibility isn't happening, either — at least, not to the extent necessary. The extra money from the baby boomers is instead required to keep the federal debt situation from getting even worse than it is.

Because the United States has a large generation that will soon start to retire, it should be investing more heavily than ever. It should be devoting a smaller-than-usual fraction of its resources to consumption. Instead, it is devoting a historically high fraction of its resources to consumption. (Look again at the top line in Figure 2.1.) The accident of demographics has raised the need for savings and investment just when the inclination to save and invest is at a historic low. The call on baby boomers to sacrifice their current living standards to provide for retirement comes just as stagnant productivity is already forcing them to sacrifice. Because the baby-boom generation is so large compared with the one that follows, the vicious circle of undersaving and underinvestment is as vicious as it can be.

THE DAMAGE DONE

This vicious circle, this pit bull foaming at the mouth, what damage has it done so far? It will take more than rabies shots to resuscitate growth in U.S. living standards! Just when America needs extra capital to prepare for the baby boomers' retirement, capital growth is slower than ever.

Figure 14.2 tells just part of the story. The chart shows the growth rate of "capital per hour of labor" over ten-year periods ending in each year from 1960 to 1993 (the last year for which we have data). When capital per hour of labor grows quickly, it raises the amount that each worker can produce in an hour. It did grow quickly during the 1950s, 1960s, and 1970s. Since the early 1980s the growth rate has plummeted, and is still heading south.

Even this chart shows only what is happening in the private sector. During the same time that capital growth has been plummeting, large budget deficits and debt service requirements have been straining the resources needed for public investment. Public investment is harder to measure, but you can be sure that the growth of public capital per hour of labor has stalled, and all signs point to the situation getting even worse.

Budget cuts in the public sector, paltry savings in the private sec-

FIGURE 14.2 CAPITAL PER HOUR OF LABOR
TEN-YEAR GROWTH RATE

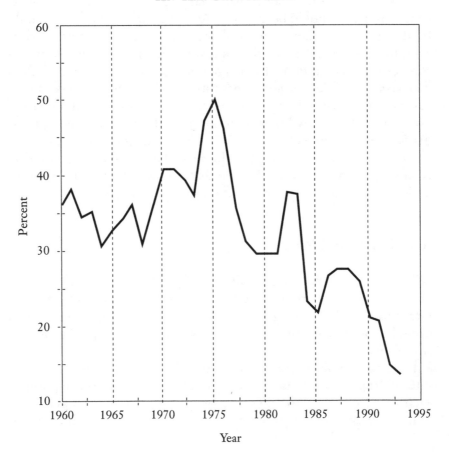

tor — all this means Americans must struggle even harder in the future. Barring a deus ex machina, there are only two ways to get out of this vicious circle. First, the United States can use its resources more fully, so as to permit more private and public investment without reducing living standards. Second, Americans can accept a lower standard of living temporarily. We'll explore these options later. Unhappily, our exploration of vicious circles is not yet through. Bear with us. There is hope.

15 ▪ Other Vicious Circles

IT GETS VICIOUSER AND VICIOUSER. The vicious circle between low saving and low growth, and the one between high debt and low productivity are the most important in the Indebted Society, but there are others.

UNHEALTHY CIRCLE

The first of these lesser vicious circles involves health care. Health care is of tremendous importance in the Indebted Society and is intimately connected with debt in a number of ways. For one thing, through programs like Medicare and Medicaid, the rising cost of health care has put pressure on the federal budget and aggravated the federal debt problem. In fact, health care spending (including Medicare) is the only category of federal spending (other than interest on the debt) that takes up a larger fraction of the national income than it did fifteen years ago.

Health care is also associated — as it always has been — with personal debt. The image of someone who has to borrow money because his wife needs an operation is an old and familiar one. In most industrialized countries, this spectacle has been all but eliminated, but in the United States, with its torn safety net, personal debt is often still the only option for some needing expensive health care. Moreover, since health insurance has become so expensive, many who have suffered occupational dislocations must go into debt simply to obtain routine health care.

Finally, health care is associated with corporate debt in ways that not everyone realizes. When a firm assumes the responsibility to finance its employees' health care, it is assuming an obligation that competes directly with its debt service obligations. Just as debt requires fixed payments in proportion to cost of the items purchased with debt, health insurance requires fixed payments in proportion to the number of employees provided with health care. When a factory purchased with debt is run at full capacity, the required debt service payments are no higher than when it is run below full capacity. Similarly, when an employee covered by a firm's health care plan works long hours, the required health insurance payments are no higher than when the employee works normal hours. In this respect, debt and health care are competing with each other as recipients of fixed payments. A firm that has taken on debt service obligations is reluctant to maintain a similar obligation by providing its workers with health care. The simultaneous increases in debt and in health care costs during the 1980s combined to put a strain on corporate resources, so that downsizing became widespread and firms became more reluctant to provide health care benefits.

Nonetheless, the most important link between health care and debt remains the public sector. Even in this country that celebrates private enterprise, public sources account for about two-thirds of the expenditures on final health care goods and services. Even our now heavily indebted federal government spends more on health care than it does on interest payments. The rising cost of health care inevitably puts pressure on the federal budget, thus increasing the government's need to borrow and reducing its ability to provide other public services, to enhance productivity, and to care for the needy.

However, in the Indebted Society, the effects of debt also tend to increase the need for health care. And as the Indebted Society becomes more unhealthy, the cost of health insurance rises. The primary mechanism by which the effects of debt place increased demands on the health care system is through personal stress. Medical researchers have increasingly come to realize that stress is a major cause of illness and a major aggravating factor in many illnesses. In the Indebted Society, stress is a way of life.

Psychologists recognize that personal debt is a source of stress. People in substantial debt are known to be more vulnerable to stress-related illness than those who are debt-free. More generally, the economic conditions created by corporate and government debt, and by the power of lenders, have made the Indebted Society a stressful place to live. Workers who live in fear of downsizing are not likely to be the healthiest of people.

Throughout the populace, feelings of impotence appear to be

much more prevalent today than at any point in the past twenty-five years. These feelings are reflected in surveys conducted by Louis Harris and Associates, Inc. Harris, Inc. provides what it labels its "Alienation Index." "Alienation" is defined including "feelings of economic inequity ('the rich get richer and the poor get poorer'), feelings of disdain about 'people with power' and 'the people running the country' and feelings of powerlessness — being 'left out of things' and 'not counting very much.'" Ever since the index was first used in 1966, it has shown a general upward trend. During the 1990s it has reached new highs and has refused to retreat from those highs.

In the age of permanent job loss, such alienation is to be expected. Since 1966 the Alienation Index has risen and fallen (mostly risen) in step with the average length of time people spend unemployed. During the late 1960s the government's survey of households typically found that jobless people had been unemployed for an average of about ten weeks. During that period the Alienation Index ranged from 29 to 36. During the 1990s the average reported duration of unemployment has risen to, and remained above, sixteen weeks, and the Alienation Index has not fallen below 60. The attitudes reflected in the Alienation Index are the ones that make people more vulnerable to stress-related illness.

THE PARANOID SOCIETY

The alienation found in a society in which the power of debt has come to exceed the power of humanity leads to another vicious circle — the circle of mistrust. When people feel they have no power, when people see the expectations they had taken for granted dashed to the ground, they are apt to begin viewing most institutions with suspicion. Unfortunately, when it comes to economic institutions such as corporations, most people really do have very little power. In a democracy, however, people do have some power with respect to political institutions. Whether or not those institutions are particularly worthy of people's suspicion, they provide a natural focus for frustration. In the United States the ever distant federal government bears the brunt of that mistrust. Just as cooperation becomes impossible in a group whose members do not trust one another, effective government becomes impossible in a Union rife with mistrust.

Unhappily, the federal government is the only institution in the Indebted Society that is equipped to provide a safety net for its citizens and to undertake actions for the general good. States, communities, families, and other less universal social units are inevitably in competition with one another and cannot be expected to cooperate, especially when mistrust suffuses the nation's atmosphere. Yet a faraway national government with its own ways and attitudes cannot or will not provide a remedy for the people's unhappiness. Because people cannot see the federal government as part of the solution, they come to see it as part of the problem. They see its protections as intrusions and its attempts to provide for the common good as a waste of precious resources.

The help the federal government can provide is not apt to address directly people's immediate concerns. It can undertake public investment that should ultimately enhance productivity, but it cannot, in the short run, reverse the decline in living standards. It can provide retraining for displaced workers but cannot force the private sector to provide jobs for those retrained workers. It can give help to the poor but cannot give the middle class an assurance against becoming poor. It can set standards for the treatment of workers but cannot guarantee the availability of gainful work. A frustrated and alienated populace rejects the seemingly ineffective help of the federal government. As a result, the people lose a potential force for economic progress, and they reduce the chances that the future will be more secure than the present.

Outside the government, the circle of mistrust operates as well. Cooperation among workers, and between workers and management, becomes difficult or impossible. Management and stockholders find themselves at odds. Everyone expects the worst from everyone else. As government becomes ineffective, civil lawsuits abound. The atmosphere clearly is not conducive to rising productivity. Trust, a valuable social and economic resource, becomes vanishingly scarce. Thus, the possibility of transcending this sad condition further dissipates.

LENDERS AND MORE LENDERS

Meanwhile, the lender-friendly policies of the Indebted Society push it deeper into debt. The power of lenders, and the economic ideas that have flowed from this power, produce policies designed to minimize the risk of increased inflation. However, given the uncertainties involved, the only way to minimize the risk of increased inflation is to push for disinflation. If the inflation rate must not go up, then it will most likely go down. Debts that were contracted on the expectation of a certain inflation rate become more difficult to service when the inflation rate is lower. Because of disinflationary policies, the dollar value of the nation's total product rises more slowly than expected, but the dollar value of debts is unchanged. Those debts become more important in relation to the size of the economy. As a result, lenders become more important, and their power increases.

Those who make a living by lending their money also benefit from having high real interest rates. Lenders can be expected to encourage policies — such as tax cuts without corresponding spending cuts — that tend to push real interest rates higher. Given the law of supply and demand, the policies that raise real interest rates are generally those that involve more borrowing. Since the real interest rate is the price of borrowing, it rises when the demand for borrowed funds rises. Therefore, the policies encouraged by lenders are those that result in additional debt. As a result, lenders become still more important, and their power further increases.

As the Indebted Society goes deeper into debt, its interest burden increases, and it must borrow more to service its existing debt. Consequently, it goes even deeper into debt.

The deeper the Indebted Society and its members go into debt, the less their resources can support that debt. As the debt increases relative to those resources, so does the risk that the debts cannot be repaid. Creditors therefore demand higher interest rates to compensate them for the higher risk. The debts then become more difficult to service, and the cycle of debt upon debt is intensified.

THE WRONG WAY OUT

A nation that is developing a larger and larger problem with debt may be tempted to attack that problem head-on by refusing to pay. Obviously, if the nation is still dependent on continued borrowing, this "cold turkey" approach can be dangerous. For a nation like the United States, which has spent two hundred years developing a good reputation with creditors, giving up that reputation can hardly be worth the cost. For the world, a default by the United States, which sits at a critical point in the international financial system, could be an unmitigated disaster. Since everyone realizes this, a serious, straight-out default by the United States is unlikely. (The unfortunate possibility of temporary default due to a contest of political brinkmanship cannot be ruled out.)

What is more worrisome, given the apparent U.S. dependence on foreign capital, is that nationalistic sentiment may drive the United States to precipitate a flight of foreign capital by more subtle means. The means may be more subtle, but the results can still be disastrous.

As long as the issue is the U.S. "debt" to foreigners in the strict sense of the word "debt," the danger is small. Americans will not simply refuse to pay. However, as we noted in chapter 10, much of America's "indebtedness" to the rest of the world is not "debt" in the strict sense. Much of what foreigners have invested in the United States takes the form of direct ownership rather than loans. Unlike loans, which have an impersonal quality, this direct ownership can excite a certain resentment among Americans. Foreign ownership of U.S. assets such as land and factories may seem to imply a certain loss of sovereignty. A political reaction against foreign ownership is a real and potentially very dangerous possibility.

A movement to interfere with foreign investment in the United States could set off a sudden and extremely vicious circle. As it currently stands, the opportunity for foreigners to invest directly in U.S. assets (rather than simply lending money) provides an "escape hatch" for those who worry about the value of the dollar. Because such direct investment is possible, the United States can attract foreign capital without having to be too overzealous about inflation. When foreign investors worry about inflation, they need not stop investing in the United States; they can simply shift their U.S. assets from inflation-vulnerable bonds into hard assets. If this escape hatch is removed, foreign investors in the United States are at the mercy of American monetary policy. As a result, the spectre of a free-falling dollar becomes more palpable, and the Fed's already overzealous attitude toward inflation becomes almost maniacal. Interest rates skyrocket.

Very high interest rates intensify all the vicious circles we have described so far. Ironically, attempts by Americans to preserve their economic sovereignty might have exactly the opposite of the intended effect. The United States may find itself trapped in circles so vicious that the only hope is to ask for a loan from an international organization such as the International Monetary Fund (IMF). Such loans come with stringent conditions. Right now Congress and the president debate whether and how much to cut programs like Medicare, Medicaid, and Social Security. In the context of a conditional loan from the IMF, international bureaucrats would tell them exactly how much had to be cut. It may sound unthinkable that the nation which leads the free world could find itself at the mercy of international bankers and bureaucrats. You might remember that Great Britain was once the leader of the free world. In 1976 Britain took a loan from the IMF — and the conditions that came with it.

As long as Americans can resist the temptation to bite the hand that feeds them, the United States can avoid this doomsday scenario. Nonetheless, if current conditions continue, the vicious circles described will continue. The result may not be catastrophic, but it will be increasingly painful. America is sinking. Unless a change is made, America will continue to sink.

Part Four

THE ROAD BACK
TO AFFLUENCE

16 ▪ Undetected Slack

C AN AMERICA EXTRACT ITSELF from this quicksand? Is there a rope or a branch that America can grab to pull itself out? The answer is yes. Opportunities exist for the Indebted Society to get its feet back on solid ground and to begin the journey back to affluence. To see these opportunities, the Indebted Society must clear away the mist that has obscured its view. America has slack resources available that can be used to invest in tomorrow while maintaining and enhancing living standards for today. These slack resources are hidden from view by the fear of inflation.

This may sound odd. Most Americans worry about keeping their jobs, about paying for their children's education, about planning — or lack of planning — for their eventual retirement. They don't lose much sleep over the possibility of rising prices. Lenders, however, do worry about inflation. The economists and policy makers who serve the lenders' needs have allowed the spectre of inflation to obscure their view. Americans have been told that all available resources are being used, even though this would seem to contradict the evidence of their senses. Politicians and self-promoters have exploited the resulting confusion by offering scapegoats: big government, immigrant labor, unfair foreign competition, an out-of-control legal system, the decay of family values — you name it. The fact is, America does have slack resources, and the decision not to use those resources is deliberate. That decision is being made by unelected and unaccountable officials at the Federal Reserve and is being encouraged by the vast majority of economists at America's universities. It is motivated — there is no question — by a fear of inflation.

Why are economists so fearful of inflation? Partly, because of a narrow-minded focus on the unemployment rate as the critical indicator of inflationary pressure. Before taking a broader look at America's resources, let us briefly examine the historical sources of the economists' neuroses — unemployment obsession and inflation-phobia.

The Psychopathology of Economic Life

Unemployment obsession and inflationphobia can be traced to two historical events — the Great Depression of the 1930s and the "Great Inflation" of the 1970s. In 1933, at the height of the Great Depression, fully one out of four American workers had no job. Before the Great Depression, most economists had seen unemployment as a necessary, tolerable, and relatively unimportant element in the capitalist system. During the 1930s it became clear that the problem of unemployment required greater attention. The great economist John Maynard Keynes, writing in 1936, provided the intellectual framework for dealing with the problem of unemployment.

After World War II the ideas of Keynes went through various refinements and modifications. Economist A. W. Phillips found an apparently stable inverse relationship between unemployment and wage growth in Great Britain. His results were quickly extended to other countries, including the United States. Observing that prices were primarily determined by wages, economists came to see the "Phillips curve" as a trade-off between unemployment and inflation. In the 1960s economists, suffering from unemployment obsession and a sort of manic overconfidence, thought they had nailed down a very precise relationship. Policy makers, it was thought, need only consult their expert advisers about the trade-off and then make a decision about how much unemployment or how much inflation to tolerate.

Then came the 1970s. Snowballing inflation — coexisting with rising unemployment — shattered the hubris of economists. High unemployment, it became clear, did not necessarily mean low inflation. However, economists retained their obsession: the unemployment rate, they insisted, was still the center of the universe. Inflation revolves around unemployment, just as the sun revolves around the earth.

Rather than abandon their unemployment dogma, economists came up with more complex explanations for the failure of the old Phillips curve. First, it was said, rising prices had become a self-fulfilling prophecy. In the late 1960s there had been some inflation, but nobody had known whether it would continue; by the late 1970s everyone expected inflation to continue, and everyone raised their prices accordingly. Second, it was argued, economists had underestimated the natural rate of unemployment; it was really closer to 6 percent, rather than the previously fashionable 4 percent. Finally, an external force — OPEC's huge oil price increases — had produced inflation and caused the U.S. economy to behave perversely. Thus was born inflationphobia, with its attendant compulsions: we must monitor market expectations at all times; we must keep unemployment above 6 percent; and we must always beat down commodity prices.

There was considerable misery in the United States during the 1970s. Many older people on fixed incomes found themselves impoverished by rising prices. Many people lost their jobs. Many young people had difficulty finding the jobs they had hoped for. But the unemployment of the 1970s was completely different from that of the 1930s. Most of the job losers in the 1970s were on temporary layoff; their jobs had not disappeared. Most were unemployed for only a few months. Moreover, throughout most of the decade, virtually anyone willing to move to Dallas could find a job. Few economists noticed, but the nation's newspapers carried record numbers of want ads during the 1970s. American economists were depressed, but the U.S. economy was not. The inflation was not an aberration; it was normal for a turbulent but — in many respects — booming economy. Just possibly, if economists had discarded their unemployment obsession and taken a broader view, they would never have come down with inflationphobia.

Economists, of course, protest this characterization. They are not obsessed with the unemployment rate. They look at many other indicators: "industrial capacity utilization," "factory order backlogs," "sensitive raw material prices," "manufacturing employment growth rate," "inventory-to-sales ratios," and so on. A lot of numbers, but not a lot of information. All these numbers answer the same question: How is the manufacturing sector doing? For the less obsessed inflation watcher, a simpler answer is possible: Who cares? Forty years ago the United States was a nation of factories. Today less than 9 percent of adult Americans work in manufacturing. Those who worry about inflation should instead concern themselves with services. Anyone who has recently bought a computer and paid a hospital bill realizes this.

THE NEW UNEMPLOYMENT

When we focus on services, we focus once again on people — secretaries, nurses, teachers, programmers, police officers, accountants, salespeople, economists. Whereas manufacturing is largely automated, services are still performed primarily by people. The cost of services depends mostly on what these people expect to be paid. Our nation's ability to produce services depends largely on whether people are available to perform them. Recent surveys show that more than 7 million Americans are actively seeking work. Another 2 million are "available" but not actively looking. Countless others are unavailable because they have found better opportunities in the "informal sector" (particularly in communities that cannot afford — or have not chosen — to invest in police protection). Should these potential workers be written off as a sacrifice to the gods of inflation?

The real question becomes, How much human sacrifice do the gods of inflation require? During the 1970s they showed a seemingly insatiable hunger. In 1974 the unemployment rate averaged 5.6 percent, and consumer prices rose by 12.3 percent. The high priests prepared the altar. Not until the unemployment rate reached double digits in 1982 did the gods finally quiet their thunder. In the 1950s, however, the inflation gods seemed much less hungry. In 1954 the unemployment rate averaged 5.5 percent — lower than in 1974 — yet consumer prices actually fell. (Yes, the inflation rate was less than zero!) During 1953 the unemployment rate had dipped as low as 2.5 percent, yet inflation was not a problem. Is today's unemployment more like that of the 1970s, or is it more like that of the 1950s?

Consider the profile of the typical 1990s job seeker: male, older than thirty, married, previously employed but old job was terminated, unemployed for over two months, finding few new jobs advertised, expecting to take a cut in pay. These characteristics contrast vividly with those of the typical 1970s job seeker, who usually was either an employee on temporary layoff or a young person seeking a first job. The characteristics of the typical 1950s job seeker are less clear, because the government didn't keep the same statistics in those days. However, there is no question that our 1990s profile is closer to that of the 1950s than that of the 1970s.

In one respect, today's job seekers, and today's job holders, are very different from those of the 1950s: they are less than half as likely to be represented by a union. In the 1970s the labor unions — still powerful, although in decline — received their share of blame for the "wage-price spiral." Today it seems inconceivable that U.S. labor unions would be able to exploit a mildly tight labor market by pushing up wages. The sacrifice of organized labor may satisfy the inflation gods for many years to come.

In general, it is the employed — not the unemployed — whose behavior affects the inflation rate. Unemployed people don't get pay raises. Unemployed people don't become more (or less) productive. Unemployment acts as a check on inflation only because it influences the behavior of employed workers and their employers. Today's employees and employers do not need the spectacle of high unemployment to keep wages and prices down. Employees are scared of losing their jobs to restructuring. Employers are scared of losing their markets to foreign competition. Fear keeps prices down. With fear so plentiful, America cannot afford to waste 6 percent of its available manpower!

The New Underemployment

America's supply of slack human resources includes more than just those who have no job and are available for work. It also includes the many Americans whose potential abilities are being wasted in work that does not make use of their personal resources.

Even as preachers and politicians emphasize the importance of getting an education, statistics show record numbers of college-educated Americans in jobs that do not require a college degree. Clearly there is a severe shortage of jobs for people without a college education. But there is also a shortage of jobs for people with a college education. Certainly the United States should invest in the future by educating its children (and adults) more. This is a task for individuals, families, communities, and elected governments. But America should also invest in the present by promoting economic growth with expansionary macroeconomic policy. That is a task largely for economists and unelected policy makers. It may require nothing short of a revolution in economic thought. America's economic experts, who already have Ph.D.s, must be educated by the American people!

Another pocket of unexploited human resources is the burgeoning army of self-employed Americans who must spend more time on promoting their businesses than on doing the work they want to do. For workers who are employed by others, statistics show — as they always have — that millions of part-time workers would like to be full-time. For self-employed people, there are no statistics. Yet the United States now has over 10 million self-employed people, and surely most of them can accommodate more business without straining their resources. Naturally, there are some self-employed people who have too much business, just as there are some skilled workers that are in overwhelming demand. In a dynamic economy, this situation would be true even during recessions. The point still stands: the Indebted Society has resources that it is wasting and that it cannot afford to waste.

Another source of undetected slack is the truly phenomenal growth in temporary employment. Many (though not all) of these temporary employees would like to be permanent. Many would count themselves lucky to find a stable working environment. By treating these people as disposable employees, the Indebted Society not only deprives them of security and fulfillment, it also deprives itself of the skills these people could develop and apply by building their careers upward instead of sideways.

Finally, consider the overall quality of jobs in the Indebted Society. Since 1975 the mix of jobs in the United States has had a general downward trend in average quality. For example, there has been a large increase in the demand for low-paid personal service workers (who typically do not receive fringe benefits), and there has been a large decrease in the demand for relatively high-paid motor vehicle assemblers (who typically receive substantial benefits). The overall trend of declining job quality is the net effect of two opposing trends: a shift toward higher-paying occupations — managers and professionals — and a shift toward lower-paying industries — services and retail trade. Incumbent politicians have made much of the occupational shift, but they have tended to ignore the industry shift — which often turns out to be more important.

The shift to lower-quality jobs means that less of people's potential is being utilized. Jobs that pay well and offer generous benefits do so because they enable people to contribute more to society's total product. As those jobs disappear, people lose that opportunity. Some jobs will always disappear in a dynamic economy, but there is no need for those jobs to be replaced with lower-quality jobs. The quality of new jobs depends on the kind of spending that a society does. In the Indebted Society, a consumer-oriented culture, politically motivated tax cuts, and a too-tight monetary policy have combined to produce the kind of spending that yields low-quality jobs. In the next chapter, we show what the United States must do to start taking advantage of its slack resources and creating more good jobs.

17 ▪ Smart Stimulus

T
O BEGIN USING ITS slack resources, the Indebted Society needs some kind of economic stimulus — something to produce demand for those additional resources. However, different kinds of economic stimuli often have different effects. The classic example of a deliberate economic stimulus is a government program to build roads and bridges. This immediately provides a demand for construction workers; then the newly hired construction workers spend their pay and produce demand for whoever makes what they buy. Another common example is a personal tax cut. A tax cut doesn't directly increase demand, but it puts more money in the hands of individuals, so they are likely to spend more.

Notice several differences. First, as noted, the highway program is a direct stimulus, whereas the tax cut is indirect. A direct stimulus has the advantage of being more reliable and predictable; an indirect one has the advantage of giving people a choice. Second, the highway program produces something that will clearly have some value for the future: more roads and bridges will make transportation more efficient and society more productive for years to come. The tax cut will most likely cause people to spend more on things that make their lives better only in the present. Finally, the two stimuli create different kinds of jobs. The highway program first creates jobs in construction, which typically pays well and has good fringe benefits. The tax cut could produce many different kinds of jobs. But experience shows that people tend to spend the money on services (housecleaning, for example) and retail purchases (going to the mall). Most of the jobs created tend to be the low-paying kind in services and retail trade.

FISCAL AND MONETARY POLICY

T
he two examples have at least one thing in common: they are both what is called "fiscal policy." That is, they are both changes in the

government budget. Numerous such "fiscal stimuli" are possible: military spending, tax credits for corporate investment, welfare programs, export subsidies, and so on. There are a couple of big problems with fiscal policy in the Indebted Society. First and most obvious, the government is already borrowing huge amounts. To launch an additional fiscal stimulus, even more would have to be borrowed. It might be worth it, at least in theory, especially if the fiscal stimulus also increased productivity for the future. It can't do much harm to hire people and use resources that would have been wasted otherwise.

That brings us to problem number two: fiscal policy won't work unless the Federal Reserve cooperates. Remember that the Federal Reserve wants to keep the unused resources out of use, in order to prevent inflation. If Congress passes a tax cut, the Fed will see (or anticipate) the increase in demand and will counteract that effect by raising interest rates. Higher interest rates discourage businesses from investing and discourage individuals from buying houses and autos. Also, higher interest rates will probably strengthen the dollar, discouraging people from buying American products. The Fed will keep raising interest rates until it has choked off enough demand to balance out the new demand created by the tax cut. What is the net effect? More demand for house cleaners, baby-sitters, salespeople, and Korean VCRs; less demand for factory equipment, houses, and American automobiles.

The other major type of economic stimulus is monetary policy. This, of course, requires not only the cooperation but the active involvement of the Federal Reserve, which has essentially unlimited control over monetary policy. Monetary policy, by definition, is the process by which the Fed controls the supply of money. It does so by changing interest rates. Ultimately, most economists now agree, the money supply itself is not what matters. Interest rates are what matter. When the Fed cuts interest rates, several things happen. First, it becomes cheaper for people to buy houses and autos, so more people buy houses and autos, and more jobs are created in the housing and auto industries. Second, firms' interest costs are reduced, so there is less pressure to lay off middle-aged employees. Third, as people shift their money toward foreign currencies with higher interest rates, the value of the dollar falls, and American goods become cheaper (and thus more attractive) relative to foreign goods. Finally, for a number of reasons, it becomes more advantageous for firms to invest in new plant and equipment, so that more jobs are created in industries like computers and machine tools.

This last effect, stimulating private investment, is the most important and the most complex. On a direct level, lower interest rates make it cheaper for firms to borrow money with which to buy new plant and equipment. They also have some indirect effects. Lower interest rates mean that a firm earns less interest on its own uninvested funds, so that it has more incentive to use them for something productive. Lower interest rates also encourage people to buy stocks instead of earning interest, thus making it easier for firms to raise money for investment by selling stock. Rising stock prices make it worthwhile for entrepreneurs to offer stock to the public in order to launch new ventures, which typically use the money to purchase new plant and equipment. In all these ways, lower interest rates encourage private investment.

JOB QUALITY AND ECONOMIC STIMULI

Different kinds of economic stimuli produce different kinds of jobs. This point is obvious, but policy debates seem to ignore it. In fact, we can actually measure the quantity and quality of the jobs produced by different kinds of spending. Specifically, we can measure the number of jobs created by each dollar of a certain kind of spending, and the average quality of those jobs. To do so, we first classify jobs according to industry (e.g., health services, insurance, motor vehicle manufacturing) and occupation (e.g., salespeople, administrators, mechanics). For each job so classified we have information on average pay and fringe benefits, which we call "job quality." Now, for each type of spending (e.g., personal consumption, defense, education) we know what industries and occupations are involved, both directly and indirectly. (For example, residential-construction spending involves the construction industry directly and the timber industry indirectly.) We also know how many people are employed per dollar of a given kind of spending. Thus, we can compare the employment effects of different kinds of spending.

Table 17.1 presents such a comparison. Specifically, it compares the numbers of jobs created, the average quality of jobs created, and the total quality (number times average quality) of jobs created by different kinds of spending. Personal-consumption spending has an assigned value of 100, with which we can compare the other values. The first thing to notice is that most of the numbers in the table are greater than 100, especially in the "average quality" column. In other words, most other kinds of spending create better jobs than does personal-consumption spending. Spending money at shopping malls and fast-food restaurants creates jobs for sales clerks and burger flippers — not the kind of jobs that Americans wish for. At the other extreme is "public safety" — in other words, cops — with a total job quality score of 167. Public-safety expenditures typically go directly to hiring police officers, who make a lot more than sales clerks and burger flippers. Another interesting category is "national defense" — with the lowest "number of jobs" score and the highest "average

TABLE 17.1 JOB MARKET "SCORES" OF VARIOUS PRIVATE AND PUBLIC EXPENDITURES

Type of Spending	Number of Jobs Created Per Dollar (Index)	Average Quality of Jobs Created Per Dollar (Index)	Total Quality of Jobs Created Per Dollar (Index)
Personal consumption expenditures	100	100	100
Private investment: Total	95	127	121
Producers' durable equipment	100	132	132
Construction — nonresidential	90	128	115
Construction — residential	92	120	110
Exports	62	128	80
Imports	−65	127	−83
Federal government purchases: Total	76	140	106
Defense (excluding pay of armed forces)	74	142	105
Nondefense	81	135	109
State and local purchases: Total	125	120	150
Education	146	113	164
Health and hospitals	108	122	131
Public safety	127	132	167
Highways	94	129	122
Water and air facilities	90	128	115
Transit utilities	87	132	115
Other	109	127	139

Source: J. Medoff, Smart Stimulus, Center for National Policy, 1993.

quality" score. Defense spending creates some jobs for highly paid engineers, but much of defense spending goes instead to expensive hardware. Five-hundred-dollar toilet seats don't create jobs for anyone.

Which is more important, number of jobs or average job quality? They are both important, but for different reasons. First, think about the actions of the Federal Reserve in the Indebted Society. Suppose the president of the United States tried to pursue a policy to maximize the *number of jobs*. What would happen? Given how the Fed usually behaves, the policy would be completely ineffective. The Fed would fight the policy by raising interest rates, until it got the number of jobs back down — and the unemployment rate back up to about 6 percent. Now, suppose the president tried to pursue a policy to maximize *average job quality*. What would the Fed do? Nothing. (Obviously, this is a little oversimplified.) The Fed is concerned only that too much labor demand — *too many jobs* — might produce inflation. In terms of inflation risk, good jobs are no more dangerous than bad jobs. A "more jobs" policy would have failed, but a "better jobs" policy will succeed. As long as the Fed insists on fighting that phantom inflation, average job quality can be improved, but number of jobs cannot.

Why do we care at all about the number of jobs, if the Fed is going to limit that number anyway? Here there is a more subtle reason, one that is particular to the Indebted Society. A government without any debt could say, "Who cares how many jobs our spending produces? If it's not enough, we'll just spend more." That attitude was typical during the 1960s. A government deeply in debt, on the other hand, does not have the option of "just spending more." To avoid exploding the national debt, the government must pinch every penny. Thus, at those rare times (as in 1992) when the Fed seems willing to accommodate a fiscal stimulus, the indebted government must be very cautious to maximize "bang for the buck" — the most jobs per dollar spent.

ECONOMIC STIMULI AND THE FUTURE

Another obvious difference between various kinds of stimulatory spending is in their long-run effects. Hamburgers and VCRs don't help much in the long run; roads and factories do. Policy debates now recognize this point. Each politician refers to his or her own priorities as "investments" and to everything else as "wasteful." But "investment" is not just a political catchword. It is true that some kinds of spending will make America more productive in the future and other kinds of spending won't. In the long run, the quality of jobs and the quality of life will be determined largely by how much of America's resources are devoted to investment.

Economists, politicians, and demagogues hotly debate the value of public investment — and which government spending should properly be labeled investment. However, there is no debate about the value of private investment. Everyone agrees that private investment is good and should be encouraged. A glance at Table 17.1 confirms that private investment spending also creates good jobs. Good jobs in the present, and better jobs in the future — sounds like a good deal! Why doesn't our society do more private investment? We return to this question later.

For now, let us weigh in on the side of those who also favor public investment. To be productive in the future, we need economy-wide technological advances — which depend on government-funded research. We need an educated workforce. We need to protect people and businesses from crime. We need efficient highway and public transportation systems. We need effective systems for retraining workers and matching workers with jobs. None of these things automatically give us a productive society, but all these things enable and enhance the productivity gains derived from private investment. The trick is to raise private investment without reducing public investment.

Another point about public investment is that it must — to the greatest extent possible — be a nationwide effort rather than a state-by-state or city-by-city effort. A nationwide effort — if possible, a global effort — is needed because the benefits of public investment are nationwide (and frequently global).[48] A community that invests heavily in education will soon see the fruits of its investment move to other communities and to other states, as its well-educated progeny search the country for the best jobs. A state that invests in scientific research will see its discoveries put to use by firms on the other side of the country — or the other side of the world. Americans' disenchantment with the federal government is most unfortunate. Only as a whole nation does the United States have the incentives that will lead to needed government investment. To ignore these incentives because of a mistrust of politicians and bureaucrats is both foolish and dangerous.

What Should We Do Now?

What is the smartest stimulus? In terms of both short- and long-run effects, public and private investment are the most beneficial types of spending, and personal consumption is the least. Private investment is also less controversial than public investment. What kind of policy produces more private investment?

One answer is often suggested by the politically conservative but fiscally liberal wing of the Republican party: tax breaks for the rich. "Cut capital gains taxes." "Stop taxing interest and dividends." "Reduce marginal tax rates." "Institute a flat tax." Although these policies would clearly benefit part of America's population, there is no evidence that they would actually increase investment. In fact, if we reduce these taxes without raising some others, the resulting government borrowing will take resources away from private investment. That is the lesson of the Reagan years. Of course, we could make tax breaks "revenue neutral" by raising taxes on labor income at the same time. Any votes for cutting taxes on the rich and raising taxes on the middle class? In any case, it still won't work. Do you really think someone will give up buying a yacht and buy stock instead, just because his or her taxes go down?

A more effective way to encourage private investment is to give tax breaks directly to corporations that invest. "Investment tax credits" and "accelerated depreciation" are typical examples. Although these cuts can be expensive in terms of lost revenue, they do seem to encourage investment. Again, they can backfire if the revenue loss means more government borrowing, reducing the funds available for private investment. Of course, corporate investment incentives can be combined with increases in overall corporate tax rates, but this strategy increases the incentive for firms to go into debt. Direct investment incentives also pose a difficulty in that the government must decide what constitutes "investment" for purposes of the tax break. Does a new building count, or just the equipment inside it? If just the equipment counts, then what about office partitions? History shows that the government never manages to cover all bases; there are always loopholes. Another problem is that Congress has a tendency to change its mind about the investment tax credit. An on-again, off-again investment tax credit, such as we have seen in the past, doesn't do a whole lot to encourage investment; it just means that firms wait until the credit is "on again" before they buy new equipment. Nonetheless, the investment tax credit (and other direct investment incentives), if done carefully and consistently, can be a very smart stimulus.

Unfortunately, no stimulus will end up creating more jobs unless it has the cooperation of the Fed. Monetary policy thus becomes a necessary ingredient in any stimulus package that can hope to be a net job-maker. As it happens, monetary policy by itself can also be a very smart stimulus. As we noted earlier, the most important effect of a monetary stimulus (i.e., a cut in interest rates) is to increase private investment. It does so at no cost to the public. In fact, a monetary stimulus helps the indebted government by reducing the cost of borrowing.

Granted, monetary policy is not precise and doesn't always work. Sometimes even a zero interest rate is not enough to stimulate private investment. The United States has not experienced such a low interest rate since 1938. Right now there is plenty of room to cut interest rates. The more relevant problem with a monetary stimulus is that the Fed is usually too cautious. Even when the Fed decides that such a stimulus is necessary, as in 1991, it is very slow to cut rates. (As 1994 showed, the Fed is not timid about raising interest rates.) Monetary policy "doesn't work" for the same reason that 8 million American job-seekers "don't work" — because the Fed is afraid to use it.

When monetary policy does work — when it's good, it's *very* good — it not only creates jobs but creates *good* jobs and encourages private investment, which increases productivity and creates even better jobs in the future. Unless you are a lender, low interest rates are "good and good for you."

A Dark Side to Low Interest Rates?

Skeptical readers may perceive a logical difficulty when a book about the ill effects of debt recommends cutting interest rates. Won't lower interest rates encourage people to take on more debt?

You might think so, but the evidence suggests otherwise. To understand why, we must consider separately the three types of debt — government, consumer, and business.

To understand the situation with government debt, ask, "Why is the national debt still rising?" Is it because the federal government is spending more on its programs than it receives in taxes? No. In fact, federal government revenues are almost equal to noninterest expenditures. The national debt is growing because the government must borrow more money to pay the interest on its existing debt. If interest rates come down, the national debt will grow more slowly, not more quickly.

Now consider consumer debt. Are consumers inclined to borrow money when interest rates are low? The historical facts recounted in chapter 2 show otherwise. Throughout the period from 1950 to 1980, as interest rates rose, Americans borrowed more and more. In the 1980s, when declining inflation rates sent *real* interest rates to record highs, consumer borrowing exploded — despite the fact that nominal interest rates paid by consumers (e.g., on credit cards) remained extremely high even as other nominal interest rates were falling. Apparently, high interest rates encourage banks to find borrowers, rather than discouraging people from borrowing. Similarly, low interest rates make banks less aggressive at making loans and may actually reduce consumer debt.

Finally, consider business debt. Businesses are famed for their cold calculations of profit and loss. Won't low interest rates make it more profitable for businesses to borrow? Yes, but . . . borrowing is only one way that businesses can finance their projects. They can also issue stock. Historically, stock prices have responded in an exaggerated manner to changes in interest rates. When rates come down, the cost of borrowing goes down, but stock prices go way up. Firms that were considering borrowing are therefore more likely to issue stock than to borrow.

So low interest rates don't really encourage borrowing. From the point of view of the Indebted Society, the only dark side of low interest rates is the fear of inflation they generate in the hearts of lenders. As we have already argued, that fear is not well founded and is given too much credence by economists and policy makers. The most important part of the smart stimulus prescription can be summed up in three words: *cut interest rates!*

But How?

"Cut interest rates" is easier said than done. The consensus among economists still holds that the Fed *should* remain vigilant against the phantom inflation. The Fed is not elected and has been deliberately (although not always effectively) shielded from politics. These days, presidents appointing members to the Fed's Board of Governors usually seem more concerned with how financial markets will react than with how voters will react. With good reason: voters don't seem to care.

It is not a simple matter to change the consensus among economists or the power of entrenched interests in the Indebted Society. But there is a place for every citizen in this war of ideas. If the American people learn to understand the issues involved, they can make their voices heard. There is certainly a place for political leaders who will bring these issues into the open rather than hiding behind the advice of experts. At present, the old consensus remains powerful, largely because it has no credible opposition. A contrary but informed consensus among the American people can change this situation.

18 ▪ Read Our Lips: Raise Taxes

A S WE HAVE ARGUED, to escape from its vicious circles, the United States must increase investment. To do so, it must increase saving, which is what makes resources available for investment. Saving, by definition, is equal to income minus consumption. In the past two chapters we have presented arguments for how to increase income. In principle, increasing income might be all that is necessary. Nevertheless, whether or not we can shift monetary policy toward a more income-enhancing stance, it would also be valuable to increase saving by limiting consumption — both private and public. Under today's circumstances, the most obvious line of attack is toward the federal deficit, which now allows both the government and individuals to consume more without paying for it.

Originally this chapter was entitled "Read Our Lips: No New Debt" — a deceptive title and rather an impractical objective. The ideal of "no new debt" cannot quite be achieved (any more than Bush's promise of "no new taxes" could be achieved). A nation cannot make an instantaneous transition from borrowing $200,000,000,000 per year to borrowing $0 per year. Nor would such a transition be desirable, even if it were possible. The sudden removal of the federal budget deficit would wreak havoc with the economy. A huge, sudden decrease in government spending and/or increase in taxes would cause a precipitous drop in demand for private-sector products. This drop in demand, along with the uncertainty in the wake of such an unprecedented policy shift, could produce a recession so sudden and severe that the Fed could not effectively counteract it. Moreover, individuals and businesses would not have time to adjust to the sudden change in federal activity, and tremendous hardship would result. A true "no new debt" policy, therefore, would be the very opposite of a smart stimulus.

Still, it is reasonable to have a balanced budget, or even a budget surplus, as a goal. It is also reasonable to take immediate and fairly drastic steps to achieve that goal. The transition, although not impossible, will be painful. However, as long as the transition occurs at a reasonable pace, the Fed should be quite able to handle the economic side effects.

Before we discuss why and how the United States should move toward a balanced budget, remember that a budget deficit is sometimes a good idea. In fact, one of the reasons to move toward a balanced budget now is to provide the flexibility to increase the deficit, should it become necessary in the future. President Franklin D. Roosevelt balanced the budget in 1938, and it was the worst mistake he ever made. After his New Deal programs had almost defeated the Great Depression, his balanced budget brought the depression back with a vengeance. In that situation, the interest rate had already reached zero, so monetary policy could be of little help in stimulating the economy. (Another devaluation of the dollar might have helped, but it might also have pushed the rest of the world back into a depression.) The outbreak of World War II in Europe the following year provided a much needed excuse for a return to deficit spending. In learning the lesson of the 1980s, let us not forget the lesson of the 1930s.

That said, let us note here that today's interest rate is still far above zero, so there is still considerable scope for a monetary stimulus. Moreover, in today's world of flexible exchange rates, an exchange-rate-oriented monetary policy might be effective even if the interest rate were zero. But let's get back to the federal budget.

WHY REDUCE THE DEFICIT?

There is one very big reason to reduce the deficit, and a lot of smaller but still important ones. Most important, deficit reduction will help get us out of the vicious circle of low saving and low growth. Deficit reduction will force the nation as a whole to save more. Individual Americans may save a little less, but, as discussed in chapter 14, net savings are the important measure, and net savings equal the difference between total saving and total borrowing. As the deficit decreases, net savings increase. More resources are then available for private investment, so the economy can grow more quickly. As we saw in chapter 17, private investment also creates a lot of good jobs in the short run.

We have to be careful here, though. If we cut the deficit by cutting public investment, then we are just robbing Peter to pay Paul. Cuts in police protection or scientific research or education or highway maintenance may very well make the vicious circle even worse. If anything, these things should be increased, not cut. Getting out of the vicious circle by increasing saving is a very good reason to undertake a rational deficit-reduction program, but not a good reason to make random cuts in federal spending.

Now for reason number two. Cutting the deficit will reduce our dependence on foreign capital, so we will no longer have to run large trade deficits. American firms can start beating the competition without bringing a nasty response from the Fed. Foreigners will stop buying up U.S. assets, because the United States won't need to sell those assets anymore. Our children will no longer face the prospect of a large national debt owed to foreigners. If we cut the federal deficit and thereby raise domestic saving, we can accomplish all this without lifting a single hostile finger against our trading partners. The danger, maybe, when the shoe is on the other foot, is that Japan and Europe and Korea will start accusing the United States of unfair trade practices.

Another reason to reduce the deficit is that the sight of a nearly balanced budget will ease the anxieties of those who fear inflation. This may sound like a silly reason, but it is very important, perhaps even more important than increasing national saving. Reduced inflation anxiety will have three extremely beneficial effects. First, if the Fed perceives less risk of an inflationary crisis, it will not feel so strongly about always pushing down the inflation rate in preparation for such a crisis. The Fed will therefore be willing to allow a higher level of employment than it now finds acceptable. Second, reduced inflation anxiety will reduce the "inflation risk premium" demanded by bond buyers. With a future of low inflation a little more certain, bond buyers will be willing to lend the same amount at lower interest rates. Third, reduced inflation anxiety by foreign lenders will mean less downward pressure on the dollar, enabling the Fed to reduce interest rates further without risking a potentially inflationary free fall.

A final reason to reduce the deficit is that reducing the deficit now will give us more of a chance to increase it in the future. This sounds a little bit like, "I like getting drunk so much that I'm going on the wagon, so I can get even more drunk when I start drinking again." But it actually makes a lot of sense for the economy. The 1991 recession was so stubborn partially because the already huge federal deficit made it inconvenient to use additional deficit spending to beat the recession. If the budget had been balanced in 1990, the federal government could have produced a strong recovery by early 1992, instead of waiting two more years for the private sector to respond to a half-hearted monetary stimulus. In particular, starting from a balanced budget, the federal government would have a lot of leeway to launch a "smart stimulus" — for example, law-enforcement grants to states and localities — instead of having its hands tied by existing obligations.

For all these reasons (and for others that we have probably forgotten), cutting the deficit — and doing so in a rational manner — is an important part of the road back to affluence. Many people argue, however, that the deficit is either irrelevant or good. Let's take a look at those arguments.

ARGUMENTS AGAINST DEFICIT REDUCTION AND WHY THEY ARE WRONG

The "Don't Worry, Be Happy" Argument

George Bush's attitude toward the deficit was "If you ignore it, it will go away." It is true that if you could really freeze federal spending, the economy would eventually outgrow the deficit. However, problems arise when trying to translate this idea into real-life policy. First, freezing federal spending is a much taller order than it sounds. For example, with health care costs rising and the population aging, a freeze in Medicare spending would be almost impossible. Just to slow the growth of Medicare spending significantly would require either draconian cuts in benefits or massive cost-shifting toward the private sector (which would actually be an unofficial tax on health care). Second, freezing federal spending is not a good idea. To do so without killing any sacred cows, the government would have to make massive cuts in public investment. Third, even if you did freeze federal spending, it would take many years to outgrow the deficit. With private investment crippled by deficits (and tight money) and public investment crippled by a spending freeze, the economy would grow quite slowly. In the long run, the deficit would disappear. "In the long run," as John Maynard Keynes said, "we are all dead."

The "Ricardian Equivalence" Argument

"Ricardian equivalence" is sort of an academic variation on the "don't worry, be happy" argument. Practical people find the idea hard to take seriously; but in academia, it just won't go away. The Ricardian equivalence theorem holds that deficits make no difference, because any change in taxes will be matched by an opposite change in private saving. If the government cuts taxes, households will realize that eventually the government will have to raise taxes again to pay back the additional debt. Households will therefore save every cent of the tax cut in anticipation of when they will need the money to pay the higher taxes. The additional private saving will exactly satisfy the government's additional borrowing needs, and there will be no net effect on the economy. Thus, in the Ricardian equivalence model, government spending always draws resources away from consumption, whether or not the government spending is paid for with taxes. Households know they will have to pay for it — either now or later. The level of tax revenue (at any particular time) is irrelevant, so the deficit (the difference between spending and revenue) doesn't matter.

The first problem with Ricardian equivalence is that, in the United States right now, people don't seem to be saving a whole lot. If people are anticipating higher taxes in the future, then they should be saving a lot. Instead, they seem to be saving even less than usual. The Ricardian equivalence people have two answers for this. First, maybe people are expecting that government spending will be drastically reduced, in which case the government won't have to raise taxes. Second, maybe people just don't want to save anything for the future. Either of these answers might be true, but there is a bigger problem.

Ricardian equivalence makes a very elegant theory, but it is inconsistent with recent U.S. political experience. If the level of taxes at any particular time doesn't matter, then why are people so anxious to have low taxes right now? In the Ricardian world, George Bush would have promised "no new spending" in 1988 rather than "no new taxes." In that world, Bill Clinton's 1992 promise of "some middle-class tax relief" would have been "some additional spending cuts on everyone *except* the middle class." In that world, Walter Mondale's 1984 promise, "I will raise your taxes," would not have assured his defeat. Ricardian equivalence simply does not make sense in a world of voodoo politics.

The "Product Demand–Investment Accelerator" Argument

While some argue that the deficit doesn't matter, others argue that it is a positive good. The argument is based on three premises. First, much of government spending is public investment, which is good, because it increases America's future productive capacity. We agree. Second, our nation needs to utilize its resources more fully. We heartily agree. Third, private investment is determined primarily by what firms expect to be able to sell. Because deficit spending produces a demand for products of the private sector, the direct effect of a deficit is to increase — not decrease — private investment. Again, we agree.

Although the premises are all correct, the conclusion falters because it ignores the role of the Fed. Since the Fed is determined to limit the economy's resource utilization, and since both public and private investment use up resources, the potential salutary effects of the deficit on private investment only cause the Fed to redouble its efforts to choke off that investment. As the government spends more on public investment, the Fed reacts by raising interest rates sufficiently to discourage an equal amount of private investment. If the stimulus from the government spending leads to more private investment, the Fed will simply raise interest rates even further until the investment finally dies out.

To appreciate what the Fed is willing to do, consider an analogy from the Marx Brothers' movie *Coconuts*. Groucho Marx hires Chico Marx to bid up land prices at an auction. However, Chico doesn't realize that he must stop raising the bid before he outbids all the other customers. He is quite content to continue doing just as Groucho has instructed him: when someone says a number, give a higher number. As Chico exclaims during the auction, "I got plenty higher numbers!" As the Fed showed in the early 1980s, it, too, has plenty of higher numbers. Ten percent . . . 15 percent . . . 20 percent . . . The Fed will keep raising the interest rate until all the bidders give up.

The "unstoppable Fed" argument works in reverse, too (although, some say, less effectively). If the government raises taxes and thereby reduces personal consumption, the Fed will react by cutting interest rates sufficiently to encourage enough investment to offset the decline in consumption. Again, if the reduced consumption discourages investment by reducing product demand, the Fed will keep cutting interest rates until the investment comes back. If rates went down all the way to zero, which is unlikely, it would be quite easy for Congress to institute an emergency tax cut. (We should have such problems!)

Even if we convince the Fed to start accommodating deficit spending, it will be better to move toward a balanced budget. If the Fed is willing to accommodate deficits, it will be even more willing to stimulate the economy with low interest rates when the deficits are gone.

The "Recession" Argument

A variation on the "accelerator" argument is the "recession" argument: a cut in the deficit will be a drag on the economy and will cause a prolonged recession. This argument seemed quite cogent in 1991, after the meager 1990 deficit-reduction package seemed to precipitate a recession. However, in 1993 and 1994 exactly the opposite happened. In August 1993 the Clinton administration pushed through a deficit-reduction package with tax hikes steep enough to produce audible groans from Beverly Hills to Kennebunkport. Wall Street traders were convinced that the United States would go into the deepest recession since the 1930s. What happened? You probably remember: seven months later, Wall Street traders were convinced that the economic boom would produce the worst inflation since the 1970s. They were wrong again, of course, but the point is that the link between deficit reduction and recessions is a tenuous one at best.

Nonetheless, deficit reduction probably does increase the risk of a recession, all other things being equal. Fortunately, the Fed knows this and will act preemptively to prevent that recession by cutting interest rates. In fact, since the Fed is in favor of deficit reduction, it should be willing to try extra hard to avoid that recession, so as not to give deficit cutting a bad name. If the president and Congress agree to reduce the deficit, they should expect a quid pro quo from the Fed in the form of lower interest rates. With a lot of pressure and a little bit of luck, the Fed may overdo the economic stimulus (just as it did after the stock market crash in 1987), and we'll finally get the easy-money policy that we have needed all along.

How to Reduce the Deficit

By now we hope you're convinced that cutting the deficit is a good idea, although you probably didn't need convincing. Now comes the hard part. All politicians seem to be for deficit reduction these days, but when asked how they are going to do it, they run into trouble. Don't have any illusions: unless the Fed has a miraculous conversion, smart deficit reduction is going to hurt. As a matter of fact, a fiscal deficit-reduction program's not hurting is a pretty good sign that it was done the wrong way. We hope that most of the pain will be felt by those who can afford painkillers.

To get an idea of the size of the problem, let's look at what it would take to balance the federal budget in one fell swoop. The pie charts in Figure 18.1 summarize the 1994 budget (including "off-budget" items like Social Security). The first thing to notice here is the slice labeled "Borrowing" in the "Sources of Federal Money" chart. Compare the size of that slice with those in the "Federal Expenditures" chart. The only expenditure slices that are substantially larger than the "Borrowing" slice are those labeled "Social Security" and "National Defense." The following are possible "one-step" solutions to the budget deficit shown in these charts:

1. Cut Social Security benefits by 64 percent.
2. Cut national defense by 72 percent.
3. Cut health care spending by 81 percent.
4. Cut income-security programs by 95 percent.
5. Repudiate the national debt. ("Net Interest" is almost exactly equal to "Borrowing.")
6. Completely eliminate the rest of the federal government. (This wouldn't quite do it.)
7. Raise personal income tax revenues by 38 percent (an average of about $2,000 per household).

Obviously, there is no need for a "one-step" solution to the deficit, but this should help to put the real task in perspective. Let's consider each expenditure category.

Social Security The Social Security system was supposed to be independent of the federal budget. However, the United States has been lucky that a large surplus in the Social Security system has been available to help plug the huge deficit in the remaining federal budget. There is a reason for this surplus, but it's the same reason why the surplus won't last. The surplus was created in anticipation of the large number of Americans that will be retiring over the next thirty years. When and if these potential retirees start to collect Social Security benefits at presently mandated levels, the system will move into deficit, and a surplus in the official federal budget will be needed to

FIGURE 18.1 SOURCES OF FEDERAL MONEY

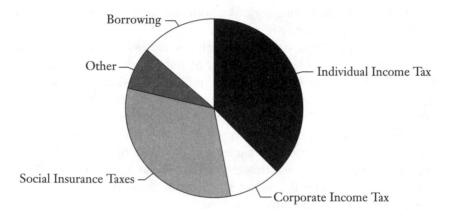

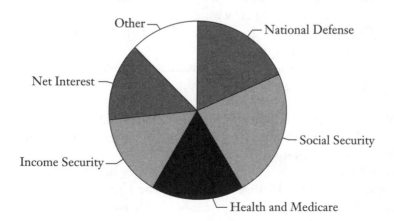

FEDERAL EXPENDITURES

cover this deficit. Cuts in Social Security benefits — perhaps a phased-in reduction in payments to higher-income beneficiaries or a gradual increase in the retirement age — are almost a sine qua non for a substantial reduction in U.S. borrowing, but these are only the beginning.

National defense It may surprise some readers to learn that defense spending has already been falling (in real, inflation-adjusted terms) at an average rate of 5 percent per year since 1989, even as the economy has grown. There are certainly arguments to be made for cutting it further, although the state of Russian politics today is hardly encouraging to those who hope for a continued peace dividend. To many of our liberal friends, defense cuts are *the* solution to the deficit problem. However, we doubt that even *they* would want to cut the defense budget by another 72 percent, especially when untrained military recruits are already receiving near-poverty wages. In principle, we do think that national defense should receive fairly severe cuts — or at least, we used to think so. Recently, our research has uncovered a strikingly high (and robust) correlation between defense spending and productivity growth in the years since World War II. Until the reason for this correlation becomes clearer, we would urge some caution in cutting defense.

Health care There is a consensus that the United States must reform its health care system. The system simply costs too much. How this might be done is the pressing issue. Probably the most cost-effective alternative for health care reform would be a single-payer system similar to the Canadian model. A good idea in our opinion, but given recent experience, we are not optimistic about its political prospects. In any case, although it would help, it wouldn't solve the deficit problem. Even if Americans were willing not only to reform the health care system but also to accept a reduction in health care quality down to the level found in Great Britain, the United States could perhaps hope to reduce its health care budget by 67 percent. This would not erase the deficit.

Income security Today's income security programs are already inadequate — at least, that's what bleeding hearts like us think. But insufficiency doesn't mean those programs won't be cut some more.

The national debt Nobody would seriously suggest that America deliberately default on its debt. Tarnished reputation aside, a serious default by the United States would most likely result in a collapse of the world's financial system.

The rest of the federal government Undoubtedly, Rush Limbaugh would say, "Cut it all." As we mentioned, this drastic step won't quite eliminate the deficit. And, well, yes, we still do believe in something called "public investment," and "the rest of the government" is where most of it takes place. Good luck finding all that fraud, waste, and abuse we're always hearing about.

Taxes Finally, we come to the subject of taxes. Frankly, though, $2,000 per household doesn't sound like the end of the world to us. It isn't peanuts, admittedly. It would hurt a lot. But compared with the other options, it doesn't seem like such a big deal. And remember, this is real life. Nobody seriously wants to balance the budget by 1997. A four-year phased-in tax hike of about $1,000 per household on average, combined with some economic stimulus from the Fed to raise the tax *base*, wouldn't be unbearably painful (especially to the rich).

Many have argued that Americans are already overtaxed. Americans certainly *feel* overtaxed. But the very reason that Americans feel overtaxed is why they are actually undertaxed. Compare the United States with Japan. (Japan is one of the few other industrialized nations that does not have a publicly financed health care system, so it serves as an appropriate standard of comparison.) The Japanese pay a much lower portion of their income in taxes than do Americans. This has been the basis of arguments that Americans pay too much in taxes. There is one critical difference, however, between the United States and Japan: Japanese households save a very large fraction of their income, whereas American households save very little. Because the Japanese save so much, their government can run a large fiscal deficit while the country as a whole remains a net lender. Even though Japanese households pay little in taxes, they finance their government by lending it money directly. As we have maintained throughout this book, for the economy as a whole, it does not matter whether payments from citizens to the government are called "taxes" or "savings." American citizens, however, do not make large payments to the government in the form of savings. Therefore, in order to stop borrowing as a nation, the United States must oblige its citizens to make larger payments to the government through taxes. This contribution will hurt. It will hurt for the very same reason that it is necessary: in order to live comfortably, Americans must consume a large percentage of their income. To stop borrowing, Americans must give up living comfortably.

Who Should Pay?

It is somewhat misleading to say that "Americans" must give up living comfortably. Most Americans are already uncomfortable, and a few could live comfortably with much less than they now have. There are also many Americans who have more than most others but who wouldn't be comfortable giving anything up. Obviously, it would be silly to assess an extra tax of $1,000 on each household, regardless of its particular circumstances. It might be economically efficient, but it would also be morally repugnant and politically impossible.

Call us communists if you must, but we think that people who make a lot of money should pay most of the new taxes. As of 1993 the top fifth of American households received nearly half the aggregate household income. To balance the budget, we don't even need to touch the other four-fifths. Moreover, the top 5 percent of American households received 20 percent of the income — about $800 billion. If Uncle Sam could get his hands on another $200 billion of that, the deficit would be history.[49]

An extra 25 percent might sound confiscatory, but it does not seem so to us. Today the top marginal income tax rate is 39.6 percent. Even doubling it would not approach the 91 percent top marginal tax rate that prevailed throughout the 1950s and the early 1960s.

In the backs of our minds, we hear voices murmuring about incentives to save and invest. Won't high marginal tax rates reduce those incentives just when we need them the most? We doubt it would make much difference — but we'll be magnanimous. Against our better judgment, we are willing to exempt interest, dividends, and capital gains from any *increase* in marginal tax rates. That would leave us the bulk of the money earned by those with high incomes. We can still balance the budget without laying a finger on the bottom four-fifths of the population.

Of course, even if such capital income is exempted, high marginal tax rates on the well-to-do may reduce incentives to engage in high-income labor. Ronald Reagan reportedly experienced this very disincentive back when the top marginal tax rate was 91 percent. Apparently, we are given to understand, Reagan would have made more movies if only he could have kept more of his earnings. So we have to ask the question, "What would life be like without *Bedtime for Bonzo*?" We suspect it would not be very different from what it is now.

Bedtime for Bonzo might seem like a contrived example. What about the innovative scientist who discovers a cure for diabetes or the computer whiz who revolutionizes information processing? Should America risk losing these national treasures to emigration because their incomes are too highly taxed? Or, worse yet, should we risk losing them to idleness and lack of motivation? We don't really think this is a problem for a few reasons. First, even if our greatest scientists and innovators all move to Monaco, we will still be able to use their discoveries. For a price, of course; but there is already a price. As far as we know, Microsoft charges the same price for Windows 95, no matter what the purchaser's nationality. There is no reason to believe that the average American would be any worse off if Bill Gates were a citizen of some other nation.

Second, we would ask the reader to consider the experience of the 1950s and early 1960s, when tax rates were much higher than those we are suggesting. American innovation and initiative did not grind to a halt during the 1950s. On the contrary, despite all their social problems, those years were something of a golden age for technological progress in the United States. Readers who are older than we are may remember a time when polio was still a major public health problem and the word "computer" was not in the vocabulary of most businesspeople. If anything, it was not until the late 1960s and the 1970s, after tax rates were reduced, that the desire to accomplish great things seemed to go out of style.

Third, consider how the U.S. economy has changed over the past forty years. Advances in information technology and telecommunications have brought about a situation in which a few high-earning individuals — and often just one — can serve a very large market. For example, one financial guru can fax his or her latest prognostications to thousands of customers in a matter of minutes. One software designer can create a program that runs on any of millions of existing personal computers. One entertainer can appear in millions of living rooms at once in wide-screen full-color stereo, and in millions of other living rooms at diverse times on videotape. One management consultant can attend videoconferences in New York, Chicago, Los Angeles, London, and Zurich, all before lunch. As a result of this situation, there is a very large premium on being the best, even when the second or third best would do almost as well. When the best can be spread so thin, there is often no need for the second or third best.

If higher taxes discourage people from working in potentially high-income occupations, we may lose the best, we may even lose the second best, but the third best will be almost as good. When only a few are needed to serve a very large market, only a small incentive is required to entice enough good people into an occupation.

Fourth, we would ask the reader to consider how much of the work of high-income earners is used in attempts to redistribute wealth rather than creating it. Lawyers are the obvious example: for the most part, a lawyer's business is to bargain and argue with another lawyer about whose client gets the bigger share of the pie. Similarly, business executives seem to expend most of their talent trying to extract more from workers for less money or trying to capture market share from one another. Mutual fund managers and numerous other financial functionaries spend their time in a hopeless struggle to outperform one another. In principle, whenever there is a large body of wealth, a lot of people will try to get their hands on it, and whoever does the dirty work will be well paid.

Granted, there are some well-paid individuals who do perform obviously useful functions that are not easy to replicate. Doctors would be the obvious example. However, it seems that the usefulness of a high-paying occupation is inversely related to the degree of pecuniary motivation of those who undertake it. Performing an obviously useful service is inherently rewarding and does not require a large financial incentive. If our country does develop a shortage of doctors, or some such profession, because of high taxes (a possibility that would surprise us), then we can always offer a tax break to the particular profession that is in shortage. All in all, if there was ever a real case to be made against progressive taxation, that case is weaker now than in the past. We submit, therefore, that heavy taxation of the rich is an idea whose time has returned.

ALTERNATIVES TO HIGHER TAXES

Politicians these days are quick to criticize the rich but slow to tax them. Bill Clinton's 39.6 percent marginal rate barely made it through a Democratic Congress. Two years later even Clinton seemed to apologize for the tax hike. Taxes just aren't cool these days, and everyone, including us, has suggestions for cost-cutting measures.

Some measures that we endorse include reductions in Social Security benefits for those in upper income brackets; raising the Social Security retirement age; reforming the health care system; and, above all, an easing up by the Fed.

We could make other suggestions for budget cuts. We could undoubtedly come up with enough cuts to balance the budget, but the problem is that everyone would disagree with some of the cuts. Anyone can come up with a list of expenses they think are useless and must be cut. But everyone's list is different. For better or worse, the United States is a democracy. Democracies require compromise. We personally want to see *more* spending on public safety, public education, basic research, and worthwhile antipoverty programs, but others have different priorities. If the United States is to get the public investment it needs, then pick-and-choose budget cutting is not a real alternative to raising taxes.

One alternative that may be realistic is tax-sheltered savings. This is an alternative — not just to higher taxes but to deficit reduction in general — that deserves close attention. The deficit is a problem only because private saving is not very high. If private saving were high, as it has been in Japan, then this saving would leave plenty of resources for private investment even after financing the deficit. It does not matter whether the funds that make their way from citizens to the government are mandated, direct payments in the form of taxes or voluntary, often indirect payments in the form of savings (which, at some level of the chain, will be used in part to buy government bonds). Therefore, a policy that successfully raises the U.S. private-saving rate is just as good as a policy that reduces the deficit.

A common prescription to increase private saving is to reduce taxes on interest, dividends, and capital gains, so that people can reap more of a return from their savings. That's not the right way to do it. First, if the tax reduction is done without any offsetting increases in other taxes, the increased government borrowing will far outweigh the increase in saving. If there are such offsetting increases in other taxes, the problem is that they will probably fall more on the middle class, while the cuts will typically benefit the well-to-do. That brings us to the second problem: this policy produces a windfall for those who already have large pools of savings. The point is to create an incentive to save in the future, but much of the benefit will go to those who already saved in the past. This tax cut will be costly in terms of lost revenue, and there won't be any new benefit to the nation, since those decisions to save in the past have already been made. Finally, we are skeptical about whether the future incentives from such a tax cut would be very strong, anyway. Saving is just what is left over after people consume, and consumption is determined mostly by habit. We just don't think people's habits are heavily influenced by calculations of how much interest they are going to get after taxes.

To get people to save more, you have to focus their attention on the decision between saving and consuming. The way to do this is to give them an *immediate* tax break when they save. What we propose, therefore, is that savings be exempt from income taxes. That is, if you use your income to consume, you should have to pay taxes on it now, but if you save it, you shouldn't have to pay taxes on it until you take it out of savings.

We have to be a little careful here, though. A limited tax break along these lines has been available for a long time in the form of Individual Retirement Accounts (IRAs). But there is a very big loophole: nobody checks to see where you got the money when you put it in an IRA. A lot of people get it by borrowing, and that defeats the whole purpose. If you borrow money to put in an IRA, you don't do any new net saving. To be effective in encouraging real saving, a tax break for new saving has to subtract out anything that is borrowed. Keeping track of people's borrowing may prove to be difficult and intrusive. Nonetheless, it may still be more acceptable than a straight-out tax increase.

Not that a savings exemption would mean no tax increase. Some taxes would have to be raised to make up for the revenue lost when people save their money and take the tax break. However, for a couple of reasons, this tax increase would be less troublesome than one needed to offset a reduced tax on investment income. First, there is no windfall for people who saved in the past. Second, the savings exemption and the offsetting tax increase could be structured in such a way as to benefit middle class people more than the well-to-do.

There are still problems, of course. For example, what do you do about buying a house? Is that saving or consumption? Does it depend on whether the house is unnecessarily opulent? If so, how do we measure that? What about buying a car? Since the car should run for many years, in a sense, someone who buys a car is saving for the future. But what if they plan to sell it in a couple of years? All sorts of thorny problems present themselves. Still, if Americans cannot accept an overall tax increase and the Fed cannot accept high employment, then a saving exemption may be the best America can do to get out of the vicious circle.

Exempting saving from income taxes is an example of a change in the Rules of the Game. To move away from being an indebted society, America will need many such changes.

19 ▪ New Rules

A MERICA'S RULES ARE THE RULES of an indebted society. If America is to transcend its indebtedness, it can no longer operate with the rules that let it fall into debt and allowed the effects of debt to become so disastrous. With appropriate changes in the Rules of the Game, the United States can once again have debt its servant rather than its master.

In this chapter we propose several changes in the rules. Some are specific; others are just sketches. Some are profound; others are merely incremental. None of these proposals is entirely new, but all deserve a new look. None of these proposals need be accepted lock, stock, and barrel, but the issues they address must somehow be attacked.

Change the Rules to End the Rule of Lenders

The most critical need of the Indebted Society is to emerge from under the yoke of the lenders. Lenders should receive a fair return, but society should not go out of its way to protect them. The battle to restore this balance may be fought largely on an intellectual field, among economists and technocrats, but there are some specific changes that can be made to start things moving quickly in the right direction.

Cure Lenders' Neuroses by Issuing Inflation-Adjusted Bonds

As things now stand, those who have money to invest must choose between clearly risky investments, such as the stock market, and supposedly safe investments, of which bonds are a prime example. Bonds as they currently exist are safe only if one can be confident that the inflation rate will remain low. There is no reason, in principle, that the safety of bonds needs to be so qualified. The U.S. government can and should issue bonds that provide explicit protection against inflation (as described in chapter 8). If the bonds themselves contain such protection, the Fed will no longer have to provide it by making sure that too many people are out of work. [As this book was going to press, we were delighted to read in the *Wall Street Journal* that Treasury Secretary Rubin had reversed his earlier opposition to inflation-adjusted bonds and that the U.S. Treasury was now planning to issue such bonds. It's nice to know that public policy is already starting to move in the right direction.]

Having the government issue inflation-adjusted bonds may seem like a very small step. After all, the federal government is only one of many bond issuers, and we cannot be sure that anyone will follow the government's lead. However, in today's sophisticated financial markets, a substantial move toward inflation-adjusted bonds by the federal government would have a disproportionate impact. With both inflation-adjusted and unadjusted bonds available on the market, arbitrageurs would find it profitable to trade futures contracts in price indices. Once a highly liquid market develops for these futures contracts, all fixed-income investors will be able to insure themselves against inflation. This insurance will come at a price, of course. Investors will know exactly how much it costs them to be safe. If investors are not willing to pay the price to insure themselves against inflation, they will no longer be able to ask American workers to pay the price.

The only real question about inflation-adjusted bonds is why the government has not already issued them. With $5 trillion in U.S. bonds outstanding and none of them indexed, you can bet that investors — especially foreign investors — are asking the same thing. They can certainly be forgiven for suspecting that the United States is planning to inflate away its national debt. Would you lend money to someone who promises to pay you back in pretty pieces of paper and reserves the right to print as many of those pieces of paper as he or she needs? If only the United States would issue inflation-adjusted bonds, there would no longer be a reason for suspicion. America would no longer have the option of inflating away the debt, because the value of the debt would rise with inflation. With the suspicion gone, the United States could start to conduct monetary policy to ensure high employment rather than to assuage the fears of investors.

Again, why hasn't the government already done so? We don't know. In fact, nobody knows. The question truly puzzles economists. Hendrik Houthakker, another economist at Harvard, thinks it has to do with America's Calvinist heritage. When the Pilgrims landed in

America, they were sure that right was right and wrong was wrong, and there was no compromise possible. In the view of America's lending establishment, perhaps, inflation-adjusted bonds would seem to be a pact with the devil. (To lenders, of course, inflation is always the work of the devil.) Issuing inflation-adjusted bonds would be like saying, "Okay, Mr. Satan, we'll work with you. We might give in to temptation, but we're going to make sure it doesn't hurt anybody." When you think about it rationally, this mind-set doesn't make any sense. As a matter of fact, we've searched the Scriptures assiduously, and we still haven't found a commandment that says, "Thou shalt not inflate." Inflation-adjusted bonds are not a pact with the devil; they are just a convenient way of dealing with a potential economic problem. Ignoring the need for inflation-adjusted bonds makes no more sense for modern America than going around in hats with buckles and putting all the Baptists in the stocks.

Make the Fed Accountable for the Effects of Its Policies

Issuing inflation-adjusted bonds would deal with the problem of lenders' power by taking away the conflict between the needs of lenders and those of broader society. Another approach, which should be undertaken simultaneously, is to challenge lenders' power directly. As is discussed in chapter 8, Fed officials have many incentives to consider the interests of lenders and none to consider the interests of workers. Legislation, including especially the Humphrey-Hawkins Act of 1978, directs the Fed to consider employment in its decisions, but the Fed has no real reason to take these laws seriously, especially since the specific goals given in the Humphrey-Hawkins Act were — nearly everyone now agrees — grossly unrealistic. (For example, the act called for reducing the unemployment rate from 6 percent to 4 percent within five years, while reducing the inflation rate from 9 percent to 3 percent. Either might be possible, but not both.) In addition, the natural rate theory — if accepted at face value — provides an ideological justification for the Fed to ignore employment because Fed policy (according to the theory) cannot affect employment in the long run.

However, the natural rate theory is only a theory. Academics can afford to take actions based on the assumption that a certain theory is correct, but when the future of the country is at stake, it is just common sense to allow for the possibility that the theory is wrong. Imagine if the Pentagon were to conduct wars based on just one particular theory. That's not how the United States became the world's strongest military power, and it won't help the United States become the world's strongest economic power. Successful business leaders take into account that their theories may be wrong, because they have incentives to do so. The Fed must be given such incentives.

Right now, the Fed has the wrong motivation. As long as potential future employers are satisfied with the achievement of consistently low inflation, Fed officials will avoid taking any risks with inflation, even when the payoff for the country may be very high. In effect, Fed officials behave like the managers of a highly indebted corporation. Just as those managers further their careers by avoiding bankruptcy at all costs, Fed officials further their careers by avoiding inflation at all costs. The United States desperately needs to change these incentives.

One way to do so would be to pay large bonuses to Fed officials based on U.S. economic performance. To satisfy natural raters, the period over which the performance criteria apply for a particular official should extend far beyond that official's time in office. That way, if the natural rate theory is true and any changes in the inflation rate are permanent, Fed officials will still be encouraged to take that permanence into account. Meanwhile, it is important that the criteria include factors relevant to the well-being of Americans. In particular, the criteria should include some measure of job market conditions (most likely the unemployment rate, although that wouldn't be our first choice) and some measure related to long-run productivity growth (for example, the ratio of investment to the GDP). The exact details are not critical, and we do not present a detailed proposal here. What is critical is that the Fed somehow be made accountable for the effects of its policies.

CHANGE THE TAX RULES TO DISCOURAGE DEBT AND ENCOURAGE INVESTMENT

The Fed is not the only institution in the Indebted Society that has the wrong incentives. The tax system, as currently constituted, encourages the use of debt financing by corporations and does too little to encourage investment by both corporations and individuals. Past efforts at tax reform have made baby steps in the right direction, but overall those efforts have paid too much attention to the lost cause of tax simplification and too little attention to feasible improvements in taxes' incentive effects. To the extent that past tax-reform efforts have improved incentives, they have usually done so by reducing government revenues and thereby promoting deficits or by unnecessarily transferring the tax burden from the rich to the middle class. The kind of real tax reforms we think are necessary to pave America's road back to affluence are presented below.

Restructure Corporate Taxation to Eliminate the Debt Subsidy

Above all else, we need to end the artificial subsidy for debt financing that has always been implicit in the way corporations are taxed. This reform cannot be accomplished just by tinkering with the corporate tax code, as Congress did in 1986. What is needed is a wholesale change in the philosophy of corporate taxation.

One way to effect this change — although it might be politically impossible — is to abolish the corporate tax altogether and shift the burden to high-income individuals. After all, they are the ones who ultimately receive most of the profits anyway. Some of the profits, though, go to small investors who don't have very high incomes. By taxing the corporation, the system is punishing fat cats and small investors equally; frankly, that doesn't seem fair to us. The current system also taxes the retained portion of profits, which is not paid out to investors. If the burden of taxation were shifted from firms to high-income individuals, then firms would have more retained earnings to invest in future productivity. They would also have a larger cushion against financial difficulty, so they would have less need to protect themselves by downsizing. Economically, the only major disadvantage of transferring the tax burden from corporations to individuals would be that corporate managers would have more freedom to pursue their own interests rather than those of stockholders — just like back before the Days of Debt. That doesn't really sound too bad to us. All in all, the advantages of taxing individuals rather than corporations far outweigh the disadvantages.

However, there is one problem: individuals vote, and corporations don't. Today, with record profits and record downsizing, corporations have a bad reputation among voters. The idea of reducing corporate taxation while increasing personal taxation would be a very hard sell. Ironically, that policy would actually reduce the incentive for downsizing and, even though it would increase profits, would prevent richer stockholders from keeping those extra profits. Furthermore, since top corporate managers make very high salaries, which would be taxed more heavily, those downsizing bigwigs would be net losers as well. If only voters would focus their anger on the *people* who are making out well while workers suffer, instead of on abstract institutions like "big government" and "big business," there would be a basis for positive change.

We hope that change will occur, but we don't expect it. Instead, we offer a more modest, though still mildly revolutionary, proposal: change the corporate profits tax into a corporate *capital returns* tax. In other words, instead of having firms pay taxes on bottom-line profits, have them pay taxes on "earnings before interest and taxes" (EBIT, as the accountants call it). Under this system, corporations would no longer be able to deduct interest payments from taxable income and would no longer have an incentive to finance unnecessarily with debt. Obviously, such a change would have to be phased in over a number of years; a sudden, drastic change in the tax rules would wreak havoc. Also, corporate tax rates would naturally be reduced as the tax base is expanded to include interest payments, so that firms would end up, on average, paying the same amount in taxes.

Such a change to reduce the incentives for debt could affect the balance of power within the firm. Workers would win, because lower-debt firms could be more generous and less heartless with workers. Managers would win, because lower-debt firms would give them more flexibility. Stockholders might lose, because they would no longer have as much "discipline of debt" to force workers and managers to do their bidding. However, the productivity-enhancing effects of financial flexibility might outweigh the decline in discipline, even for stockholders. The result would be a win-win situation, with workers and managers as the big winners and stockholders coming out slightly ahead. In any case, a reduction in the incentives for debt financing could break the vicious circle of high debt and low productivity.

Institute Direct and Permanent Investment Incentives for the Private Sector

If the United States is going to continue taxing corporations, at least it should take maximum advantage of the corporate tax law by giving firms incentives to do what is best for the country. The one (and only, as far as we can see) big benefit of corporate taxation is that it gives the public a lever to influence corporate policy. The public should use that lever by giving corporations more incentives to invest.

There are several ways to do so. One possibility is the investment tax credit discussed in chapter 17, which would allow firms to take a direct tax break proportional to the amount they invest. The overall tax rate could be increased to compensate for the lost revenue. (As you can imagine, we prefer that the personal tax rates for the rich be raised instead.)

Another possibility is liberal expensing rules. In other words, a firm buying a new machine could deduct the entire cost from its taxable income that same year instead of deducting depreciation charges over a long period of time. This modification would make investment less of a drain on corporate cash flow, so high debt levels would have a less vicious effect on productive investment. Again, some tax rate somewhere would have to be raised to make up for the lost revenue.

Whatever their particular form, corporate investment incentives should be undertaken as a permanent change in the tax law, not just a temporary push for the economy. Although it is theoretically possible for America to invest too much, there is no reason to expect anything like that to happen during our lifetime — or ever, for that matter.

At times the nation's resources may be strained, and consumers and government may be unwilling to reduce their spending, so that reduced investment would be the only alternative to higher inflation. This problem would be temporary and could (and, we are all too sure, would) be handled quickly by the Fed through the interest-rate mechanism. Although Congress may try several times before getting the investment incentives right, it should not try using those incentives to fine-tune the economy. Because the process of motivating, passing, and implementing legislation is so slow, previous fine-tuning efforts of this sort have been very badly timed, and there is no reason to expect them to be more successful in the future. If Congress is to do any fine-tuning, it should do so by adjusting public investment, which has more immediate and predictable effects, rather than by playing with private-sector incentives. The time for private-sector investment incentives is "now and forever."

Change Personal Taxation to Reward Saving Without Giving the Rich a Windfall

In order to increase investment without angering the Fed or raising the trade deficit, the United States has to increase its saving. "Increased saving" is really just another way of saying "reduced consumption (compared with the national income)." This reduced consumption (or, more optimistically, increased income) would free up resources to be used for investment. As we discuss at length in the previous chapter, the most effective way to reduce consumption is to raise taxes so that people have less disposable income to consume. As we also mention, another possibility is to change the tax law to allow sheltering of savings while increasing tax rates to keep revenues unchanged. Even *with* an overall tax *increase*, it would be good to put more savings incentives in the tax law, provided these incentives are effective and equitable. The form of a possible savings incentive is outlined in chapter 18.

MAKE THE LAW (JUST A LITTLE BIT) WORKER-FRIENDLY

There are other ways in which U.S. labor law should be revised to provide better protection for workers in these difficult times.

Change Employment Law to Protect Older Workers

Under the law as currently written and interpreted, protection for older workers is illusory. Even though a firm cannot terminate older employees specifically because of their age, it can get rid of them, for example, because their pensions are about to vest or because their salaries are higher than more junior employees. The law now protects employment more effectively for lawyers and courtroom experts than for older workers. We're certainly not going to complain about the demand for expert economists, but we would like to see the law provide real protection for older workers as well. Congress should amend the law to make it clear that firms cannot terminate older employees because of seniority, salary, and other factors (such as pension eligibility) that are direct consequences of seniority, salary, or age (except, of course, when those factors interfere with job performance). Downsizing to cut costs by eliminating senior workers and giving their duties to lower-paid younger workers should not be an option for corporations. This type of downsizing doesn't increase productivity or efficiency; it only enriches shareholders at the expense of terminated employees. Because of the loss of trust, and because losing a job hurts older employees more than a little extra profit helps shareholders, society as a whole is a big loser when firms downsize in this way. If firms are really restructuring to improve productivity, that's fine. But now firms have a strong temptation to use restructuring as an excuse just to dump higher-paid senior employees. Congress should take away this temptation.

Fix the Unemployment Insurance System

Today's unemployment insurance (UI) system does little of what it should and much of what it shouldn't. In the past, it has proven a very effective inducement for cyclical businesses to engage in temporary layoffs. Harvard economist Martin Feldstein once described such periods of temporary layoff as "UI holidays." Despite the incentive for temporary layoffs, such UI holidays are no longer common. Although the UI system provides little incentive for permanent downsizings, it also provides little help to people who are victims of those increasingly common events.

Currently, federal and state legislation provides for extension of the benefit period during times of high unemployment and/or recession. Typically, the extension period is triggered when the unemployment rate reaches a certain level. However, a problem exists, whereby the unemployment rate might be low overall, but the length of time that workers remain unemployed could be long. A more equitable and realistic trigger for extended benefits, therefore, would be the average length of unemployment among the unemployed population rather than an arbitrary level of the unemployment rate. This is the most critical change that needs to be made as more workers suffer permanent layoff and encounter difficulty obtaining reemployment. Benefits for these workers, who in the Indebted Society account for a fair proportion of the jobless, run out before a new job is secured. If the workers are "lucky" enough to be out of work during a period of high unemployment, they are eligible for extended benefits. But if the unemployment rate is low, these workers are just out of luck.

Other valuable changes would include more job training for displaced workers and changes in the incentives given to workers and firms by the UI system. We don't discuss these in detail here. America's leaders must understand, however, that job training is *not* a substitute for economic stimulus. Some politicians seem to believe in a sort of *Field of Dreams*, in which, "If you train them, firms will come!" In fact, retraining is of no value unless there are jobs for the retrained workers. While changing the rules of the UI system, our leaders should remember that this is only one part of the solution to America's jobs problem.

Raise the Minimum Wage

Last in our list of the rules of the labor market is one that economists have wrongly accused of destroying jobs. Although polls show broad public support for raising the national minimum wage from its current $4.25 per hour, polls of economists have shown that 90 percent would expect employers to react to a higher minimum wage by cutting employment. This belief is based on standard economic theory, but it completely contradicts the evidence. A recent book by economists David Card and Alan Krueger shows that, in study after study, a higher minimum wage seems, if anything, to *increase* employment. Apparently, some of the assumptions underlying the standard economic theory are just plain wrong. (In particular, the assumption that workers have a choice about where to work appears to be quite suspect.) In any case, the conclusion — that a higher minimum wage will reduce employment — is clearly wrong.

While the minimum wage is not as big a deal as some people think, it certainly has a role in increasing incomes and reducing poverty. More important, perhaps, it has a symbolic role in showing that America is a society where work is rewarded. Whatever the advantages and disadvantages of welfare reform, it is absurd to try conquering poverty by getting people to work when working won't earn them enough to keep out of poverty. If America is serious about welfare reform, part of it should be a substantial increase in the minimum wage.

Change the Way the Government Does Business

Finally, in addition to changing the rules for the private sector, the federal government should put its own house in order. There is no shortage of proposals for reforming the federal government: mostly one hears either "slash and burn" proposals from the Republicans or "tune and tinker" proposals from the Democrats. We leave this grand debate to others, but here we suggest the changes that are most important to get America on the road back to affluence.

Change Federal Budgeting Procedures to Account Explicitly for Public Investment

When a business keeps its books, it makes a critical distinction between expenditures for long-term investment and expenditures for day-to-day expenses. When a business makes a long-term investment, such as buying a new factory or a companywide computer system, no expense shows up immediately on the firm's accounts. Rather, the firm is said to have acquired an asset, which it then writes off gradually over the useful life of the asset. The idea is to match the expenses with the revenue they generate. A new factory doesn't generate most of its revenue in the first year of production. Typically, it lasts for many years and continues to generate revenue until it is taken out of service. Therefore, to present an accurate picture of the firm's profits, accountants apply what is called the "matching principle." Day-to-day expenses show up immediately in the firm's profit-and-loss statement, but long-term investments show up gradually over their useful life.

The federal government does things very differently. In the federal budget, expenses for roads, bridges, and scientific research — things that can be expected to produce long-term benefits — are treated just like congressional salaries and the Energy Department's advertising budget. There is no distinction between long-term investments and day-to-day expenses. Essentially, every federal expenditure is treated as if it were a day-to-day expense, thereby creating the misleading impression that the government is wasting a lot of money. After all, any business that has a trillion dollars a year in day-to-day expenses obviously isn't being managed very efficiently. Furthermore, the current federal budgeting system effectively forces Congress to concern itself purely with government cash flow rather than long-term costs and benefits. Any successful businessperson will tell you this is not a good idea. It is almost as if we have a law saying that the government is required to be penny-wise and pound-foolish.

President Clinton's solution is to refer to any expenditure that he supports as an investment — which doesn't really solve the problem. First of all, President Clinton's priorities, although we personally agree with many of them, do not have anything remotely approaching general acceptance. Second, just because an expenditure is a good idea doesn't mean that it is an investment rather than a day-to-day expense. Third, no matter how the president refers to expenditures in his speeches, they still show up in the official budget as if they were day-to-day expenses. In budget debates, the bottom line is still the current deficit. The government is like a corporation that issues a cash flow statement but no profit-and-loss statement. Ironically, the federal government is also the one institution for which cash flow per se is really of no importance. Unlike a private firm, if the government runs out of cash, it can always borrow or print more. Government bookkeeping is 100 percent backwards.

Although this silly way of keeping books is fairly standard for national governments (which often take U.S. practice as a model), the United States cannot afford to continue it. To make rational decisions about government expenditures, Americans and their leaders need to be able to see how well the government is really doing, not just how much cash is coming in and going out. The objective of federal budget policy should be to make the government "more profitable," not just to reduce the deficit. To treat capital expenditures (investments) just like current expenditures is to say we don't care about the future. Americans do care about the future. There will be a lot of problems to resolve in designing capital budgeting procedures for the federal government, but the result will be well worth the trouble.

Collect and Use Job Vacancy Statistics

Another less ambitious but possibly equally valuable change that the federal government could make would be to begin collecting job vacancy statistics, as we suggest in chapter 7. How can the Fed — or any other policy makers — know whether it needs to create more new jobs if it doesn't know how many new jobs are already out there? How can we know whether job-training programs will help people unless we know whether there are jobs to train them for? Most industrialized countries do collect vacancy statistics, and research shows that these statistics can be very useful in assessing whether business conditions are depressed or inflationary. They can also help tell us how badly people without jobs are hurting. If you want bang for the buck — a small increase in government expenditure with a big payoff — this is it.

Don't Give Up on Health Care Reform

Last but not least, we return to the subject of health care reform. We are certainly not experts in this subject, but it is so incredibly important that we have to mention it again. The federal government alone spends more on health care than it does on national defense, and that is only the beginning of the problem. With the population aging, the government's problem is set to increase, even aside from the increasing cost per person. Meanwhile, private-sector health care costs have intensified the effects of the corporate debt service culture, and many people remain uninsured. In addition to having inadequate health care, these people tend to use the health care system in an inefficient manner, which makes health care more expensive for everyone else. Rising health care costs are also a drag on job creation, not just because of the cost to employers but also because they provide another source of inflation for the Fed to worry about. (In fact, outside of the health care sector, there is almost no inflation today.)

As health care technology improves, health care becomes more expensive for everyone because insurers, for fear of being called inhumane, must offer the up-to-date best in care, and they pass these costs on to customers. Life is infinitely precious and, as medical technology improves, begins to become infinitely expensive. Somehow we have to stop health care costs before they become infinite. If the Clintons' plan wasn't one that Americans could live with, let's go back to the drawing board. In the long run, if America is to take the road back to affluence without getting crushed, we must somehow stop this juggernaut.

New Rules for the World?

Health care is one problem that the rest of the industrialized world seems to have solved more effectively than the United States. Some other problems, although they are far from being solved here, are even more difficult for other countries. For example, unemployment seems still to be a much bigger problem in Europe than in the United States. Most of the problems discussed in this book are not unique to America, and the way in which we handle these problems will have implications for the rest of the world. The prescriptions that are offered so far tend to ignore the effects of U.S. actions on the rest of the world, and they have only lightly touched on the role of the rest of the world in the success of these prescriptions.

Although the United States certainly cannot make rules for the rest of the world, it can, by its example and by persuasion, urge the rest of the world to change its ways. In the next chapter we look more closely at the role of the United States and other countries in each other's economies, and how those relationships affect our prescriptions.

20 ▪ Saving the World

W E ARE NOT ALONE. Thirty years ago Americans could act as if the U.S. economy existed in a vacuum. Today they clearly cannot. The recognition that other nations' policies affect the U.S. economy has tended to focus public attention on trade policy and trade negotiations. We believe this attention is misdirected. The most important relationships are not in the rules of trade but in the way nations conduct macroeconomic policy — that is, interest rates, taxes, public spending, and exchange rates.

In fact, even thirty years ago, the United States was not alone. However, policy makers governed its economy in such a way that the importance of the rest of the world was not easily visible. In 1960, when Richard Nixon blamed his presidential defeat on Fed Chairman William Martin, he might just as reasonably have blamed the rest of the world. When Martin refused to cut interest rates, he was not just trying to get a Democrat elected. He was reacting, at least in part, to international financial conditions — trying, one might say, to protect the illusion that the United States was alone in the world.

In other chapters of this book, we argue for lower interest rates and a more balanced budget. This prescription is not very different from what Nixon and Eisenhower wanted in 1960.[50] Unlike Nixon, however, we do not ignore the international consequences. We now discuss those consequences, what they mean for the United States, how they affect other countries, and how the United States and other countries should handle them.

WHY THE FED VOTED AGAINST NIXON IN 1960

F or U.S. economic policy, the late 1950s were a conservative time. In 1959 the country ran a budget deficit of $12.8 billion (equivalent to about $70 billion today, adjusted for inflation), and that was too much for President Eisenhower. Determined to leave office with a balanced budget, Eisenhower vetoed one spending bill after another and allowed tax revenues to rise sharply as income growth pushed people into higher tax brackets. The balanced budget proved to be a drag on the economy. The Fed might have offset that drag by cutting interest rates, but it chose not to do so until it was too late to prevent a recession. Why was the Fed so cautious about cutting rates? Partly, as usual, the Fed wanted to prevent inflation. Partly, however, it must also have been concerned about the international financial position of the United States.

Under the system then in place, America was committed to maintaining the dollar's foreign exchange value. This fixed exchange rate effectively enabled Americans to ignore the rest of the world, because the terms of international competition did not change from year to year. To enforce its commitment to a fixed dollar, the U.S. Treasury stood ready to buy or sell unlimited amounts of gold at $35 an ounce. When U.S. interest rates fell, this would set off a chain of events that would force the United States to sell off some of its gold. First, in response to an interest rate cut, global investors would move their assets out of the United States in search of higher returns. In the process, they would exchange their dollars for other currencies. Foreign central banks would be left with a surplus of dollars, which they would then bring to the U.S. Treasury to exchange for gold.

Although the United States had plenty of gold to sell, it used up over 20 percent of its reserves from 1958 to 1960. During 1958, to get the country out of a deep recession, the Fed had allowed some interest rates to fall below even 1 percent, and as a result, America had been forced to sell gold. Gold had continued to flow out during 1959. If this outflow were to continue year after year, it would deplete U.S. reserves, and the United States would eventually have no choice but to devalue the dollar. The Fed did not want to hasten that prospect. Therefore, until the Fed was sure it had a good reason to cut interest rates, it refused to do so. By the summer of 1960, that good reason appeared. With the economy clearly sinking, the Fed started to cut rates — but it was too late. The recession had already begun. Not coincidentally, Nixon lost the election.

Thus far we have ignored the role of other nations in the problems of 1960. If other countries had been willing to cut their interest rates along with the United States, investors would have had no incentive to take money out of the country, and gold outflows would not have been an issue. Instead, with strong economic growth continuing in Europe, most interest rates there were still rising during the early months of 1960. If this had not been the case, then the Fed might have started to cut rates earlier. Perhaps it would have tipped the balance in favor of Nixon on Election Day.

The point here is not to explain why Nixon lost, but to show the way in which nations are interdependent. Even though, with a fixed exchange rate, the average American could ignore the rest of the world, conditions in the United States and conditions abroad were closely intertwined. Given its fixed dollar policy, America could not easily cut interest rates, because interest rates abroad were rising. Today, with a dollar that can bounce up and down like a yo-yo and change the terms of competition in an instant, the average American cannot ignore the rest of the world. The nature of international relationships has changed, but the basic fact of interdependence has not.

The United States in the World Economy Today

So much for 1960. It is now 1996. The problem now is to fix the Indebted Society; and the solution is to cut interest rates and raise taxes (or raise personal savings). What will happen — in the context of the world economy — if the United States does so?

This is one of those cases where economic theory has a definite answer, but practical people (including most economists) aren't so sure. The theoretical answer is clear: just as in Eisenhower's time, lower interest rates will cause investors to sell dollars and try to move their assets to other countries. Since it no longer needs to support a fixed exchange rate, the U.S. Treasury will not sell any gold. Instead, the value of the dollar will go down until investors decide it's such a bargain that they can live with the low interest rates.[51] American goods will become more competitive, and U.S. industry will boom. Also, a rise in import prices and a rise in the pricing power of U.S. firms could possibly cause a bout of inflation. Remember, though, all this is just theory. The theory might well turn out to be right, but there are reasons to suspect other possibilities. We'll call this theory-supported scenario the "export boom."

Why might that theory be wrong for the United States today? Because it wasn't designed for an indebted society. For a country that has been sending IOUs abroad for years, the reaction to a tax hike or a rise in personal saving may be very different from what the theory predicts. As we noted in chapters 10 and 15, foreign investors are understandably nervous about the increasing indebtedness of the United States. They are afraid America will be tempted to "inflate away" its foreign debts. Also, because the United States is so big, its debts make up a large fraction of the world's assets. With more and more bonds coming out of America, global investors worry about having too many eggs in one basket. (After all, if the United States were a small nation, and U.S. bonds were only a small part of global investors' portfolios, the risk of a decline in their value wouldn't be a big deal for those investors.) A major move toward higher taxes or a higher saving rate would mean that the United States intended to stop borrowing. This would immediately make dollar assets look a lot safer. Despite lower interest rates, investors might try to *buy* dollars, not sell them.

Then the Fed could cut interest rates even more without worrying much about inflation. The dollar wouldn't fall, and import prices wouldn't rise. This outcome would not be the best for American industries that compete internationally, but it would be excellent for the country as a whole. The low interest rates would stimulate private investment, thereby generating good jobs for today and raising productivity for tomorrow. We'll call this the "unsinkable dollar" scenario.

We can't really say which scenario is more likely. The United States — and the rest of the world — must be prepared for either the export boom scenario or the unsinkable dollar scenario. Each scenario has its own set of advantages and its own set of problems — both for the United States and for the rest of the world.

The Export Boom Scenario

Advantages, Problems, and Solutions for the United States

The export boom scenario has two great advantages. First, it will revive industries that have been hurt by international competition, and will do so without going back on any trade agreements — thereby eliminating the distraction of the trade issue and letting Americans focus on more important problems. Second, the export boom scenario provides a strong stimulus to final demand, thereby giving firms two reasons to invest more: lower interest rates *and* higher product demand. Therefore, we don't have to worry that the improved federal budget and higher personal saving will backfire and produce a recession.

The big potential problem with the export boom scenario is the risk of inflation and the way the Fed will react to that risk. A declining dollar will tend both to raise import prices and to give U.S. firms the opportunity to raise *their* prices, because the competition will be weaker. This is just a risk; it's not a certainty. The dollar has already fallen quite a bit since 1985, and import prices have not risen as much as many feared. Even if such price increases occur, they can be offset by lower prices for consumer goods and services, since a higher national saving rate will mean less demand for those items. Even the general inflation rate's rising a little bit will not be a major disaster, in our opinion. Unfortunately, the Fed may feel differently. Once the dollar starts to fall, the Fed may hold the line on interest rates, so that the pickup in private investment will be minimal. With little increase in private investment, the United States will lose much of the long-run advantage from increased saving.

We have three solutions to this potential problem. The first is the president's appointing Fed governors who don't think that 5 percent inflation is a major disaster. The second is aggressive U.S. intervention in foreign exchange markets so as to moderate the dollar's decline. We suggest actually selling gold in the process. With the budget and trade deficits under control, selling gold will not scare international investors as much as it may under present circumstances. The United States has the world's largest gold reserve — three times larger than second-place Switzerland and ten times larger than currency-powerhouse Japan. All that gold doesn't do us much good just sitting there in Fort Knox. Our third solution is the most radical — so radical that it was used by that damn commie, Richard Nixon. We don't think Nixon gave wage-price controls enough of a chance. Admittedly it's an extreme solution, not a popular one with economists, and it shouldn't be used unless the situation warrants it. Nonetheless, looking back from 1996, 1972 doesn't seem like a bad year at all.

Of course, the best solution to the potential inflation problem in the United States is for other countries to lower *their* interest rates so that the dollar wouldn't fall too far. This might also have advantages for them. America should encourage such policies abroad, to the extent possible. Unfortunately, the United States can't save the world all by itself.

Advantages, Problems, and Solutions for the Rest of the World

The U.S. export boom scenario has two major advantages for other countries. First, making American products more competitive without changing the trade rules will get U.S. trade officials off those countries' backs. Second, making American goods cheaper will aid other countries in their (sometimes misguided) attempts to reduce inflation.

The biggest overall problem with the U.S. export boom scenario is that it will tend to depress foreign economies. The cheap dollar will make their products harder to sell, so that they lose where the United States gains. For this reason, a weak dollar policy is sometimes called a "beggar thy neighbor" policy.

However, this problem has an easy solution. If other countries don't like the cheap dollar, they can cut their interest rates, and the dollar will strengthen again. If their interest rates are already close to zero (as Japan's have been recently), they can intervene aggressively in the foreign exchange markets to weaken the dollar (as Japan has done recently with apparent success). Unlike U.S. intervention to support the dollar, foreign intervention to support the dollar is effectively unlimited, because other countries can support the dollar using their own currencies. Trying to support its own currency, the United States has to use up foreign currency reserves (or potentially use up gold), of which it has limited supplies. Trying to support the dollar, which is to them a foreign currency, other nations need only print more of their own currencies. America could run out of foreign currency and even possibly run out of gold, but Germany, for example, need never run out of deutsche marks (just as the United States, if it were trying to support, rather than weaken, the deutsche mark, need never run out of dollars).

The real problem is that many other countries may be too worried about inflation to undertake the necessary policy changes. After all, the United States is not the only country with powerful lenders. We hope those countries also have maverick economists that will write (or at least translate) books urging changes in policy. Again, America can't save the world all by itself.

The Unsinkable Dollar Scenario

Advantages, Problems, and Solutions for the United States

The scenario in which the dollar refuses to weaken in the first place presents an altogether different set of advantages and problems. The tremendous advantage is that, because there is little inflation risk, there is no major barrier to policies that encourage private investment. Private investment, as we have said before, is what the United States needs most to help get it out of the vicious circle.

The problem — or more precisely, the danger — from the unsinkable dollar scenario is that it does not guarantee sufficient product demand to support investment. If national saving increases heavily and the dollar stays strong, product demand can plummet and firms may refuse to invest. The Fed can keep cutting interest rates to encourage investment, but it can't get interest rates to go below zero. The United States in 1938 and Japan in 1995 both experienced this problem of "exhausted interest rate policy."

And they both eventually found solutions. America solved the problem by starting to run big budget deficits again. Japan is solving it by aggressively buying foreign currency, so as to weaken the yen. Of course, neither of these solutions may be right for the United States if it should face the same problem again. Going back to a large budget deficit will seem rather like backsliding, and buying foreign currency may have unpleasant effects on other nations' economies.

But there are other solutions. Instead of running deficits, the United States could run a balanced-budget stimulus — for example, a highway program financed with a gasoline tax. This will still increase product demand.[52] Instead of buying foreign currency, the United States can buy gold — or anything else — just to produce some benign inflation, so that firms will start investing instead of hoarding dollars. If America starts on the road back to affluence, the solutions will appear faster than the problems do.

Advantages, Problems, and Solutions for the Rest of the World

Problems and solutions may also appear for the rest of the world, although both the advantages and the problems associated with this unsinkable dollar scenario are likely to be smaller for the rest of the world than those associated with the U.S. export boom scenario. The main difference that other countries are likely to see is that their firms will be able to finance more cheaply in the United States. Also, barring the "exhausted interest rate policy" problem described above, they may see some increase in exports, as a stronger U.S. economy imports some of its investment goods. Both of these differences will have the effect of stimulating their economies. If they are worried about inflation, some countries may seek to counter that stimulus by raising their interest rates, in which case their currencies will strengthen, and the United States will move closer to the export boom scenario.

Or they may seek to counter it with fiscal policy — raising taxes or cutting public spending. For nations like the United Kingdom and Australia, which seem to be in "low saving, slow growth" vicious circles similar to that of America, this policy can have the beneficial effect of shifting resources toward private investment. In that happy event, the United States may truly be helping to "save the world."

21▪The Virtuous Circle

T HE CITIZENS OF THE Indebted Society are bruised and scared. They are like someone driving a car on an icy road. The way to avoid a crash is to steer into the skid.

There are several ways in which this is true. Most important, in order for their standard of living to start rising again, Americans may have to accept a modest standard of living today. If Americans use the discipline of taxation to enforce temporary restraint in their material well-being, they can choose to impose that restraint on the rich and the upper middle class. Otherwise, Americans of all income levels must cut back on their own consumption. If Americans have the serenity to accept a modest standard of living today, then they will find over time that a much higher one will be within their reach and that of their children.

In another respect, America has to "steer into the skid" in its foreign trade conditions. However, as pointed out in chapter 20, we don't yet know which direction the skid will go. Lower interest rates depressing the value of the dollar may appear to be an intensification of an already troubling trend. But if the Fed resists the temptation to raise interest rates again to defend the dollar, our trade conditions will improve, and other countries will have a reason to join our prescription for affluence by cutting their interest rates as well. On the other hand, if global investors react to a higher U.S. national saving rate by buying instead of selling dollars, and if the rest of the world's economies remain weak, we may find that trade conditions will continue to be difficult. Then the skid will be in the direction of difficult international competition. If we are wise, we will turn into it by taking the opportunity to invest the available foreign capital for improved productivity in the future. When the world's other economies recover, the United States will then be in a better position to compete in the expanding markets that result. This will set the stage for a worldwide increase in productivity, which will ultimately increase both U.S. and foreign living standards.

GOOD DEBT AND BAD DEBT

Another sense in which America has to steer into the skid is by allowing debt to play a large role in the transition back to affluence. Although we hope and expect that incomes will grow faster than debts during the transition period, we also expect that debt will be an important part of the process. Two conditions are necessary for the transition to be successful. First, debt must be used only to make investments whose returns to society exceed the cost of the debt. Since lower interest rates reduce the cost of debt, this first condition is quite consistent with an increase in debt levels, but not with an increase in debt burdens. Low-cost debt used to finance high-return projects does not become burdensome. Government debt to finance improvements in the nation's infrastructure and corporate debt to finance new plant and equipment may well end up meeting this condition. Even personal debt may be valuable, if it is used to shift consumption away from nondurable items, such as restaurant meals and stylish clothes, toward things with longer-term value, such as new cars equipped with the latest safety, efficiency, and antipollution features.

The second condition for a successful transition is that debt must be used as a tool to achieve the broad objectives of society rather than as a threat to enforce the narrow interests of particular groups. To see how this condition may apply, consider the example of corporate debt. After corporate debt exploded in the 1980s (partly in response to existing tax incentives), it was used to justify the harsh treatment of workers and thereby to enforce the interests of capital owners against those of workers. Most of the corporate debt undertaken during the 1980s was not used to finance new investment but to replace existing financing for old investment. Under the reforms that we envision, firms would have an incentive to reverse that shift — that is, to replace existing debt financing with equity financing. This change would improve the balance of power within firms, but it would also serve society's interests by reducing the incentive to conserve cash at all costs and by arresting the breakdown of trust within firms. Although the proposed tax changes give firms an incentive to shift from debt to equity, low interest rates give firms an incentive to undertake financing for new investment. Much of this financing may be in the form of debt. Thus, while debt-equity ratios will decline, total capital (debt plus equity) will increase — possibly meaning an absolute increase in the amount of debt. Since this increase will finance new investment, it will be in the broad interests of society.

Government debt provides another example. As used during the 1980s, government debt was really part of a scheme to shift resources from the poor and the general public to the rich. The more clever individuals among the supporters of Reaganomics recognized this arrangement. They knew that debt incurred to finance tax cuts (which mainly benefit the rich) under high interest rate conditions would ultimately require interest payments (also mainly benefiting the rich) that would reduce the funds available for public services and for helping the poor. However, under conditions of low interest rates, and particularly if interest rates were to approach zero, government debt could be used to provide an economic stimulus that would be broadly beneficial to society and that would not involve a large long-term expense to society. Especially if such low-cost debt were used to finance public investment, it could turn out to be an extremely good deal for the broader society.

Although debt will likely play a role, possibly even a leading role, in the transition back to affluence, we must not allow debt to become the director. The big problem of the Indebted Society is that it has gotten itself into a position where debt can dictate its actions. Lower interest rates, higher taxes, and appropriate changes in the rules will probably not reduce the *amount* of debt, but they will reduce the *power* of debt. Debt will no longer be a weapon that one group in our society uses against another. Instead, it will be a servant of society's interests.

The insidious power that debt seems to have today is partly a consequence of the way we think about it. As Shakespeare's Hamlet says, "There is nothing either good or bad, but thinking makes it so." Just as Denmark was a prison to Hamlet, debt has been a prison to America, because it has been used to legitimate antipoor and antiworker policies by firms and government, and sometimes even by individuals. If Americans refuse to let debt be used in this way, they can break free from the prison.

A Philosophical Plea

In this regard, we urge that, despite the fiscal difficulties of the federal government, the nation should resume an active war on poverty. We cannot argue convincingly on purely economic grounds that helping the poor is a critical step on the road back to affluence. In a philosophical sense, however, we believe that helping the poor is important to affirm our resistance to the dark power that debt is exerting, to show that America is breaking free from its prison. The typical American will certainly see some economic benefits — reduced crime, for example. We cannot say whether those benefits will be sufficient to offset the costs. But we can say that a society which cares for its underprivileged will be a more humane society. Programs for the poor should be reformed, not with an eye to saving money but with the goal of improving their effectiveness at helping the poor. If federal antipoverty programs are to be transferred to the states, let it be with the strong condition that the funds involved be used truly to fight poverty, and let us make sure that the federal government can enforce this condition. Fighting poverty should be one of our society's broad objectives, if only because it helps our society become what a society should be.

Fighting poverty may require the continued use of debt. Will this be consistent with the condition that debt must be used only to make investments whose returns to society exceed the cost of the debt? Can helping the poor realistically be considered an investment? Perhaps not in the strict sense. Nonetheless, if we measure the return in terms of social welfare — in terms of how much good it does for people — rather than in terms of mere production, then that return will surely exceed the cost. If helping the poor is not a critical step on the road to becoming an affluent society, it is surely a critical part of being a good society.

The Virtuous Circle

Still, those who have sympathy for the poor, as we do, must realize that the United States cannot likely be or remain a good society unless it also becomes once again an affluent one. We have already enumerated the policy changes necessary to move the country in that direction. Americans, be they bleeding-heart liberals or fiscal conservatives, will benefit as a nation when those changes begin to bear fruit.

If we start making the necessary policy changes now, we can reverse the vicious circles and move into a virtuous circle. Low interest rates and better tax policies will encourage investment and reduce the burden of debt. Investment will raise productivity, which will raise incomes. A "smart stimulus" fiscal policy will also raise incomes. Rising incomes will provide more for savings and reduce borrowing. High saving will make more resources available for investment, and growth will accelerate. High saving and fast growth will increase international confidence and thereby encourage foreign investment in the United States. However, if we save enough ourselves and use our resources fully, that foreign investment will no longer be a necessity, and America can once again become a real source of capital for the growing nations of the world rather than a drain on the world's capital.

Lower debt burdens will also reduce the power of lenders, so there will be less pressure to avoid inflation at all costs, and policy makers can once again explore all possibilities for growth. Better tax policies will encourage firms to move to a more equity-oriented capital structure, which will allow them to pursue long-run productivity without paying excessive attention to cash conservation. Higher productivity will enable them to increase retained earnings without reducing the share going to labor, so they can invest more in future productivity without borrowing and without harming workers. A more secure working environment and a smaller debt burden will reduce stress, and health will improve. Americans will begin to trust one another again, so they can work together for the common good. With growing and more secure incomes, Americans will no longer see foreigners and immigrants as a threat.

Once America starts in the virtuous circle, the possibilities are limitless. Given the right stimuli, technology can improve more rapidly than ever. Given the right stimuli and the right attitudes, that technology can be harnessed to improve people's lives and to make workers more productive rather than displacing them from their jobs. Economic growth in the United States can even exceed that experienced during the former Age of Affluence. When growth proceeds that quickly, it is almost a foregone conclusion that nearly everyone in society will participate and benefit.

THE ROAD AHEAD

There are many battles to be fought as America makes its way toward the virtuous circle. Some battles will take place within individuals, some will take place in the political arena, and others in the intellectual arena. Americans as individuals will have to fight their tendency to try to solve their problems by consuming more. Americans as citizens will have to fight for the policy changes necessary to bring us to the virtuous circle. Americans as thoughtful people will have to fight for ideas that do not foreclose a future of growth.

Today in the Indebted Society we are already seeing a few hopeful signs that America may be beginning to move in the right direction. Recent data from retirement accounts and mutual funds suggest that Americans are finally beginning to save more. The booming stock market, which partly reflects the success of firms in raising profits at the expense of workers, may also reflect this increase in saving. Politicians of all parties and inclinations have begun at least to recognize the problems of job insecurity, wage stagnation, and economic inequality — although most still offer the wrong solutions. Mainstream economists, although still committed to the natural rate theory, now seem open to the idea that a structural change in the U.S. labor market has reduced the natural rate of unemployment. Some polls are showing that Americans would support a tax increase if it were used to reduce the deficit. Will Americans have the courage to follow through on these tentative first steps? Let us hope so.

Many of the early steps down the road to affluence will be difficult ones, and many of the benefits will be slow to appear. Middle class standards of living will not immediately start to rise. Downsizing will not come to an immediate end just because tax and employment laws are improved. Americans will spend some years in the wilderness before the promised land becomes visible. Unfortunately for those hurting in the Indebted Society, we must pass through it before going beyond it.

Notes

1. Our definition of "habit" is based on a simplified version of one used by John Y. Campbell and John H. Cochrane to study stock market behavior. See Campbell and Cochrane, "By Force of Habit: A Consumption-Based Model of Aggregate Stock Market Behavior," mimeo, Harvard University, December 15, 1994.

2. This theory is associated with James Duesenberry, who, coincidentally, was the former occupant in John Campbell's Harvard office.

3. This index was formulated from a combination of the Help Wanted Index kept by the Conference Board and Bureau of Labor Statistics data on payroll employment. The Help Wanted Index measures the level of help-wanted advertising in the United States and is "normalized" by dividing it by an index derived from Bureau of Labor Statistics payroll employment.

4. Quoted in Robert Lekachman, *The Age of Keynes* (New York: Random House, 1966), 43.

5. Nineteen fifty-one is the first year for which the Help Wanted Index, an indicator of job availability, was produced.

6. Some of the decline in manufacturing employment would have occurred anyway as employers made very profitable "labor saving" technological changes.

7. Reagan's negative attitude toward unionism was evident when he fired the nation's striking air traffic controllers in 1981 and hired permanent replacement workers.

8. Although the Johnson tax cut "worked," it was not necessarily the best method for stimulating the economy. The tax cut stimulated the economy by encouraging consumption, which has only short-run benefits. The same effect could have been achieved through increased government investment (in roads, research, education, etc.), which would have long-run benefits. The same effect could also have been achieved by cutting interest rates and thereby encouraging private investment, again with long-run benefits. It may even have been better to accept a weak economy, leaving more resources available for the increasingly demanding military operations in Southeast Asia. As it turned out, the Vietnam War, along with the simultaneous War on Poverty, strained the economy's resources and brought about inflation and high interest rates.

9. Margaret M. Blain, ed., in *The Deal Decade: What Takeovers and Leveraged Buyouts Mean for Corporate Governance* (Washington, D.C.: The Brookings Institution, 1993), posits that restructuring and leveraged buyouts in the 1980s disproportionately affected manufacturing firms. As is pointed out in chapter 3 and is discussed throughout this book, the jobs with higher wages and benefits have typically been in manufacturing. Thus, the loss of these jobs due to reorganization is important to the future of workers in the United States.

10. Despite the tax advantages, firms have historically been reluctant to finance with debt. One factor in this reluctance was the belief that debt increased the stockholders' risk. However, in 1958 economists Franco Modigliani and Merton Miller showed that the increase in stockholders' risk was an illusion and that the only difference between high-debt firms and low-debt firms was taxation. See "The Cost of Capital, Corporation Finance, and the Theory of Investment," *American Economic Review*, June 1958.

11. Here is the explanation, for those who have enough patience to follow it. First, consider the firm *without debt* in an inflationary environment. We are now going to assume that the share price is $7.50 instead of $10, because this assumption will end up producing the same 10 percent real return as in the example without inflation. Since the dollar value of the firm's assets rises with inflation, its annual profit (before interest and taxes) will be $300,000 ($200,000 real profit plus $100,000 because of inflation). The interest rate will be 20 percent (10 percent real interest plus 10 percent to compensate for inflation). Before borrowing, the firm makes $300,000 per year and pays half in taxes, leaving $150,000. Dividing by the 100,000 shares gives a profit of $1.50 per share — a 20 percent nominal return on the $7.50 share value. Adjusting for inflation, the real return is 10 percent. Now, the firm borrows $375,000 at a 20 percent interest rate and uses the money to buy back half its outstanding shares at the market value of $7.50. It's annual interest expense is $75,000. This leaves a pretax profit of $225,000. After a 50 percent tax, the firm is left with $112,500 of after-tax profit. Dividing by the 50,000 shares outstanding gives a profit of $2.25 per share — a 30 percent nominal return on the $7.50 share value. Adjusting for inflation, the real return is 20 percent.

12. Peter Lynch, in his popular book *One Up on Wall Street* (New York: Simon and Schuster, 1989), uses the term "diworseification" to refer to unproductive diversification that ultimately reduces a firm's real value.

13. This premise is given exhaustive treatment in Margaret M. Blain, ed., *The Deal Decade: What Takeover and Leveraged Buyouts Mean for Corporate Governance* (Washington, D.C.: The Brookings Institution, 1993).

14. Ibid. at p. 3.

15. Steven Sharpe, "Financial Market Imperfections, Firm Leverage, and the Cyclicality of Employment," *American Economic Review*, September 1994.

16. Michael C. Jensen, "Agency Costs of Free Cash Flow, Corporate Finance, and Takeovers," *American Economic Review*, May 1986.

17. Andrei Shleifer and Lawrence H. Summers, "Breach of Trust in Hostile Takeovers," in Alan J. Auerbach, ed., *Corporate Takeovers: Causes and Consequences* (Chicago: University of Chicago Press, 1988).

18. *The Wall Street Journal*, May 4, 1995, p.1.

19. American Management Association

20. Bennett Harrison and Barry Bluestone, *The Great U-Turn, Corporate Restructuring and the Polarizing of America* (New York: Basic Books, Inc., 1988).

21. Bureau of Labor Statistics, Worker Displacement During the Early 1990s.

22. Harrison and Bluestone, p. 126.

23. Gary Burtless, *A Future of Lousy Jobs? The Changing Structure of U.S. Wages*. (Washington, D.C.: The Brookings Institution, 1990).

24. Ibid. at p. 2.

25. Department of Labor, *Report on the American Workforce*, 1995.

26. Harrison and Bluestone, p. 126.

27. "Maine's Money Managers," *Maine Times*, June 23, 1995.

28. Steve Bailey and Steven Syre, "Fidelity's High-Tech Escape Pays Off," *Boston Globe*, January 12, 1996, p. 75.

29. Private banks can and do create new money, but only by using money that has already been created. The U.S. Treasury can coin money, but coins are a tiny part of the total money supply.

30. The definition of a "high" inflation rate has changed over the years. In 1957 the Fed precipitated the 1958 recession in response to an inflation rate of 3 percent, which was quite high by the standards of the time. In 1974 the Fed precipitated the 1975 recession in response to an inflation rate of 12 percent. In 1981 the Fed precipitated the 1982 recession in a determined (and very successful) effort to bring inflation down from its 13 percent level of 1980.

31. A fixation that it shares with the majority of macroeconomists.

32. With the vacancy rate, the picture is of course turned upside-down. Vacancy rates below the natural rate would be disinflationary, and vacancy rates above the natural rate would be inflationary.

33. For example, Japan's data is difficult to interpret because there is very little variation in the unemployment rate. (Until recently it always stayed very close to 2 percent.) Data from France and Germany are difficult to interpret because their vacancy rates and unemployment rates move more or less in lockstep, so there is no basis for deciding which is a better predictor of inflation.

34. Although we disagree with prevailing Federal Reserve opinions about what the objectives of monetary policy should be, we do admire the increasing success with which the Fed meets its objectives. Although the unemployment rate, in our opinion, has been too high in recent years, it has also been more stable than in the past. Moreover, several potential financial crises have passed with little adverse effect. (The 1929 stock market crash and the banking crises of the early 1930s remain vivid in the minds of economic historians decades later. The 1987 crash and the savings and loan crisis of the late 1980s have already been almost forgotten.) The Fed's success is a tribute to the advancement of monetary economics. We only wish they would pay more attention to labor economics.

35. We are grateful to John Kenneth Galbraith for pointing out to us the effect that increased debt levels have on the importance of lenders and their influence in society.

36. This is one way to structure such a loan. Another possibility is that the interest rate could vary according to the level of the inflation rate.

37. The actual market value of the bond at the end of the first year might be different, but this change would not concern a long-term lender.

38. When interest rates rise, a new bond buyer can get a new bond with a higher interest rate. The new bond buyer will not be willing to pay full price for an old

bond, which carries the old, lower interest payments. Therefore, the prices of existing bonds fall when interest rates rise. Similarly, when interest rates fall, existing bonds, with their old, higher interest payments, become more attractive, and their prices rise.

39. If the unemployment rate is too low, then (according to the theory) the rate of inflation will keep rising and never stabilize. Prior to the acceptance of the natural rate theory, economists thought (perhaps rightly) that, even if the unemployment rate were very low, the inflation rate would eventually stop rising and stabilize at some higher level.

40. This is not quite true, because our tax code does not make complete allowances for inflation. As economist Martin Feldstein pointed out during the 1970s, high inflation rates effectively raise the taxation of returns to capital, because you have to pay taxes on the part of the return that merely compensates you for the increase in prices. However, we regard this issue as a problem with the tax code, not a problem with inflation.

41. We are grateful to Lawrence Summers for pointing this out to us.

42. As noted in chapter 3, there is an exception to the rule that revenues go up and down with tax rates. This exception, which applies to the Kennedy-Johnson tax cut, occurs when there are slack resources in the economy and monetary policy makers are willing to cooperate with the stimulative effect of a tax cut. Unfortunately, raising spending after the economy reaches full employment, as Johnson did later in his administration, the beneficial effect of the tax cut disappears, and we end up with inflation and high interest rates.

43. The phrase "user interface" refers to the way a computer and a user communicate. A "graphical" user interface is one that uses pictures rather than words. This is usually easier to use, because it is not necessary to learn and remember a lot of names and commands. Before graphical user interfaces were invented, there were only "text interfaces," which required more training to use and placed greater mental demands on the user.

44. Much of this capital is provided by central banks — the Bank of Japan in particular — that are trying to revive their economies while preventing the dollar from dropping further. A falling dollar exacerbates their economic problems by making their products harder to sell.

45. With the inflation rate declining, the Fed may not have to raise nominal interest rates. Eventually, however, businesses will realize that it is not worth their while to invest if prices are not going up.

46. The Matcham article appeared on page 1 of the *Boston Sunday Globe* on June 4, 1995. It was under the following headline: "Hectic on the homefront: Families in the '90's face a vastly changed landscape where time is short and sense of connection is fragile."

47. Saving figures cited in this and the following paragraph are based on the International Monetary Fund's definition of saving, which takes into account such things as fluctuations in the exchange rate. These figures may not be directly comparable with saving figures cited elsewhere in this book.

48. A global effort at public investment — probably too much to hope for — would involve national governments' pooling their resources to finance things like scientific research and environmental improvement.

49. We realize that adding 25 percentage points to the tax rates would not do the trick, because people would find new ways to move their income out of U.S. jurisdiction. Even the realistic Laffer curve is not quite linear. Our point is only that the required rise in tax rates would not be outside the feasible range. In any case, we do not seriously propose to get all the new revenue from the top 5 percent of taxpayers.

50. The situation is complicated by the fact that Nixon and Eisenhower didn't want the same thing. Nixon, who wanted to get elected, urged Eisenhower to spend more on defense in order to stimulate the economy. Eisenhower, who wanted to balance the budget, refused. Nonetheless, Nixon blamed the Fed, not the president, for his defeat.

51. Technically, the dollar must go down far enough so that investors will expect it to come back up over time. Since the dollar can still be used to buy the same goods and services in the United States, investors will expect its foreign exchange value to rise again if it goes down very far. This gradual increase in the value of the dollar will compensate investors for the lower interest rate. The idea that a currency must go far enough down so that it can come back up is referred to as "overshooting" and is associated with economist Rudi Dornbusch.

52. The spending side of the program would increase product demand directly, as well as putting more money in the hands of the people working on it. The tax would reduce demand, but by a lesser degree, because people would not reduce their spending one-for-one with the amount taken in tax. This is an old idea called the "balanced budget multiplier." It hasn't gotten much press in recent years, but it still works.

Index